T0098794

"Neuroscience researcher Mark Waldman and business professor Chris Manning have mapped out an original model showing how the human brain moves through four stages to achieve any desired goal: motivation, decision-making, creativity, and awareness. The experiential exercises in this very useful book will help you, and your brain, function at its very best…a practical approach for applying the insights gained from the emerging field of neuroscience." —RICHARD STAFFORD, PHD, Associate Dean and Director, Executive MBA Program, Loyola Marymount University

"In this book, the authors demonstrate how to engage in brief exercises—some which take only a few seconds to complete— that have the power to improve your productivity and enhance the quality of your work. They also describe how you can use your intuitive and creative powers to solve problems more rapidly and to build stronger, more meaningful relationships with others. The *NeuroWisdom* strategies in this book are now included in the Executive MBA NeuroLeadership curriculum at Loyola Marymount University." —DENNIS W. DRAPER, PHD, Dean of the College of Business Administration, Loyola Marymount University

"*NeuroWisdom* is the perfect recipe book for self-transformation. The authors brilliantly distill insights from brain research to show you how to lead a more fulfilling and extraordinary life." —JOSIAH HULTGREN, Senior Lecturer, California Lutheran University and Founder/CEO of MindFullyAlive.com

"Applying mindfulness and positivity as you work toward achieving important life-transforming goals is one of the most important breakthrough discoveries of the 21st Century. Grounded in the newest brain research, this book makes an important contribution to the business community as it guides the reader toward a values oriented lifestyle." —NEIL SCHUITEVOERDER, PhD, Clinical Psychologist, founder of the Center for Advanced Human Development

"Everyone in all walks of life and professions needs to read and re-read this material, and the lessons to be learned are important in personal interrelationships. I highly recommend *NeuroWisdom*." —DON EPLEY, CEO, Coastal Economics; past president of the American Real Estate Society

"*NeuroWisdom* is a cornucopia of up-to-date information integrating the latest findings in brain science, human behavior, and the essential strategies needed to insure business success. If you practice the experiential exercises in this book, you'll train your brain to become more focused, confident, empathic and socially responsible. Both scholarly and entertaining, this is a must read book for anyone seeking long-term life-satisfaction." —ROBERT COFFMAN, Clinical Psychologist and Business Coach

"Once again Mark Waldman hits it out of the park with *NeuroWisdom*. As both an avid student and teacher of personal development for over forty-five years, I found this book to be packed with powerful tools that will help people retrain their brains and take command of their lives." —KEN COSCIA, International Training Director, Silva Method

"*Neurowisdom* is brilliant, thought provoking and refreshingly practical. It's very rare you can read a book about neuroscience and walk away with a set of tools that absolutely will change your brain and your life if you put them to good use. NeuroWisdom is that book. Best read of the year for me." —JEFFREY GIGNAC, Clinical Hypnotherapist and creator of Passive Brain Fitness

NEUROWISDOM

NeuroWisdom

The New Brain Science of
Money, Happiness, and Success

MARK ROBERT WALDMAN
& CHRIS MANNING, PhD

DIVERSIONBOOKS

Books by Mark Robert Waldman & Andrew Newberg, MD

How Enlightenment Changes Your Brain
Words Can Change Your Brain
How God Changes Your Brain
Born to Believe

Books by Mark Waldman

Archetypes of the Collective Unconscious, Volumes 1–4
The Spirit of Writing
Love Games
Dreamscaping
The Art of Staying Together

Diversion Books
A Division of Diversion Publishing Corp.
443 Park Avenue South, Suite 1004
New York, New York 10016
www.DiversionBooks.com

Copyright © 2017 by Mark Robert Waldman & Chris Manning, PhD
All rights reserved, including the right to reproduce this book or portions thereof in any form whatsoever.

For more information, email info@diversionbooks.com

First Diversion Books paperback edition June 2019.
Paperback ISBN: 978-1-63576-668-4
eBook ISBN: 978-1-68230-304-7

In memory of
Jeremy P. Tarcher
(1932-2015)
Publisher, Mentor, and Friend

NeuroWisdom

n(y)o͞o-rō-wiz-dəm

Neuro: relating to the nervous system and the brain
Wisdom: the ability to use your knowledge and
experience to make good decisions

Tucked away behind the folds of the neocortex are two of the newest evolutionary structures of the human brain: the insula and the anterior cingulate. They contain special neurons that give you profound powers of perception. They enhance your ability to be self-directed and socially aware, but they remain largely underdeveloped in your brain for many decades. Recent brain-imaging studies have proven that you can consciously strengthen these neurons and the connections between your social brain, your decision-making brain (your frontal lobes), and the emotional centers that shape your desires and your level of happiness.

When you stimulate these complex circuits through mindfulness and self-reflection, something remarkable happens: negative feelings and thoughts are transformed into optimism, your motivation and creativity increase, your decision-making skills are enhanced, and your ability to empathize with others rapidly grows. Compassion increases, self-love soars, and a new "voice" can be heard, one that will guide you toward greater awareness and serenity. We call this NeuroWisdom. It is your inner teacher and spiritual compass; and when fully embraced it will help you to achieve your financial and emotional goals, and bring more passion and satisfaction into your relationships and work. The exercises in this book will stimulate this delicate circuit in your brain. Nurture it daily, and it will enlighten and enrich your life.

Contents

PREFACE   1
What this Book Can Do for You and How to Use It

CHAPTER 1   5
Happiness or Wealth: What Do You *Really* Want?

CHAPTER 2   17
How to Manage Your Busy Brain:
Superlearning and the Four Pillars of Wealth

CHAPTER 3   44
Preparing to Succeed:
60-Second Strategies for Warming Up Your Brain

CHAPTER 4   63
Motivation—The First Pillar of Wealth:
Money, Pleasure, and the Desire to Acquire *More*

CHAPTER 5   83
Turning On the M-Drive:
Nine Strategies to Stimulate Motivation and Desire

CHAPTER 6   108
    Decision Making—The Second Pillar of Wealth:
    Turning Desires into Conscious Goals

CHAPTER 7   123
    Sharpening Your Decision-Making Skills:
    Six Strategies to Increase Optimism and Performance

CHAPTER 8   145
    Creativity—The Third Pillar of Wealth:
    Imagination, Daydreaming, and Intuition

CHAPTER 9   158
    Thinking Outside the Box:
    Nine Strategies to Increase Creativity at Work

CHAPTER 10   170
    Awareness—The Fourth Pillar of Wealth:
    Fairness, Empathy, and Generosity

CHAPTER 11   202
    Developing Your Social Brain:
    12 Strategies to Deepen Communication,
    Empathy, Kindness, Forgiveness, and Gratitude

EPILOGUE   233
    Putting it All Together

Acknowledgments   243
Appendix: NeuroWisdom 101   245
Endnotes   247

PREFACE.

What this Book Can Do for You and How to Use It

We are born into this world already possessing a hidden stockpile of wealth, and it is free. It's your incredible brain. If you want to "have it all"—money, happiness, and success—you must first understand the power lying dormant within your brain and then develop it using the strategies and exercises presented to you in this book. This will enable you to have both inner and outer wealth: friendship, love, health, power, possession, a meaningful career, and long-term, lasting contentment.

To achieve any important goal in life you need to develop four neurological processes in your brain: motivation, decision making, creativity, and awareness. We call these the "Four Pillars of Wealth" and each one is essential to master if you want to unlock and realize your fullest potential. Each pillar is based on groundbreaking neuroscientific discoveries that have completely changed the way we understand human nature and our biological drive to seek money, happiness, and success.

Following our discussion of each of the Four Pillars of Wealth, we have created a complementary chapter that will guide you through experiential exercises proven to build stronger neural connections throughout your brain. These "NeuroWisdom strategies," as we call them, will reduce harmful stress, significantly boost your energy, increase your ability to concentrate and stay laser-focused throughout the day, and improve your overall health and sense of well-being. They will help you to acquire new skills more quickly, and they will help you to build more satisfying relationships with others—at work and at home. They will help you transform negativity into optimism, enabling you to create practical solutions to virtually every problem you face.

By spending only a few minutes several times a day practicing these experiential exercises and strategies, your sense of confidence and self-esteem will grow. You'll discover that you have a wealth of intuitive wisdom that can assist you in making wise decisions. In the process, you'll discover what *really* motivates you. You'll find that inner passion that makes your life more purposeful and meaningful. In addition:

1. This book will show you how to better manage people, your business, and your time.
2. It will assist you to become a better salesperson, entrepreneur, and innovator within a larger company.

3. It will enable you to deal more effectively with toxic people in the workplace.
4. It will assist you in developing better relationships with family, friends, and colleagues.
5. It will improve your daily focus and increase your ability to be more productive and efficient with your time.
6. This book will help you to recognize which of your current thinking habits exhaust you and lead you in circles, and it will show you how to build new habits that eliminate emotional turmoil.
7. You'll also learn how to experience more pleasure and satisfaction, even when you are carrying out difficult tasks.

To get the most from this book, we recommend that you first read chapters 1 and 2 together as an overview. But read them slowly, and don't skim over the experiential exercises. Take the time to understand the theory underlying each of the Four Pillars of Wealth and make a commitment to integrate the eight principles of brain-based experiential learning. Think about how you can bring these pillars and principles into your work and home environments. When you get to chapter 3, take your time experimenting with each of the exercises, which have been proven to enhance the performance of your brain, and then practice a few of them throughout your workday, adapting them to your personal and professional needs.

The remaining chapters in this book alternate between theory and practice, first introducing you to the most recent neuroscientific discoveries in motivation, decision making, creativity, and awareness, and then guiding you through specific exercises designed to give you the inner *experience* of each of the Four Pillars of Wealth.

At the end of this book Chris Manning will share with you how he has personally made use of these NeuroWisdom techniques to enrich his life, and we hope that it will serve as a model and impetus for you, the reader, to take action and create your own NeuroWisdom strategies as you build greater inner and outer wealth.

Finally, we suggest that you do one more activity while reading this book. Share some of the principles with your trusted colleagues and teach some of the exercises to your friends. You'll discover even deeper layers of personal and professional intimacy that can increase harmony, cooperation, and happiness for everyone. After you have finished, keep the book on your coffee table and revisit your favorite exercises frequently, because each time you do them you'll discover something wonderful and new as you create your own unique brand of success in life.

Authors' Note: The principles and strategies described in this book are grounded in extensive neuroscientific and psychological research published in peer-reviewed journals, which we have referenced throughout this book. We have made the material as user-friendly as possible but generalizations often leave out important subtleties. For those who want to explore the topics in greater detail, you can review the references by going to **www.pubmed.gov**, the database of the National Institutes of Health and the US National Library of Medicine.

CHAPTER 1.

Happiness or Wealth: What Do You *Really* Want?

If you were given a choice between happiness and wealth, and you could only have one of them, which would you select? Circle your answer below.

WEALTH   HAPPINESS

If you are like 90% of the people we've surveyed over the past decade[1] you probably picked happiness over wealth, and it probably took you less than five seconds to make your decision. After all, what good would all that money be if you were miserable? In fact, many people believe that happiness is the key to creating wealth, but the newest economic research disagrees. It's the other way around: wealth *predicts* happiness, and the more you make, the happier you actually become.

Before we explore this controversial finding, I'd like you to think about your choice from a perspective called *mindfulness,* a self-reflective strategy that shifts the neural functioning of your brain so that you can access deeper layers of consciousness. Most people make their decisions by relying on unconscious memories that reflect their old habits. They are using their past experiences to predict future events, barely aware of the thoughts and feelings that govern their actions. Mindfulness, however, will instantly bring you into the present moment, where you can see yourself and the world in a fresh new light. This is where your intuitive awareness—what we call "NeuroWisdom"—allows you to make better decisions and choices. But first you need to be mentally and physically relaxed.

Begin by closing your eyes and taking 10 very slow, gentle, deep breaths. As you inhale, feel the cool air entering your nostrils, and as you exhale, pay attention to the warm air flowing out. Immerse yourself in this experience for 30 seconds as you focus on all the subtle feelings and sensations in your body.

Next, stretch out your arms and legs—in super slow motion—relaxing all of the muscles in your shoulders, neck, and face. Slow your movements down more and take a full 30 seconds as you turn your torso from side to side. You'll notice that the slower you go, the more you'll become aware of subtle aches and pleasures.

Remain still for another 5–10 seconds. Does your body feel lighter or heavier? Does your mind feel more calm or alert? Do your senses—your hearing, vision, etc.—feel heightened or dulled?

A combination of relaxation and mindful awareness

eliminates physical and mental stress, and this allows you to solve problems more easily and attain goals more quickly. In fact, spending just one minute every hour to enter a conscious state of relaxed attentiveness will increase your work productivity and enjoyment.

It also allows you to become more aware of what you *really* want, so let's return to the topic of happiness versus wealth. Take a few more seconds to relax more, and then allow your mind to deeply reflect on this question:

"What would it feel like for you to be
the happiest person in the world?"

Visualize yourself being as happy as you possibly can be. What do you see yourself doing? In our survey, most people imagined themselves doing something pleasurable, like lying on the beach, or traveling to some exotic or romantic place. However, few people saw themselves engaged in a money-making activity, and many envisioned themselves doing nothing at all. When the human brain experiences pleasure and contentment, it wants to take a nap, not unlike your pet after it's been fed well and cuddled. In other words, the happier you feel, the more your brain turns *off* its motivation circuits.

Now I want you to consider a third question. But first, make sure you are mentally and physically relaxed, and then pay attention to the thoughts and images that come to mind as you ponder this question:

"What would you do if you were
the wealthiest person in the world?"

Think about all the things you could do with that

money, and all the people you could help. Visualize the changes you could make in your life and how you could improve the lives of those around you. Notice how these thoughts make you feel.

Now, from your new, more relaxed thoughtful perspective, ask yourself again: Which would you rather be? The happiest person in the world, or the wealthiest?

When our survey participants mindfully contemplated what they wanted to accomplish with great wealth, and were asked again which they would choose, more than 90% selected wealth over happiness. What happened? Why did so many people change their preference? Sandy's response was typical: "I thought about how much good I could do for the world—funding hospitals, doing cancer research, helping my parents—and that thought made me feel really happy!"

Tom expressed similar feelings: "Hands down I'd choose to be the wealthiest man alive! If I had unlimited funds, I would be incredibly happy being in service to others and I'd be serving myself at the same time."

George, who was unemployed but considered himself fairly happy, also changed his mind after reflecting on the questions posed above: "I thought about my kids, and I realized that if I were broke, and they got sick, my happiness would disappear if I couldn't pay for their medical bills. I now think money makes it easier to be happy."

George's response mirrors hundreds of studies conducted throughout the world:[2] money gives a person access to resources that are essential for maintaining happiness, security, and lifelong satisfaction.[3] Contrary to popular belief, wealth is the secret to happiness and well being.

Still, the question of choosing *either* happiness or

wealth is unfair. After all, why can't you have both? You can, and you deserve it because your brain is biologically programmed to pursue anything and everything that will enrich your health, your checking account, and your psychological well-being. The poorest person wants more happiness and wealth, and so do the richest people in the world. Students want more. Secretaries and stay-at-home parents want more. Managers and CEOs want more.

But there's a catch. While the pursuit of money appears to be one of the strongest neurobiological impulses humans have, the pursuit of happiness *as a goal* can actually lead to feelings of loneliness and misery.[4] As psychologists at the University of Denver discovered, the more highly you value happiness, the *less* happy and *more* depressed you may feel.[5] On the other hand, making and spending money in *meaningful* ways is one the surest routes for achieving deep and lasting satisfaction.

What, Exactly, Is Happiness?

Whereas money is understood even by a four-year-old, who will work harder and longer on any task that promises the reward of even a single coin,[6] the concept of happiness can take a lifetime to grasp. In fact, the word has a plethora of meanings in different cultures, and its meaning has changed throughout history, although it was often cited as brief moments of pleasure that one would stumble upon by chance.[7] It was Thomas Jefferson who, in the Declaration of Independence, gave Americans the idea that we all have the unalienable right to "life, liberty, and the pursuit of happiness." However, few people today realize that Jefferson was actually referring to the Greek and Roman philosophies that tied happiness to the social virtues of courage, moderation, and justice, not simply to the pursuit of personal pleasure.[8]

Contemporary definitions of happiness include various combinations of the following words and phrases: pleasure, contentment, joy, bliss, satisfaction, pride, serenity, hope, faith, trust, confidence, optimism, relational connectness, and a harmonious integration between living systems.[9]

The above definitions are of happiness as an ideal. But if you ask yourself what has made you happy in the past, you'll instead recall events that have given you that pleasurable sense of well-being: romantic encounters, new experiences, specific forms of entertainment, or simply marveling at the beauty of nature. Furthermore, if you were to ask yourself the question "What would make me happy today and in the future?" you'll discover a very different range of desires. When we asked our survey participants that question we received hundreds of different responses that often reflected the person's deepest values and ideals:

- Discovering the fullness of my entire being
- Removing the veils of ignorance
- The place between laughter and tears
- Inner peace which comes from God
- Doing work that I love
- Feeling strong and vibrant
- Liberation
- People being kind to one another
- The ability to manifest all my desires and dreams
- Freedom from guilt and shame

Neuroscience continues to shed light on this elusive state of mind: happiness, it seems, is a momentary experience of pleasure that is regulated by some of the oldest structures in your brain,[10] and every organism is neurologically programmed to seek pleasurable experiences because it increases the chance of survival.[11] The bigger the brain, the more pleasures it will seek, including the pursuit of wealth. The evidence is clear: from the moment of birth, the human brain will go after as much money *and* happiness as it can procure, and every goal reached is a measure of personal success.

But happiness is not just about seeking momentary pleasure or putting dollars into your purse. It's also shaped by how you choose to make those dollars and how you choose to spend them. In other words, the pleasure you get by engaging in the activity of making and spending money through work and social activities is the secret to neurological satisfaction and *worldly* success.[12]

Who Are the Happiest People in the World?

The controversy began in 1974 when Richard Easterlin, a distinguished professor of economics at the University of Southern California, argued that there was little correlation between happiness and wealth.[13] Since then, a series of research studies have shown that Easterlin was wrong. Not only do measurements of happiness rise as your income rises, so does your sense of well-being and life satisfaction.[14] The following chart was prepared by the National Opinion Research Center at the University of Chicago, summarizing nearly 40 years of accumulated worldwide statistics between 1972 and 2010:[15]

Family Income	Very Happy	Pretty Happy	Not Too Happy
<$12,500 (bottom 10%)	21%	53%	26%
$12,500–$49,999	25%	61%	13%
$50,000–$149,999	40%	54%	6%
≥$150,000 (top 10%)	53%	45%	2%

Money *predicts* happiness. For those who earn less than $12,500, 26% are not very happy. With incomes above $12,500 and up to $49,999, dissatisfaction is cut in half, down to 13%. For those who earn between $50,000 and $150,000, unhappiness decreases to 6%, and for those who earn more than $150,000, only 2% say they are dissatisfied with their lives.

Research at the Wharton School of Business, published in 2012, found no evidence showing a satiation point; the more money you make, the more happiness you'll experience.[16] These researchers also noted that 100% of those who earned $500,000 or more a year were very happy. In related research, Michael Finke at Texas Tech University found that retirees who had saved over $2 million in non-housing wealth were some of the happiest people in the world.[17]

According to Cornell University economics professor Robert Frank, increased yearly income is the most significant way to increase happiness.[18] Richard Layard, the founder of the Centre for Economic Performance in London, concurs: in nearly every country studied, "the rich are always happier than the poor."[19] Material prosperity predicts life satisfaction,[20] and the higher the economic status you achieve, the more satisfied you'll feel with your life.[21]

The Six Qualities of Happiness

Income appears to be the most important indicator for happiness, but it isn't the only criteria. According to the World Happiness Report, published by the United Nations in 2015, the six most powerful indicators for happiness (in descending order of importance) are:[22]

1. Spending power (economic capital)
2. Friends, family, and community support (social capital)
3. Healthy life expectancy
4. Freedom to make decisions
5. Financial generosity to others
6. Absence of corruption in business and government

The report also found that those who make more money are happier, and those who are happier live longer. In addition, the World Happiness Report identified another essential quality of happiness: well-being. Well-being is defined as a life that is filled with enjoyment and feelings of safety, coupled with the absence of anger, worry, sadness, depression, stress, and pain.

The exercises provided in this book have been tailored to help you eliminate these negative mental states as you build greater confidence, self-esteem, and serenity. As reported in a 2015 issue of the *Lancet*, having an ongoing sense of well-being lowers your risk of physical and emotional disease, tripling your survival rate and extending your life.[23]

Can An Obsession With Making Money Harm You?

As we will explain in chapter 4, money is one of the most powerful motivating factors rooted in the ancient circuits of the brain. Money is a universal symbol representing anything of value, giving you access to food, medicine, education, and a host of other benefits and rewards.

But there is a dark side to money. Research shows that the more wealth you have, the more it strengthens narcissism and feelings of entitlement.[24] And when people become obsessed with making money, their relationships often deteriorate.[25] Research also shows that increased material wealth causes people to become more selfish and insensitive toward others.[26] This often occurs when corporate leaders are given larger salaries: not only do they become more narcissistic, they also become more prone to making impulsive and risky decisions.[27]

Greed, narcissism, selfishness, entitlement, and unfairness toward others—these are the risks when a person becomes overly absorbed in the pursuit of material wealth. However, research has shown that when wealthy individuals engage in values-based exercises that increase self-awareness and social awareness, their egotism diminishes. These are the people that are often recognized as great leaders. [28] In chapter 10 we'll guide you through techniques that will neurologically enhance your awareness in ways that increase empathy, fairness, teamwork, and group satisfaction. In the workplace, this becomes a win-win situation in which everyone benefits from cooperation and increased work productivity. You'll feel more connected to your colleagues, and your satisfaction with work and life will soar.

Beware of Selfishness and Greed

Making money increases happiness, but the way you spend it predicts long-term satisfaction. For example, if you make experiential purchases (vacations, cultural events, etc.) you'll be happier than if you spend it on material objects.[29] In fact, the more you spend money on shared experiences with others, the happier you'll be.[30] The reverse is also true: when researchers reviewed 259 studies comparing money and happiness, they found that the more people focused on materialistic wealth, the more dissatisfied they felt with their lives.[31]

Furthermore, if others perceive you as being too greedy or selfish, they will want you to fail, and even go so far as to sabotage you and your successes. When people feel that they've been treated unfairly, especially when it comes to money, they will take steps to punish the greedy individual, even at a cost to themselves. This reaction, known as altruistic punishment, is embedded in the neurological circuits of the brain,[32] but it will only be triggered when you *believe* that another person or business has treated you unfairly.

In summary, to be successful and achieve life satisfaction a person must create a balance between inner and outer wealth, integrating material, social, and personal desires. This is the formula for establishing trust with others and building self-confidence and self-esteem, the cornerstones for happiness and success.

CHAPTER SUMMARY

- Increased income and wealth leads to greater happiness.
- Worldwide, happiness depends on six criteria. The most important is spending power, followed by social support, physical and emotional health, personal and societal freedom, being financially generous to others, being free of corporate and government corruption, and maintaining a consistent sense of well-being.
- Spending money in meaningful ways—especially when it is used to benefit others—increases life satisfaction.
- Being obsessed with money increases greed, narcissism, feelings of entitlement, selfishness, risky behavior, and insensitivity toward others.

CHAPTER 2.

How to Manage Your Busy Brain: Superlearning and the Four Pillars of Wealth

Each year at Loyola Marymount University, a select group of CEOs, administrators, managers, and entrepreneurs enroll in our Executive MBA program. As one of the world's most demanding educational programs, it prepares highly motivated people to reap greater financial and personal rewards. If these students do not learn how to lower their stress levels and increase their productivity, their grades—along with their businesses and careers—will suffer. They will also compromise their personal happiness and self-esteem.

To help our EMBA students overcome the enormous stress inherent in achieving large goals, we created a special course called NeuroLeadership. It's based on the newest brain science showing how anyone can turn an ordinary workday into a rich and satisfying experience. But instead of using standard textbooks and traditional teaching models, we immerse our EMBA students in a unique experiential learning environment that has been proven to enhance cognitive performance, as we will document throughout this book. The course is complemented by an eight-week mindfulness and positivity training program that includes 58 NeuroWisdom exercises, many of which are featured in this book (see the appendix for more information). Since its inception in 2009, the NeuroLeadership course has attracted worldwide attention from many colleges, businesses, and community organizations. The success of this course has been documented in the *Journal of Executive Education*, and the article has become the second-most requested paper in the history of the journal.[1]

This book will help you to create more inner and outer *wealth*, which we define as the combination of money, happiness, success, and personal contentment. Outer wealth, which is what the brain is programmed to seek, includes any object or activity that you (or your brain) consider to be valuable. Inner wealth begins with the neurological desire to experience pleasure, be it through social play or the involvement in any *experience* that provides greater meaning, purpose, satisfaction, and a lasting sense of well-being. The book presents both the scientific background and a set of NeuroWisdom exercises and strategies that can be used to increase productivity and create a more meaningful and satisfying life. By spending just a few minutes each day practicing the exercises described in this book, your work will become more pleasurable and less stressful as you learn how to anticipate and solve problems more efficiently. These same strategies can also be used at home to build better relationships with your family and friends. You can use the exercises to break bad habits, to improve personal health, and to enhance your emotional well-being. The principles are simple, based on scientific research concerning the development of the human brain.

The Four Pillars of Wealth

To better achieve any important goal in life—money, success, health, love, friendship, happiness, contentment, etc.—you need to master four neurological processes: motivation, decision making, creativity, and the ability to become fully aware of yourself and the needs of others. These are the four pillars for building inner and outer wealth, and if you do not "exercise" these qualities, each of which controls a different brain function, you will limit your ability to turn your dreams into reality. The more you understand how these neural processes shape your actions and your future, the more you can harness them to achieve the goals you truly desire.

PILLAR #1: MOTIVATION

The acquisition of wealth is a neurological process that begins the moment you wake up. First your brain uses its sensory system to survey the environment. Then, when something emotionally excites you or captures your attention, your brain decides whether to move toward the object of desire or away from any perceived threat. This motivational drive is fundamental to the survival of every

4. AWARENESS
FAIRNESS - EMPATHY - SELF-KNOWLEDGE
Stronger connections between frontal lobe, anterior cingulate, and insula

3. CREATIVITY
IMAGINATION - INTUITION - DAYDREAMING
Increased inter-hemispheric activity

2. DECISION MAKING
GOALS - CONSCIOUSNESS - LANGUAGE
Increased forebrain processing and decreased limbic activity

1. MOTIVATION
DESIRE - CURIOSITY - PLEASURE
Sensory and emotional processing in limbic and midbrain activity

THE FOUR PILLARS OF WEALTH

Figure 1. The Four Pillars of Wealth.

organism. It gets you out of bed and causes you to seek out anything that promises you a pleasurable reward.

The motivation-and-reward circuit is centered in the nucleus accumbens (figure 2), located in the most ancient part of your brain. It is driven by instinct and curiosity, and when you perceive something interesting, the nucleus accumbens releases dopamine, a powerful neurochemical that wakes up the rest of your brain and prepares you to take action in the world.

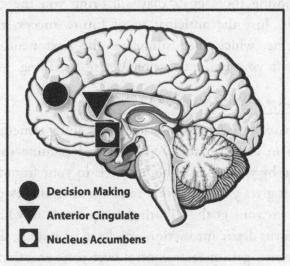

Decision Making

Anterior Cingulate

Nucleus Accumbens

Figure 2. Key areas relating to Pillars 1, 2, and 4.

Dopamine stimulates desire; without it, your mind would remain in a lethargic state. Dopamine is essential for mental health, and when it's not being regularly secreted by the nucleus accumbens, you'll gradually slip into depression, losing your desire to work toward meaningful goals and rewards.[2] That's why it's important to engage in new and interesting activities throughout your life.

However, if your brain releases too much dopamine when it perceives a potentially rewarding object or activity, it can cause you to become destructively addicted to it. Too much pleasure can lead to risky behavior that undermines your brain's ability to make wise decisions in work, relationships, and recreational activities.[3]

Every human brain is different, and the more you become aware of the activities that turn on your desire and motivation circuits, the more pleasure you'll receive by choosing those goals that will bring you the greatest rewards. Just the anticipation of future success releases dopamine, which then stimulates the next neurological process in your brain: conscious decision making.

PILLAR #2: DECISION MAKING

Once you have been motivated to acquire something or engage in a pleasurable activity, the dopamine that was released by your ancient brain travels to your frontal lobe, where it gives you the ability to plan out strategies to help you reach your goals.[4] During this process, in which the brain turns desire into action, you learn new skills, develop new habits, gain greater control over your emotions, and form belief systems that allow you to better understand the world. Here, in a very small part of your frontal lobe (figure 1, above), is where you begin to *consciously* decide what to do and how to do it.[5]

The frontal lobe helps you analyze any problem or obstacle that stands between you and your desired goal. First, your brain will sort through thousands of stored memories, searching for solutions that worked for you in the past. This process only takes a few seconds, and even though we're not aware of it, most of our actions come from this reservoir of learned habits and behaviors.

If those unconscious memories do not help you move toward your goal, then your frontal lobe begins to search for new options. The right side tends to focus on possible problems and dangers while the left side envisions positive solutions. These two sides literally communicate to each other through words, arguments, and intense subconscious dialogues. The process is known as "inner speech," and it begins in the first few years of life, as children internalize the language styles of the culture they are raised in. The right side of your prefrontal cortex generates negative thoughts and feelings, and the left side uses logic to maintain a sense of optimism as it formulates strategies to help you get what you want. If the right side becomes overly active, you'll find yourself worrying, procrastinating, and slowly slipping into depression. However, new research, which we will fully document in chapter 4, confirms that you can consciously teach your brain to lower neural activity that generates negativity and fear,[6] and also to increase neural activity that generates greater confidence and positive decision making.[7]

PILLAR #3: CREATIVITY

Staying focused on a specific task or goal, or solving a difficult problem, uses up a lot of neural energy, and the harder you work, the more quickly the brain tires. In fact, mental fatigue begins to set in after only a few minutes of concentration.[8] Clarity and productivity decline as your mind begins to wander, which is your brain's way of taking a relaxation break.[9] If you want to maintain peak performance, you should deliberately take a 30-second break once or twice an hour to do something pleasurable and relaxing.

You can try it right now: just take a few moments to yawn and slowly stretch your body. You'll immediately feel more focused *and* relaxed as your brain begins to shift into a more creative state of consciousness. When you get into the habit of deepening your relaxation while you work, you'll significantly increase the dopamine levels needed to keep you focused and fully engaged.

When mental fatigue kicks in, your brain does something similar to daydreaming, as your mind begins to wander in a seemingly random way. Researchers believe that mind-wandering is essential for problem solving and decision making,[10] and if you don't allow your brain to enter this highly imaginative state of neural activity before a challenging task, your memory, performance, and mental health will be compromised.[11]

Daydreaming and mind-wandering are necessary for neurocognitive development in childhood,[12] and in adulthood, they give you direct access to creative talents that are unique to human beings.[13] In fact, as brain researchers at the University of California, Santa Barbara demonstrated, scheduling positive daydreaming time into the workday will improve these four core processes that build long-term satisfaction and contentment:[14]

- You'll increase your learning capacity
- You'll enhance your creative problem-solving skills
- You'll make better plans for the future
- Your work will become more personally meaningful

The science of mind-wandering is a delicate art: too much and you'll feel disorganized, but too little can lead to work burnout, mood disorders, and other health risks.[15] But by consciously shifting back and forth between focused attention and constructive daydreaming, you harness the power of your creative imagination.[16] Your motivation will increase while your stress level remains low.[17]

PILLAR#4: AWARENESS

For the first few years of life, your brain is concerned primarily with outer goals that bring immediate pleasure and satisfaction: the acquisition of toys, food, pleasure, comfort, and security. These pursuits are largely self-centered, with only minimal attention given to other people's needs. In fact, the neural circuits involved in self-awareness and social awareness, the insula and anterior cingulate (figure 1, above), won't become fully functional until a person is well into his or her third decade of life.[18] This explains why many young adults are oblivious to how their actions influence others. They have weak organizational skills and take greater risks, and since they have not fully developed the neurological capacity for empathy and moral reasoning, they often make costly mistakes when it comes to relationships and work.[19]

However, there is a way to speed up the development of self-awareness (the conscious knowledge of your character, personality, and everything else about you) and social awareness (the conscious knowledge of how your actions emotionally influence others) through a very simple process known as *mindfulness*, a form of brief meditation that strengthens the areas in your brain involved with confidence, optimism, emotional regulation, happiness, self-love, and compassion for others.[20] Mindfulness is an awareness-enhancement strategy, and all you have to do to practice it is remain deeply relaxed, bringing your attention into the present moment as you notice the creative dreamlike processes that quietly go on in the background of your mind.

Try it right now. Close your eyes and sit quietly for a few minutes. Is your mind completely silent, or do you find that thoughts and feelings seem to automatically jump into your consciousness? The longer you sit there and allow your mind to wander, the more you'll realize there is a seemingly endless stream of thoughts and feelings flowing in and out of your consciousness. But if you are patient, observing the feelings, thoughts, and sensations without judging them—just allowing them to be present and allowing yourself to remain present as you observe—you'll slowly begin to experience a growing sense of clarity and serenity. Researchers at Wake Forest University School of Medicine found that just three or four days of practicing mindfulness improves cognition and reduces anxiety, depression, pain, and fatigue.[21] It also allows you to discern different hierarchical levels of awareness that influence nearly every aspect of your life:

1. Awareness of bodily sensations
2. Awareness of positive and negative thoughts
3. Awareness of positive and negative feelings
4. Awareness of old habits and behaviors
5. Awareness of your own self-image and self-esteem
6. Awareness of your belief systems

7. Awareness of your purpose and values
8. Awareness of other people's thoughts and feelings
9. Awareness of the social consequences of your actions
10. And finally, awareness of awareness itself

Beginning in the next chapter, and throughout this book, we'll introduce you to many variations of mindfulness, showing you how to take brief moments throughout the workday to remain calm, relaxed, and highly focused on achieving more goals with little stress. We'll show you how to use mindfulness to turn a tedious activity into a pleasurable experience, and we'll take you through a variety of mindfulness-based NeuroWisdom exercises that will transform negativity into optimism as you rapidly increase your confidence, self-esteem, and empathy toward others. In chapter 10, we'll guide you through a series of formal exercises to prepare you for the most challenging—and rewarding—of all the NeuroWisdom strategies: *social mindfulness.*

Mindfulness makes you more consciously aware of all four of the Pillars of Wealth and how they shape your life. The more you practice mindfulness, the more you begin to realize that you are not your thoughts. At that moment, you become aware that there is a different you that constantly remains observant, non-judgmental, and calm. In this heightened state of awareness, you'll begin to have small "aha" experiences that give you sudden insights into different aspects of your life. These experiences transcend everyday logic and reason, and with each insight, your brain will actually reorganize itself, becoming more functional, productive, and efficient.[22]

Mindfulness is one of the few strategies that will give you access to the intuitive powers of your brain. Intuition is very different from the type of thinking you use when analyzing problems and making everyday decisions (Pillar Two), and the process is controlled by unique neurons found in the insula and anterior cingulate, the same areas that process social dilemmas and spiritual concerns.[23] Intuitive reasoning is one of the most powerful wealth-building skills you can develop, and mindfulness appears to be the most effective way to access it.

Self-awareness opens the door to social awareness, and as you mindfully observe other people, you'll begin to intuitively grasp what they need and want. Empathy and tolerance for others will increase,[24] but if you fail to develop these social skills, others will perceive you as selfish and will often take steps to get in the way of, or sabotage, your efforts to succeed. It's a neurological process called altruistic punishment, a quality that is genetically rooted in every human brain, making sure that we, as fellow human beings, are biologically motivated to treat other people fairly.[25]

Mindfulness can also be used to help you discover what your deepest values are, and thus what gives your life more meaning, purpose, and satisfaction.[26] When your values are not aligned with your goals and work, neural stress increases, happiness fades away, and burnout is more likely to occur.[27]

In the past, this form of awareness was considered a *spiritual* quality, but because mindfulness is theologically neutral it can be easily integrated into formal education, as we do in our Executive MBA NeuroLeadership course at Loyola Marymount University. Today mindfulness exercises are being taught in many psychology and business schools, and the benefits have been so robust that programs have been created for every level of education. For example, when a five-week mindfulness-based awareness program was introduced to children in kindergarten and elementary school, classroom behaviors dramatically improved. Students increased their ability to pay attention, exhibited greater self-control, and demonstrated more care and respect for others.[28] Because these same improvements are seen in adults, many educators consider mindfulness to be one of the most important skills that busy professionals need to learn.[29] Even the founders of Google created their own mindfulness-based meditation program, which includes many of the exercises that we will begin teaching you in chapter 3.[30]

In a comprehensive overview of the research on mindfulness, the following benefits are cited:[31]

- Decreased stress
- Improved self-esteem
- Increased well-being
- Decreased reactivity to negative thoughts, feelings, and experiences
- Enhanced immune and health functions
- Improved cognition and decision-making skills
- Enhanced attentiveness and less distractibility
- Increased self-awareness and body awareness
- Compassion, empathy, and understanding of others

Mindfulness brings you into the present moment so you can fully experience this astonishing world and the amazing people you share it with. When you develop this unique awareness tool and apply it to your work and personal life, your motivation increases, you'll make better decisions, and your creativity will soar. That is the formula for creating inner and outer wealth.

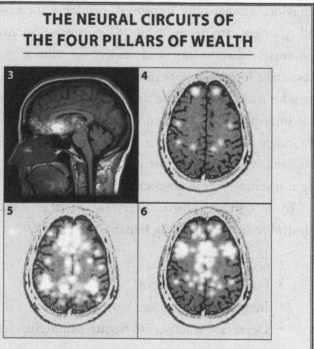

THE NEURAL CIRCUITS OF THE FOUR PILLARS OF WEALTH

Figure 3. Motivation; Figure 4. Decision Making; Figure 5. Creativity; Figure 6. Social Awareness.

These illustrations will help give you a visual sense of what parts of your brain you use for each of the Four Pillars of Wealth. Every hour, throughout the day, these neural circuits interact with each other, turning on and off as you pursue different goals, activities, and interactions with others. But remember, each person's brain is different, and each circuit can strengthen or weaken its connections with other parts of the brain.

MOTIVATION: The First Pillar of Wealth. It is controlled by the nucleus accumbens, located below the neocortex in both hemispheres of the brain (figure 3). When activated by something that is potentially desirable or pleasurable, dopamine is released, which then travels to the lower parts of the frontal lobe, preparing your brain to consciously find ways to satiate that desire. For example, when you see something or someone who is pleasantly attractive, you will feel a biological urge to approach that person or object.

DECISION MAKING: The Second Pillar of Wealth. Figure 4 (looking down through the skull at the neocortex) shows the areas that are most active as you make plans to achieve a specific goal. Many areas of the brain become inactive as the dorsolateral prefrontal cortex (the two white circles at the top of the picture) become more active. This is the center of your *conscious* awareness. Small areas in the motor cortex also begin to be activated (the small white areas in the middle of the picture), preparing your body to take action. Several areas in the parietal lobe are also active, helping you to orient yourself with the world (the four white areas in the lower part of the brain image). For example, after you initially find yourself drawn to an attractive person or object, your brain begins to imagine different ways of "acquiring" the object of desire, or solving a problem that interferes with you getting it, and the more you become conscious of these inner fantasies, the better you can consciously choose which action to take.

CREATIVITY: The Third Pillar of Wealth. When your brain needs to rest, your mind begins to wander and daydream. The decision-making centers in figure 4 turn off, and many other areas throughout your brain become more active, especially in the frontal, parietal, and visual cortex (the white areas at the top and bottom of figure 5). Also known as the default mode network, this is where imagination and creative problem solving takes place. Most people are unaware of this inner process, but if you relax and mindfully observe those seemingly chaotic thoughts and feelings, you'll often discover new ways to pursue your desires and goals. The more you consciously interact with these inner creative processes, the more you'll enjoy the challenges of creating inner and outer wealth.

AWARENESS: The Fourth Pillar of Wealth. Self-knowledge and social awareness (empathy, fairness, self-acceptance, kindness toward others, etc.) are regulated by two key structures in your social brain: the insula (the white outer areas in the upper middle portion of figure 6) and the anterior cingulate (the large white area between the two lobes of the insula). The connections between the insula and anterior cingulate extend into the frontal lobe areas of consciousness and into the emotional centers deep within your brain (the white areas in the lower half of figure 5). This is the circuitry of your social brain that takes decades to fully mature. As we'll explain in the last chapter of this book, taking a few minutes every day to reflect on how your actions influence others will insure that you *and the people you engage with* experience more satisfaction in life.

The practice of mindfulness is one of the best ways to become aware of your creativity and the social impact you have on others. Mindfulness strengthens the neural connectivity between Pillars Two, Three, and Four. The result: you'll begin to take greater interest in the welfare of others.

Brain-Based Experiential Learning and Living (BELL)

Despite the enormous advances made in science and psychology, society's approach to education hasn't changed much in the last 200 years. At the elementary and high school levels, people traditionally rely on what we call the four R's of reading, writing, arithmetic, and *repetition*, where teachers often overwhelm a child's brain with information that often has no personal meaning or immediate relevance to their life.

Yes, we are preparing these young minds to tackle the complexities of an adult world, but what about creativity, imagination, and intuition? Other than an occasional art or literature class, these core skills are rarely addressed until you enter college, where professors sometimes demand innovation and original thinking. Even at the university level, knowledge is fractured into individual subjects (psychology, business, engineering, etc.), with few models to help students integrate these disparate parts into their lives. Nobody teaches them how to reflect on their inner processes of awareness, or how to tap into the intuitive and creative processes of their brain.

Recent neuroscientific evidence suggests that there are at least eight core strategies that will enhance every work environment. We call this new education model Brain-Based Experiential Learning and Living, or BELL, and we recommend that you incorporate these principles into your daily life and work routine. Each will help sharpen your decision-making and problem-solving skills. They will also deepen your awareness and enhance your satisfaction while working. BELL begins with conscious relaxation, a strategy that is rarely brought into the classroom or work environment:

BELL PRINCIPLE #1: RELAX!

To maintain the highest levels of productivity and performance, you must briefly pause to deeply relax—even for just a few seconds—several times an hour.[32] As we explained before, the brain loses concentration quickly, and any form of stress will disrupt the normal functioning of your brain. As stress levels go down, neurological pleasure and motivation increase.[33]

There are two basic forms of stress—physical and mental—but surprisingly very few people know how to effectively relax their bodies or brains. In the next chapter, we'll show you how to do this in under 60 seconds, and briefly explain the neuroscience behind these two unusual strategies: yawning and superslow stretching. If you can remember to do just these two things several times an hour, you'll significantly enhance your capacity to work. That's why relaxation is the most important factor for managing any form of stress.[34]

Relaxation is a core strategy for increasing motivation—the First Pillar of Wealth—and it also triggers the creative circuits in your brain, the Third Pillar of Wealth.

BELL PRINCIPLE #2: VISUALIZE YOUR GOAL, OBSTACLES, AND SOLUTIONS

In order to carry out specific plans and move toward specific goals in the world, the brain heavily depends on visual cues to guide you toward pleasure and away from pain. The more you develop your ability to visualize what you desire, the easier it becomes to reach that goal, and the more you visualize obstacles that stand in your way, the easier it becomes to develop strategies to reach your intended goal.[35] Most people have discovered that writing their thoughts down (e.g. goals, obstacles, solutions, etc.) helps greatly to visualize them.

Visualizing goals and obstacles will improve your academic performance,[36] will give you more energy and stamina,[37] will help you manage difficult emotions,[38] and will facilitate concentration, problem solving, and positive changes in behavior.[39] In other words, visualization is a core strategy for decision making, the Second Pillar of Wealth.

BELL PRINCIPLE #3: CONCENTRATE ON YOUR TASK

After visualizing your goal and the steps you'll need to take to achieve it, you'll need to fully concentrate on your task. Many of the sensory and emotional processing centers in your brain become inactive and any form of distraction— or too much stress—will interfere with your performance and productivity.

Anxiety and procrastination will also undermine your ability to stay focused on your work. In the next chapter, we'll show you how to intensify your concentration in under a minute by focusing on a specific sound, object, or body sensation. Then, when you throw yourself back into work, your clarity and decision-making skills will be enhanced.

BELL PRINCIPLE #4: DAYDREAM

Daydreaming is part of the brain's creative process, the Third Pillar of Wealth, but most children are criticized by teachers when their minds begin to wander in class. These teachers don't know that this is a natural process that occurs every few minutes, one that is essential for learning new information.[40] As researchers at the University of Edinburgh discovered, just a couple minutes of restful daydreaming after learning something new will boost your memory.[41]

Mind-wandering has such a bad reputation that most people resist the impulse to daydream, especially when they are at work. Rather than fight this impulse, we encourage you to deliberately daydream for very brief periods whenever you feel stressed or are struggling with a difficult problem or emotional issue. Not only will it improve your mood,[42] when you return to your work, you'll remain focused for a longer period of time.

Mind-wandering facilitates introspection[43]—a form of awareness associated with the Fourth Pillar of Wealth—and it's also a necessary component for problem solving because it allows your brain to imagine new ways to improve future outcomes.[44] When you set aside a minute or two once an hour to consciously daydream, you'll learn quicker, you'll do better on tests, you'll solve problems better, and your overall work performance will be enhanced.[45] But don't overdo it. Research shows that too much mind-wandering impairs sleep quality and cognitive performance.[46]

BELL PRINCIPLE #5: INTUIT

Logic and reason are important elements in education, problem solving, and goal achievement, but there are additional cognitive processes that are needed to build inner and outer wealth. They involve nonverbal levels of awareness, and the only way to access this level of consciousness is to interrupt the normal way you think and feel. The neurological doorway to your intuition, as we explained earlier, is through increased awareness of yourself and others, which is the Fourth Pillar of Wealth.

Intuition is not a language-based process but more of what psychologists call a "felt sense"[47]—an impressionistic or gut-level feeling that helps the brain solve problems in a highly efficient way. Whereas most decision-making processes of our Second Pillar of Wealth involve the language centers of the frontal lobe,[48] intuition engages many neurological processes that happen "behind the curtain" of everyday consciousness. However, when you deliberately turn your attention to these subconscious whispers, you'll just seem to instantly know the right answer or action—which often turns out to be the best thing to do. Intuition transcends logic and reason, and the more you use mindfulness as a way to tap into these creative processes of the brain, the more you'll enhance all your decision-making skills.[49]

BELL PRINCIPLE #6: ANCHOR YOURSELF

Relaxing, visualizing, concentrating, daydreaming, and intuitively reflecting on the creative processes of your mind are four core learning strategies that will improve your work performance. But if you don't have an *external reminder* and an *internal cue* to engage these new tools, your brain can easily ignore the subtle symptoms of stress. The most effective external reminder is an unexpected or unfamiliar sound, like a bell.[50] For this reason, we recommend that you use one of the following websites where you can program a mindfulness clock that will ring a bell at regular intervals throughout the day:

- www.fungie.info
- www.dejal.com/timeout
- www.mindfulnessdc.org/bell

There are also dozens of similar apps that you can load onto your phone, or you can simply use the phone's timer. However, the more pleasant the sound, the more quickly you can train your brain to automatically refresh itself when you are concentrating intensely while hard at work.

The mindfulness clock is your anchor—a reminder to regularly pause, relax, and refocus on your goal. We recommend that you download the clock as soon as possible and begin experimenting with different settings. Try this one first: Have the bell ring one or two times an hour. The first two times you hear it, just pause for 10 seconds to yawn and slowly stretch. On the third ring, take 60 seconds to daydream or do something pleasurable. Then throw yourself back into work. Our Executive MBA students have found this to be one of the most useful tools for keeping their stress levels low, and a recent study confirms that focusing on the sound of a resonant bell enhances the relaxation process of your body and your brain.[51]

After using the bell for 60–90 days, these BELL strategies will become an automatic behavior deeply embedded into the memory circuits of your brain.[52] Taking these brief, restful pauses while learning and working will enable your brain to embed information in your long-term memory and solve problems with greater ease.[53]

In chapter 2, we'll show you other anchoring strategies using inner values, power words, and focusing on the sensation of your breathing. These will become inner cues that will stimulate the neural circuits described in the Four Pillars of Wealth.

BELL PRINCIPLE #7: ENJOY

It may seem obvious, but without enjoyment, life loses most of its purpose and meaning. Pleasure and enjoyment are the intrinsic rewards you reap whenever you accomplish something or reach a specific goal, and if you frequently reward yourself—physically, emotionally, socially, or verbally through expressions of self-appreciation—throughout the workday, your brain will be more motivated to work harder and pursue bigger goals.[54] Even the anticipation of a reward improves mood, motivation, and decision-making skills.[55]

Here's an exercise you can do right now that will immediately boost your mood. Create a "Pleasure Board" by listing 20–30 simple activities that give you immediate pleasure. For example: rinsing your face with cool water, dancing to a favorite tune, massaging your scalp, thinking about someone or something you love, etc. Include activities that pleasurably stimulate as many of your senses as possible, including your mind. Separately, write down 10 of the most enjoyable experiences you've had in your life.

By the time you've completed the lists, you should feel the pleasurable effects of dopamine being released into your brain, and if you keep your Pleasure Board posted by your workstation, with the internal promise that you will allow yourself to enjoy several of them throughout the day, you'll see a discernable improvement in the quality of your work. So whenever you are feeling tired or stressed out, give yourself a pleasure break and immerse yourself in one of your enjoyable activities. It takes less than a minute to refresh your brain and increase your desire to work, and if you choose rewards that bring pleasure to others as well, brain-scan research shows you'll be building long-term satisfaction and happiness.[56]

BELL PRINCIPLE #8: MAINTAIN UNWAVERING OPTIMISM

No matter what obstacle you face, the more optimistic you feel, the more motivated you'll become.[57] There are many solutions to any problem that will bring you comfort or peace of mind (including surrender and acceptance). We will teach you how to alter the naturally pessimistic tendencies of cognitive awareness and literally build stronger neural circuits of optimism. There are over 100 published studies showing that optimism is essential for physical and emotional health. For example, optimists have been found to live two years longer than pessimists.[58]

So when negative thoughts creep into your consciousness, just write them down on a sheet of paper. Then take a minute to deeply relax as you mindfully gaze at the negative words on the page. Don't react; just observe. Within minutes the worrisome feelings will subside. You'll see that most of them aren't real—they're not actually happening in the present moment—and for the few that are, you'll be able to use your imagination, creativity, and daydreaming skills to find intuitive solutions to problems that would normally be difficult for you to resolve. That's the power of using these simple BELL principles.

Motivation begins in the nucleus accumbens (**NA**) which releases dopamine to wake up your frontal lobe (**FL**) in preparation for conscious decision-making. When your brain gets tired, concentration fades and creative processes take over, stimulating hundreds of additional areas throughout the brain. If you train yourself to mindfully observe your creative imagination, the insula and anterior cingulate become activated (**I/AC**). Your self-awareness increases, selfishness decreases, and social empathy is enhanced. Stress levels drop, productivity increases, and others are more likely to trust you. Cooperation increases as mutually beneficial goals are more easily achieved.

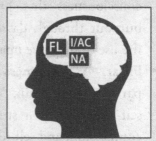

Figure 7.

CHAPTER SUMMARY

To achieve any important goal in life, you need to master four neurological processes: motivation, decision making, creativity, and awareness—awareness of yourself and your ability to be compassionately aware of the needs of others. If you do not exercise these four qualities or "pillars" of wealth-building on a daily basis, you will limit your ability to turn your goals, wishes, and dreams into reality.

- **Pillar #1: Motivation** is your brain's instinctual drive to survive and acquire anything that is new, different, and potentially valuable. When this occurs, the brain releases dopamine, a pleasure chemical that increases your conscious ability to take action and achieve your goal.

- **Pillar #2: Decision Making** happens in your frontal lobe. It involves habitual behaviors, it regulates mood, and it helps to keep you focused on your desired goal. Because decision making can be disrupted by stress, worry, and doubt, you need to train your brain to stay focused, confident, and optimistic.

- **Pillar #3: Creativity** involves a unique state of consciousness that prevents mental exhaustion and burnout through daydreaming, mind-wandering, and the use of intuitive imagination to solve problems.

- **Pillar #4: Awareness** takes advantage of the newest parts of your brain. When you mindfully engage in self-reflection, you stimulate the circuits of empathy, compassion, and self-love. You become more self-aware, more socially aware, and more spiritually aware of your values, allowing you to meet the needs of others as well as your own. Mutual trust and cooperation grow, and work becomes more meaningful, purposeful, and satisfying, enabling you to achieve true happiness, success, and wealth (both inner and outer).

The Eight Principles of Brain-Based Experiential Learning and Living (BELL) are part of a new educational model used in the NeuroLeadership course at Loyola Marymount University in Los Angeles. These strategies have been shown to reduce stress and improve performance at home and work.

1. Relax your mind and body several times an hour while learning or working.

2. Visualize your goals, obstacles, and solutions throughout your workday.
3. Learn how to deeply concentrate and maintain focus on your task.
4. Daydream once or twice an hour for 60 seconds to enhance memory and problem-solving abilities.
5. Integrate your intuition with logic and reason.
6. Every hour, anchor mindfulness in your mind and body with sensory cues and value-based words.
7. Integrate pleasure and enjoyable activity breaks into your work schedule.
8. Maintain unwavering optimism, no matter what.

CHAPTER 3.

Preparing to Succeed: 60-Second Strategies for Warming Up Your Brain

The moment you wake up, the most ancient parts of your brain begin to drive you toward specific goals that will bring pleasure, nurturance, and security. This is the First Pillar of Wealth—but we usually are unaware of this instinctual motivational process. Instead, we jump right into our hurried habits as we prepare ourselves for work, not realizing that we are missing an important opportunity to increase our workday productivity. If, however, you remain in bed for a few extra seconds to become aware of your body and your mental state, your brain will function much better for the rest of the day. You'll accomplish more goals with less stress.

Nearly every mammal and bird will do two things when

44

they awake: they slowly stretch their bodies and they yawn. The stretching eliminates any physical tension and the yawning helps their brain become more focused and alert.

We recommend that you do a similar ritual every morning. Instead of jumping out of bed the moment you open your eyes, take a few seconds to feel the sheets as you take a mental and physical inventory of your body: Do you feel calm or anxious? Do you feel tired or refreshed? Do you feel any aches or pains? Pay particular attention to the pleasurable sensations in your body because this stimulates the motivation centers in your brain, which is the First Pillar of Wealth. The more pleasure you can generate, the more your brain will want to take action in the world. Next, visualize what you want to accomplish that day and imagine yourself overcoming the obstacles that stand in your way. This simple technique has been proven to increase your physical and mental energy in ways that help you reach those goals with efficiency and ease.[1] When you take a few moments to fully visualize your intentions and the possibility of success, your brain becomes more adept at turning your intentions into reality.[2]

Now you are ready to get out of bed, and when you do, take another few moments to yawn a few times and slowly stretch. By doing this simple morning ritual, you'll be stimulating neurons in your brain that enhance the fourth Pillar of Wealth—awareness—as you build emotional resilience that will carry over into the rest of your day.

The Fastest Way to Lower Mental Stress

Olympic athletes yawn before they race, musicians and

Figure 8.

speakers yawn before they go on stage, snipers are trained to yawn before they pull the trigger, and pack animals yawn together to establish communal empathy. Yawning can even play an important role in the workplace. For example, one of our Executive MBA (EMBA) students regularly asks her argumentative board of directors to yawn before an important discussion because it brings the entire room to order in less than 60 seconds. Even the Library of Congress has documentation (figure 8) showing that yawning was an exercise used by elementary school teachers in the 1890s, and we found evidence that yawning before a test can improve your grade point average in school.[3]

Why is yawning so important? It clears away the fogginess of sleep and increases cerebral blood flow, which enhances mental efficiency and quickly brings you into a heightened state of cognitive awareness.[4] In fact, yawning appears to be the fastest way to lower mental stress and anxiety.[5] It has a similar effect as having a cup of coffee,[6] and it regulates the clock in your brain, helping you to sleep better at night!

Yawning helps you to wake up and stay alert during a stressful workday,[7] and it helps your brain quickly shift between the highly focused demands of decision making and the restful daydreaming state that gives you access to creative problem-solving skills.[8] Numerous neurochemicals that are essential for motivation, memory recall, and voluntary decision making are released during the yawning experience.[9] In fact, it's hard to find another activity that positively impacts so many of your brain's functions. So if you want to maintain an optimally healthy brain, make it a habit to yawn whenever you want to relax or enhance your ability to concentrate on a task.

---

10 REASONS TO YAWN FREQUENTLY

1. Stimulates alertness and concentration
2. Optimizes brain activity and metabolism
3. Improves cognitive function
4. Increases memory recall
5. Enhances consciousness and introspection
6. Lowers stress
7. Relaxes your upper body
8. Fine-tunes your sense of time
9. Increases empathy and social awareness
10. Enhances pleasure and sensuality

Yawning also appears to be a primitive form of empathy that can be found in many mammals, and there is even a connection between frequent yawning and increased emotional empathy.[10] That's why we recommend that you yawn a few times before entering a stressful business meeting or discussing a sensitive issue with another colleague.

Our advice is to yawn as many times a day as possible: when you wake up, when you're confronting a difficult problem at work, and whenever you feel anger, anxiety, or stress. Yawn before giving an important talk, yawn before you take a test, and yawn whenever you feel bored. But do it mindfully, paying close attention to how it affects your mood and awareness.

Conscious yawning takes a little discipline to get past our social conditioning that it is rude, along with the excuses that people sometimes use: "I don't feel like it," "I'm not tired," and a favorite, "I can't." Of course you can. All you need to do to trigger a deep yawn is to fake it four or five times. Try it right now, and you'll see how each yawn feels more pleasant and relaxing.

A Mindful Yawning Experiment

This exercise only takes two minutes, and works better if you are standing up. Begin by taking a slow, deep breath, and then yawn. You can fake yawns at first, and if you make an "ahh" sound during exhalation you should be able to trigger a series of real yawns on your fourth or fifth try.

As you continue to yawn, pay close attention to the sensations in your mouth, your throat, your chest, and belly, and don't be surprised if your eyes start watering. If you feel dizzy, lightheaded, or disoriented, stop, sit down, and rest. Continue to yawn another 10 or 12 times, and then pause, noticing the different body sensations you are having. Do you feel more relaxed and alert? If you feel tired, it probably means that you are exhausted from overwork. If you've been particularly stressed or anxious, you might find yourself yawning a great deal over the next half hour, or even throughout the day after you've tried this yawning experiment. It means that your brain needs more blood circulation to improve neural performance. Enjoy the yawns, knowing that they're a special treat for your busy brain.

> ## BONUS EXERCISE:
> ## MINDFUL AWARENESS OF OBJECTS
>
> Close your eyes, right now, and create a mental image of the room you are sitting in. See how many objects you can visualize, and as you gaze at this imaginary landscape, notice how it makes you feel.
>
> Now open your eyes and look at all the objects that actually surround you. Pick one item and study it closely, as if you were seeing it for the very first time. Immerse yourself in its shape, noticing the texture, the colors, the shadows and the contours. Close your eyes again and visualize the details of that object. Now turn your attention to your body and notice the subtle sensations you are feeling.
>
> Open your eyes and look around the room. Notice how everything seems more rich, intense, and three-dimensional. You have just used mindfulness to enhance your *perceptual* awareness of the world.

The Fastest Way to Physically Relax

When you are working hard, your brain is focusing on a specific task. Because body awareness all but disappears at these times, you won't notice when stress and tension are building up. But, if you remind yourself to do just one slow stretch and a couple of yawns several times an hour, your stress level will remain low. Yawning and stretching cause the release of dopamine,[11] the "juice" that keeps work-related motivation high.[12] Mindful stretching increases your body awareness, and this has been shown to give you greater emotional control along with higher levels of personal satisfaction and well-being.[13] The research also demonstrates that if you slowly move one part of your body, paying close attention to all the subtle associated sensations, muscle tension will diminish rapidly and movement coordination will improve.[14] Here's a simple experiment we'd like you to try:

First, turn and twist your torso in the way you would normally stretch your body. Then remain still and notice how you feel. Usually, most people will spend about 5 or 10 seconds to stretch out their neck or back, but I want you to see what happens when you take a full 30 seconds to turn your torso and your head to your right side, and another 30 seconds to turn your body and head back to center. When you do *superslow* movements you'll experience many more subtle aches and pains. This is the information your brain needs to send a relaxation signal to each of the tense muscles in your body. Take a moment to notice how different your left side feels compared to your right side.

Next, *imagine* yourself turning slowly to the left side, and then take a full 30 seconds to actually turn your body and head to the left, and another 30 seconds to come back to center. Again, notice how different everything feels. If you do this same stretch in 5 or 10 minutes, you'll notice far less pain and greater ease of movement, a fact that has been demonstrated in many slow-movement studies.[15] It is the *awareness* of your body, brought about by very slow movement, that is the key element for relieving pain and increasing your sense of well-being.[16] Other studies have shown that slow-movement exercises like yoga, Feldenkrais, and Tai Chi will reduce anxiety and depression and improve your overall mood.[17]

The Easiest Way to Enhance Awareness

Breathing awareness is another way to optimize the performance of your brain, and many people assume that deep breathing is the best way to relax. But the opposite is true: deep breathing energizes you and can even increase anxiety and stress,[18] whereas slow, regulated conscious breathing—known as mindful breathing—gives you greater control over your entire nervous system, allowing you to more fully relax.[19]

Try this simple exercise now: slowly and gently breathe in through your nose as you count to three, and then breathe out slowly, again counting to three. This has a powerful calming effect on your nervous system and has similar neurological benefits as yawning.[20]

Only One Mindful Breath a Day Is Needed

Most people believe that it takes months to become proficient at meditation or mindfulness, but brain-scan studies tell a different story: awareness can be mastered in a matter of minutes. You don't have to sit on a cushion for an hour a day, and it doesn't matter what posture you assume. All you have to do is commit to taking a single conscious breath once each day. This suggestion comes from Chade-Meng Tan, the creator of Google's mindfulness training program. His program includes leading psychologists and neuroscientists,[21] and he emphasizes this important concept: "The *intention* to meditate is itself a meditation."

The following will demonstrate this for you: Sit upright in your chair and turn your full attention to your breathing. Keeping your mouth closed, notice how the cool air feels as you breathe in, and then notice how the warm air feels as you breathe out. Do this as many times as you like, paying attention to all the subtle pleasurable sensations you experience.

Now place one hand on your chest and the other hand on your belly. As you breathe through your mouth, notice how your chest and belly rise and fall. Immerse yourself in these sensations for as long as you wish, becoming aware of the ways in which your breathing affects the different parts of your body. The more deeply absorbed you become, the more you are training your brain to remain focused and emotionally calm. It's one of the easiest ways to improve the functioning of your brain, improving your concentration,[22] reducing anxiety and depression,[23] and increasing your ability to stay focused on tasks and goals for longer periods of time.[24]

Remember, when it comes to meditation, keep it pleasurable, knowing that even a single minute of mindfulness per day will improve the quality of your life.

Anchor Yourself with a Single Word

Anchoring is one of the key principles in brain-based experiential learning, and an anchor is anything you use to remind yourself to stay calm, relaxed, and pleasurably engaged in an activity. As we mentioned in the previous chapter, having a mindfulness clock installed on your computer or cell phone is the easiest way to remind you to take several brief breaks an hour to yawn, stretch, or mindfully focus on a single breath. Any of these strategies take only a few seconds to do—that's all it takes to reduce physical stress and mental fatigue. The brain refreshes itself as dopamine is released, and this allows you to resume your work with increased concentration and clarity.

Another useful anchoring tool involves repeating a single word that holds deep meaning for you. It's one of the first homework assignments we give our Executive MBA students on their first day of class, and I think you will find it worthwhile to try right now. It combines the above steps (as will most of the exercises in this book) and then adds another brain-based learning strategy that is associated with the creative elements of the third Pillar of Wealth: listening to your intuition.

Let's begin. Close your eyes and take a few seconds to deeply relax. Bring your attention to your natural breathing. Then yawn and very slowly stretch. When your mind feels calm, ask yourself this question: "What is my deepest *innermost* value?" Don't use your analytical mind to think about the question, just pay attention to the first word that comes closest to reflecting a value that has great meaning for you. Write that word down, and then ask yourself the same question: "What is my *deepest* innermost value?" Listen for that small intuitive voice, and if a different word comes to mind, write it down. If nothing occurs to you, as will sometimes happen, don't fret. Just enjoy the quietness that comes from being mindful and momentarily thought-free. Take another slow breath, yawning and stretching to deepen your relaxation, and ask yourself the same question one more time: "What is my deepest innermost *value*?" See what word intuitively comes to mind this time, and write it down. Gaze at the three words on your paper and focus on the word that has the most emotional impact for you. Repeat it silently and notice how it makes you feel.

That's all you have to do. With our EMBA students, we intentionally don't define what a value is, nor do we offer suggestions from the hundreds of value words available. We thus encourage our busy executives to use the more creative part of their brain to generate new thoughts and ideas. We ask our students to spend one minute every morning, before going to work, to practice this "inner values exercise." At the end of the 10 days, our EMBA students are given the following questions to answer and turn in as a homework assignment:

1. What was your initial reaction to this exercise?
2. Was the exercise enjoyable, boring, interesting, annoying, etc.?
3. How long did you spend, each day, contemplating your inner values?
4. Did the exercise have any effect on other aspects of your day, work, or life?
5. How do you define the word "value"?
6. Did you discover anything about yourself?
7. Did the exercise influence the way you think about your work and business values?

Over the past six years, virtually all our EMBA students chose to do the inner values exercise and 90% came to the same conclusion: this brief 60-second exercise lowers stress levels throughout their entire day of work.[25] Nearly everyone finds the exercise useful, enlightening, and enjoyable, but it doesn't always start out that way for all students. For example, one class member—a chief operating officer at a midsize corporation—put it bluntly: "What the *#!* does this have to do with financial planning?" But by the fourth day, this same EMBA student wrote the following comment: "I found myself so focused at work I now think it should be required for every MBA student in America."

Busy executives hate to take any time off of work, which is why we've designed most of our exercises to take less than a minute. If it only takes 10 seconds to yawn or stretch or reflect on an inner value word, we get a very high rate of compliance. But we discovered—through trial and error over the past six years—that requesting anything that took longer than 60 seconds met with resistance. We also discovered that more people will experiment with these NeuroWisdom exercises if they are optional, not required, and we want to make the same recommendation to you: do only those exercises that you *want* to do, and only those that feel the most useful and pleasurable.

Some of our EMBA students have used the inner values exercise to build teamwork within their companies and to improve the quality of communication with their colleagues. They do this by asking the members of their group to share their deepest relationship and communication values. The result: you can actually see a marked improvement throughout the entire group, and when you repeat your value words before entering an important discussion, they will protect you from being knocked off balance when disagreements arise. When John, a foreman at a multi-million dollar construction firm, did the inner values exercise for 10 days, he found a new way to deal with his belligerent boss:

> I hadn't put much focus on values in the past, but as I started reflecting on love—my highest value—I realized how much animosity I felt toward my boss. By the third day of my values experiment, I started feeling kindness toward him. I began to let go of my anger because I saw that he was only doing his job. Then I started feeling gratitude, because he was the one who gave me my job.

Cheri Frootko, a South African film director and script supervisor, saw the inner values exercise on YouTube and decided to try it with her crew:

> We created a fun routine. We yawned and stretched and shook our hands. We envisioned our value words and then, in a spirit of lightheartedness, we shared them with each other. The result? Ten people, who a week earlier were total strangers, created a bond of insight and intimacy. And it wouldn't have happened without this three-minute catalyst. We would have worked well without the exercise—say, on a level of six—but with our sharing of values, the group reached a level of nine.

At a famous restaurant in Northern California, the manager did the inner values exercise with the waitresses and the cooking staff. When they shared their values with each other, a huge smile spread across everyone's face. Team cooperation instantly improved. It even works for adolescents: when students completed a 10-minute exercise describing their personal values, the researchers saw strong increases in positive social behavior that continued for three months![26] So why not experiment with our inner values exercise with your colleagues, family, and friends? You'll be surprised how this simple exercise can improve social dynamics and awareness.

According to researchers at the University of California, "Reflecting on personal values can keep neuroendocrine and psychological responses to stress at low levels."[27] It is truly amazing that a single word can improve the health of your brain and that repeating it throughout the day can turn on thousands of stress-reducing and immune-enhancing genes.[28] You'll protect yourself from burnout at work, you'll reduce your propensity to ruminate on failure, and you'll be less reactive and less defensive when someone confronts you with uncomfortable information.[29]

Power Words

There's another application of this exercise that we recommend you try. Before you begin a specific task, ask yourself what would best capture the state of mind that would enhance your productivity. Some of our students call this a "power" word and examples include: "focus," "confidence," "calm," "clarity," or "win." These words are different from those that reflect our deepest personal values, words like "compassion," "family," "God," "peace," "integrity," etc. These self-affirmations help give your life deeper meaning and a sense of purpose, whereas power words help your brain to stay anchored on a state of mind that is free from emotional distractions. As researchers at Clarkson University discovered, "self-affirmation produces large effects: even a simple reminder of one's core values reduces defensiveness" and helps you perform better at work.[30]

Here's a simple formula for creating an affirmation using your inner values and power words, a favorite NeuroWisdom exercise among our EMBA students. Think about a positive quality you want to emphasize at the beginning of each day, and a negative quality you would like to eliminate, and insert them into this phrase:

"I breathe in _____; I breathe out _____."

You can coordinate this affirmation with your breath, breathing in a positive quality and breathing out a negative quality. Or, if you prefer, they can both be positive. Repeat the expression throughout the day, and change the words to best address each new situation at work or at home. Examples:

- Feeling stressed?
  "I breathe in peace; I breathe out stress."
- Feeling angry?
  "I breathe in love; I breathe out rage."
- Feeling sad?
  "I breathe in happiness; I breathe out joy."
- Feeling frustrated with a loved one?
  "I breathe in peace; I breathe out love."
- Feeling overwhelmed?
  "I breathe in strength; I breathe out fear."
- Feeling anxious?
  "I breathe in trust; I breathe out confidence."

Anchor Yourself before Sleep

All too often we take our daily worries to bed with us, and it disturbs our sleep. To counter this neurologically detrimental behavior, there are several anchoring strategies that have been proven to enhance confidence and self-esteem. Just spend a few moments reflecting on all of the things you did well and all your accomplishments that day. Don't focus on any failure or negativity (it doesn't help to solve the problem, as we'll explain in chapter 6); just focus on the positives. Or reflect on three things for which you feel grateful. Do either or both of these exercises just before falling asleep, and your happiness and well-being will gradually increase over the next three months.[31] The author of these famous studies, Martin Seligman, who founded the field of positive psychology, also noted that these effects don't fade away. You are building permanent optimism as you prepare your mind for sleep. If you wake up at night, try repeating a value word that makes you feel relaxed, like "peace" or even "sleep."

The Basics

In 1979, when Jon Kabat-Zinn began documenting the benefits of his Mindfulness-Based Stress Reduction Program at the University of Massachusetts Medical School, students were instructed to spend 20–45 minutes each day engaging in a series of mental and physical exercises. Our research has shown that 10–12 minutes of any gentle form of meditation offers the same neurological and psychological benefits as 20–45 minutes. But busy people often balk when asked to spend 5 minutes doing a relaxation or focus exercise.

Nevertheless, of our EMBA students and the corporate teams we work with, we have found that nearly everyone will commit to one minute each morning to yawn, stretch, relax, and reflect on a personal value. We also suggest that they use their mindfulness clock at work (mentioned in chapter 2) to remind them once or twice an hour to spend 10–30 seconds to yawn, stretch, and focus on a work-related power word or value. The results: 90% make this commitment, and because they immediately feel more focused and energized, half of our students reported spending between 5–30 minutes every day creating different variations of the exercises we've described in this chapter.

So give it a try for the next 10 days: commit to 60 seconds of yawning, stretching, and values reflection. Experiment with the other strategies that are summarized below, but only do the ones that feel useful, and only do them as long as they feel pleasurable.

CHAPTER SUMMARY

Developing a peak-performance brain begins the moment you wake up. Use any of the following strategies to prepare your mind and body for a highly productive, low-stress day:

1. When you first wake up, take a moment to feel your body lying beneath the sheets. Take a brief mental inventory. Are you tired, calm or anxious? Take a few more seconds to scan your body. Does it feel tense

and achy, or relaxed? Spend a few moments focusing on various pleasurable sensations in your body.

2. Slowly get out of bed, and then yawn a few times.

3. In superslow motion, stretch your body. Select an inner value to emphasize during the day.

4. Commit to taking one mindful breath each day, paying attention to the different sensations and movements.

5. At work, select a power word that can help you stay focused on each specific goal or task. Create an affirmation with your inner values and power words: "I breathe in _____; I breathe out _____."

6. Whenever you feel stressed or tired at work, stop for 30 seconds to yawn, stretch, and reflect on your values and power words. Or do one of the activities on the Pleasure Board that was described in chapter 2. Use your mindfulness clock to remind you to take at least one stress-reduction break per hour while at work.

7. Before falling asleep, reflect on the things you did well that day and the things you feel grateful for.

The World Health Organization states that "a healthy working environment is one in which there is not only an absence of harmful conditions but an abundance of health-promoting ones."[32] They cite excessive stress as public enemy number one, and the long-term effects of stress can permanently damage your heart and brain.[33] The warm-up exercises presented in this chapter—as documented in research, classrooms, and work environments—are the fastest ways to lower physical, emotional, and mental stress in under a minute. Yawning, slowly stretching, focusing on a value or power word, or just taking a few seconds to observe a single breath or pleasurable body sensations will refresh your brain and improve the quality of your work. With practice and the help of a mindfulness clock, they can be easily integrated into your work schedule.

CHAPTER 4.

Motivation—The First Pillar of Wealth: Money, Pleasure, and the Desire to Acquire *More*

Desires.

They can be big or small. They can be easy, difficult, or sometimes impossible to attain. But without them, we couldn't survive. We wouldn't be motivated to go to work, or find a mate, or even get out of bed. Desires fuel the basic engine of the brain, and the bigger the brain, the greater the number of desires. But when it comes to the question of what we *really* desire, a very different process take place in our imagination. In fact, it's one of the most difficult questions to answer.

So aside from happiness and wealth, can you guess what someone else really desires? Interestingly, you have less than a 10% chance of guessing correctly, because everyone has a unique brain that is programmed with personal desires and shaped by unique past experiences.

Here's how some of our survey participants responded to the question, "What do you *really* desire?" Tim yearned for work that would stimulate his creative mind, and Carol longed for the soul mate of her dreams. George, who was the CEO of a large company, wished he had more time to spend with his family.

Others craved inner peace, a house by the beach, or the vacation of a lifetime. Parents wanted to see their children turn into responsible adults and retirees yearned for long-term health. Some expressed poetic and spiritual desires, like Lea, who wanted to "rest in God without expectations," or Val, who wanted to "be free from the illusions of ego." Jim, however, just wanted to be free from depression.

Others had global desires, like Jorge, who wanted to "eradicate poverty from the planet," or Selina, a North African refugee who dreamed of living in a free society. Wisdom, joy, success, fun, serenity, abundance, inspiration, purpose, passion, security, legacy, completeness, warmth, understanding—these are just a few of the desires that our survey participants said they wanted the most. And the five top desires? Love, peace, happiness, health, and wealth. But when it comes to our *neurological* desires, we really want it all, and it doesn't seem to matter how much we have. Wealthy people want more wealth, happy people want more happiness, and peaceful people want everyone on the planet to live in peace.

Desire, Greed, and Fairness

When we asked our survey participants to rate how happy they were with their lives, and how satisfied they were with their current income (using a 1–10 scale) a wide range of responses came in. A few people rated their happiness and wealth very low, a few rated them very high, and most rated themselves somewhere in the middle. But when we asked them how much *more* they wanted, nearly everyone, rich or poor, wrote down a 10 for both happiness and wealth. They wanted more of everything—money, friends, health, vacations—*much* more.

This statistic tells an intriguing tale: when it comes to filling our heart's desire, we never feel we have enough. But it's a double-edged sword, one that explains why so many people, deep down inside, feel unsatisfied with their lives. Our insatiable desire for more comes from an ancient evolutionary process—based on past threats to survival—that biases all living organisms, including humans, toward greed and selfishness. But as we mentioned in chapter 1, selfish desires do not lead to lasting happiness and a deeper satisfaction with life. Instead, they lead to behaviors that others tend to resent. Even at the age of six, selfish children are harshly punished by their peers, whereas fairness is rewarded through cooperative engagement and acceptance.[1]

Greed stimulates the motivation centers of the brain, and the more drive you have, the bigger the rewards you'll seek.[2] But when you seek wealth for your own private pleasure, you'll feel somewhat empty.[3] Those who share accumulated wealth with others feel greater emotional satisfaction.[4] As researchers at the Tilburg Institute for

Behavioral Economics Research discovered, people who learn how to better direct their instinctual greed toward the social good experience greater life satisfaction.[5]

In fact, the most recent research shows that humans are shaped by evolution to interrupt greed and establish a fair distribution of wealth for those who are less fortunate.[6] Furthermore, the more you develop your neurological capacity for empathy, the more fairly you will treat others.[7] Perhaps this explains why most of the world's religions emphasize the importance of sharing one's wealth with others.

Where Does Desire Come From?

Just as there are two forms of stress—physical and mental— there are two forms of desire: an unconscious instinctual drive to survive, and a more conscious "wanting" that is driven by optimistic fantasies about the future. Most of the desires described by our survey participants fall into this latter category of imagination and wishful thinking. The research also shows that the more you consciously think about your desires, the more motivated and skilled you will become in reaching them.[8] So by all means, think deeply about what you truly desire.

Here's an exercise that will give you a sense of what you physically, emotionally, and mentally desire. Take a couple of minutes to write down as many of your desires as you can think of for each of these five categories:

- Financial and work-related desires
- Relationship desires
- Health desires

- Recreational and pleasurable desires
- Moral/ethical/spiritual desires

After you do this, slowly stretch your body and yawn several times to enter a state of deep relaxation and clarity. Mindfully gaze at your list and circle those items that give you a sense of physical pleasure. Focus on your own bodily awareness and see if there are any additional items to add to your list. Next, circle those items that emotionally excite you. Add any additional items to your list as you reflect on past desires that brought you emotional satisfaction. Often, when we think about our deepest desires, we leave out the physical and emotional qualities that are essential for increasing motivation. Finally, circle those items that stimulate your intellect and mind.

Post your "Desire List" in a prominent place and keep revising it over the next few weeks, crossing off desires that don't have deep meaning or purpose for you and adding additional ones that do. By remaining in a mindful state of relaxed attentiveness, you'll begin to *intuitively* sense which desires really motivate you to take action in the world.

"Bottom-Up" and "Top-Down" Desires

On the instinctual level, desire is really a form of hunger, and the satiation of hunger is the primary goal of any creature with a nervous system. That is why the brain of nearly every animal is situated in the same place: *right above the mouth*. A single-celled organism doesn't need a brain because it can absorb nutrients directly from the environment. But as creatures become more complex, a feeding tube forms, stretching from one end of the organism to the other. Vascular systems form to help nurture the cells, bones stabilize its shape, and a nervous system develops to help move the animal through the environment, and the "executive" nerves congregate near the mouth to create a primitive brain. Even our senses—eyes, ears, nose, skin, etc.—are extensions of the brain, designed to improve your chances of survival.

Hunger is your first desire and goal, and satiation is the reward. As the brain gets larger, more desires are born: the search for a mate, a safe harbor to procreate, and the accumulation of any knowledge or tool that gives you an

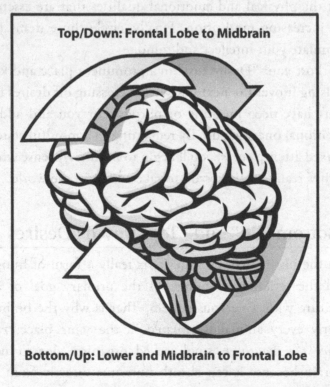

Figure 9. Top-Down and Bottom-Up processing of information.

edge over competitors. Even the most sophisticated desire is driven by a simple formula that helps your brain decide what it wants to do and what it needs to avoid: pleasure and pain. Actions that bring a pleasurable reward are turned into memories and habits, and this is what governs most of the choices we make.

In neuroscience, *instinctual* desire is called "bottom-up" processing (figure 9), and it's the primary motivator for most animals. Humans, however, have huge memory storage systems and a larger capacity to dream up creative solutions to problems. This is a conscious process governed by your frontal lobe, and it can directly influence the older, more primitive parts of your brain that motivate you to take action in the world. In fact, your thoughts can actually change the structure of other parts of the brain. This is called "top-down" processing, and most of the *conscious* desires people pursue come from these pleasurable memories and fantasies.[9]

Human imagination appears to have no boundaries, and, as a consequence, it has a very unusual effect on the rest of the brain. When you dream up something you believe will make you happy, your brain assumes that it is easy to get. In other words, the more you envision something you want or like, the more obtainable it appears to be. It's a cognitive illusion called "wishful seeing," and some scientists believe that this is the secret that drives a lazy brain—one which is primarily interested in *immediate* gratification—to work very long and hard on projects that might otherwise seem too difficult to achieve.[10]

When you simultaneously pursue both top-down and bottom-up desires, you generate more motivation and stamina in your pursuit of inner and outer wealth. You can also devise better strategies for reaching goals and anticipate outcomes before you take action in the world.[11]

Pleasure Makes Your Dreams Come True

Unfortunately, the human brain has an odd quirk: it barely registers pleasant experiences, but it overemphasizes every tiny displeasure and disappointment. This explains why so many people feel anxiety when they realize that their desires may take extra effort and work. When this happens to you, instead of focusing on the potential of a large reward, your brain may start to ruminate on fears of failure. These negative thoughts and feelings turn off the motivation circuits in your brain. Fortunately, you can use your imagination to reverse this process by consciously reinforcing the promise of a future reward.[12]

Your brain is constantly seeking immediate gratification, and motivation will decline unless it receives plenty of small rewards as you steadily move toward your larger goals and desires. This is easy to do, but many people ignore this biological need for a pleasure "fix." Managers will say, "I don't have time to take a break," and entrepreneurs will often push themselves beyond their limits working overtime to become successful and rich. But as we have stated earlier in this book, the brain tires easily, especially when there's a lot of work-related stress. That's why it's so important to administer healthy doses of pleasure throughout your workday. Fortunately this only takes a few seconds to do, and any form of pleasure can propel you to greater productivity.[13]

Here's an exercise that will immediately give your brain more energy. Write down five activities that have brought you a moment of deep pleasure. Then close your eyes and visualize one of those pleasant memories as if you were living it again. Using your imagination, take your time to savor each aspect of that past experience. Do you feel a slight tingly sensation in your body, or a sense of increased alertness? When you do this, your imagination will stimulate a tiny structure in one of the oldest parts of your brain: the nucleus accumbens.[14] It sits in the center of your motivation-and-reward circuit—the M-Drive, as we'll refer to it in this book—and when activated, the M-Drive wakes up your entire brain, preparing you to seek out anything that will bring more pleasure.

If the M-Drive gets too stimulated, a powerful craving results, similar to an addiction. For example: If you take a moment to think about one of your favorite comfort foods, you are likely to salivate. And if you picture where that tantalizing treat is stored in your house, you may find it difficult to resist the temptation to eat it now. Simply put, too much pleasure leads to impulsivity, and impulsivity can derail you from seeking goals that can bring you lifelong satisfaction.[15]

The reverse is also true. If you focus too long on your worries, fears, or doubts, you'll instantly deactivate the entire motivation-and-reward system in your brain.[16] But if you focus on simple desires and achieving *small* goals throughout the day, you can eliminate most forms of depression, anxiety, and fear.[17]

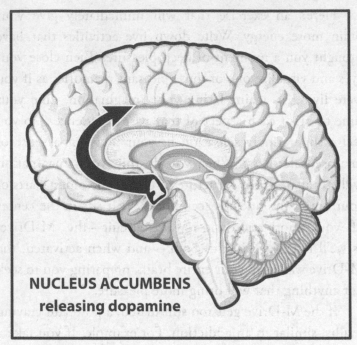

NUCLEUS ACCUMBENS
releasing dopamine

Figure 10. Motivational dopamine migrating into the frontal lobes.

Dopamine Drives Desire

The M-Drive produces some of the most pleasurable sensations in your brain by releasing dopamine from the nucleus accumbens[18] (figure 10). This neurochemical rapidly spreads into the front and upper areas of your brain, where billions of neurons are called into action for the sole purpose of helping you get whatever you desire.[19]

Dopamine enhances conscious decision making, the second Pillar of Wealth. It keeps your mind clear and focused as you develop strategies to reach your goal. It improves learning and cognition, and it helps regulate negative feelings that could interfere with your work.[20]

Dopamine is the fuel that drives the motivational engine of your brain, and if the M-Drive did not release enough dopamine, you would barely be conscious of anything. It gives you the *desire* to explore the world, and it makes you work as hard as possible so that you can continue to feel pleasure and satisfaction throughout your life.[21]

Anticipating Desire Keeps the M-Drive Going

When you study successful people, you'll discover they have two things in common: they are highly motivated *and* they love what they do. Pleasure drives motivation, and the motivation drives you to acquire more. But there is another mechanism that is built into the M-Drive of every mammalian brain: *anticipatory expectation*. In other words, when you expect a positive, rewarding outcome, your brain will be more motivated to work harder, even when difficult obstacles stand in your way.[22]

We can use this fact to make long-term goals easier to achieve by training our minds to stay focused on the future reward. Some people use a "Vision Board" to do this. They'll post pictures of what they desire, and those pictures stimulate the M-Drive.[23] However, just using a Vision Board and only focusing on the reward can also cause people to make poor decisions.[24] Research psychologist Gabrielle Oettingen at New York University provides a simple solution: after you visualize the potential reward of your desired goal, take a few minutes to visualize potential obstacles, and then visualize solutions for overcoming them. This will make it possible for your brain to solve problems and achieve goals with greater efficiency and ease.[25]

In this manner, you are integrating the instinctual motivation circuits in your lower brain (the first Pillar of Wealth) with the creative circuits of your imagination located in the upper portions of your brain (the third Pillar of Wealth). If your brain senses that you are getting closer to your goal, it will rely on your imagination to keep the promise of a future reward alive. Even when you fall asleep, your dreams will continue to feed the M-Drive with expectations of success.[26]

In with the New, Out with the Old

Pleasure stimulates motivation, and motivation drives you to seek more pleasure. But what constitutes pleasure for the human brain? First, the M-Drive is set in motion by sensations we experience in the world. Behavioral neuroscientists have identified dozens of stimuli that motivate this unconscious part of the brain. Some stimuli are physical and many are emotional, but they usually boil down to one or more of the following basic pleasures:

- Does it have pleasant taste or odor?
- Is it colorful, shiny, and pleasing to the eye?
- It is physically pleasurable?
- Does it sound pleasant or stimulate an evocative mood?

You can use this bottom-up approach to stimulate your motivational desires, keeping you joyfully productive while working hard. For example, you can play pleasant music in the background while working, which increases

BONUS EXERCISE: MINDFUL AWARENESS OF PLEASANT SENSATIONS

Because the brain is programmed to pay more attention to pain than pleasure, you have to train yourself to become more sensitive to the dozens of pleasant sensations that constantly occur in your body. As you do, negative thoughts and feelings will subside.

Here is an exercise you can do either lying down or sitting up: Make yourself as comfortable as possible. Then take an inventory of all the subtle aches and pains in your head, around your eyes and mouth, in your neck, your arms, your hands, your back, your belly, your hips, your legs, and your feet. Notice the discomfort—but don't judge or react to it. Just allow the discomfort to be there. If the pain increases, slowly and gently move that area of your body to a more comfortable position. This will usually release muscular tension after a few minutes.

Now turn your attention to the pleasant sensations in your body, beginning with your breathing. Notice the cool air traveling up your nostrils as you breathe in and the warm air exiting your nostrils as you breathe out. If it feels nice, whisper to yourself, "Pleasant." Now scan the rest of your body from head to toe. Which parts feel pleasurable? Note each one of them and whisper, "Pleasant." Gently run your fingers over your hands, arms and face as you notice which areas feel the most pleasant.

Now shift your attention to the outside world. What pleasant sounds do you hear? Do you find the sound of your own breathing pleasurable? Use your fingers to explore the texture of your clothes, the chair you are sitting on, and any object within reach. Immerse yourself in these subtle pleasant sensations.

Notice how this exercise improves your mood and increases your energy. This exercise causes the M-Drive to release dopamine, which will increase your concentration and performance at work.

motivational drive while interrupting the effects of negative emotions,[27] or you can take hourly breaks to immerse yourself in pleasant activities, sights, smells, sounds, and tactile sensations (stretching tight muscles, massaging your scalp, etc.)—all of which have been shown to increase motivation and work performance.[28] The bonus exercise below (Mindful Awareness of Sensations) will help you to enhance your sensory perception of your body. You'll feel better and you'll be more motivated to pursue your growing list of desires.

One of the most important components for pleasure—in humans and animals—can be summarized in three words: Is it new? Put a mouse in a maze filled with objects it has never seen before, and as long as the object is not perceived as a threat, the mouse will take great interest in it.[29] Then it will do something amazing. It will hoard the object away, hiding it in a safe place, because it has an instinctual sense that anything new may have value in the future. Old acquisitions bring less pleasure than new ones, so the healthy brain will always turn its attention toward something new.[30]

Humans are no different, and novelty is one of the strongest motivators in our lives. In fact, every time you encounter something new, a dozen different processes are triggered in your brain. Awareness and perception are increased, you'll feel a greater desire to learn, and your memory will be enhanced.[31] Thus, one of the secrets to happiness and success is to remain continually curious when it comes to seeking new sources of knowledge, activity, and social interaction.[32]

As your brain explores the world, it looks for these motivational cues: Is it new? Is it cool? Does it look or taste or smell interesting? Does it make you feel good or excite you in a pleasurable way? Neuromarketing experts use these instinctual pleasure-drivers to entice you to buy nearly every type of product on the shelves.[33] Auto dealers spend millions finding the right smell for a new car, and women will spend fortunes on a perfume to attract a well-dressed mate. Retailers know that if they can stimulate the pleasure centers in your brain, you'll instinctually want it—and the reverse is equally true. The slightest hint of anything bitter, sour, painful, noisy, shadowy, dull, broken, or worn out will send signals that immediately turn off a prospective customer's M-Drive.

The same holds true for personal relationships. Your brain will seek out people who exhibit qualities that promise pleasure or a future reward.[34] So keep your relationships fresh. Engage in new activities. Explore new levels of intimacy and experiment with new ways to communicate with each other. In chapter 11 we'll show you how to have mindful dialogues that will strengthen the circuits of the social brain.

Pain and Fear Turn Off the M-Drive

Pleasure, novelty, and curiosity will motivate the brain to take action. But if the experience triggers displeasure or pain, neurochemicals are released that immediately shut down the M-Drive. If you experience pain, your body freezes, and the decision-making circuits in your frontal lobe get turned off so your ancient, instinctual brain can use its survival-based programming to take evasive action.

As we've mentioned earlier, pain and pleasure are the primary motivators for every animal with a nervous system.

Pleasure will make you move toward a desirable object and pain will make you avoid it. This mechanism also underlies the learning system of the brain. In 2000, Eric Kandel earned the Nobel Prize for showing how a single nerve cell in a sea slug could be taught to become more inquisitive or more fearful through exposure to a pleasant or unpleasant stimulus.[35]

Neurons can be trained to become more motivated to learn new skills, which strengthen neural connections throughout the entire brain. But you can also condition your brain, through chronic worry or fear, to believe that the world is unsafe. When this happens, the M-Drive shuts down, and neurons throughout your brain begin to disconnect from each other. Your mental clarity and problem-solving skills are compromised, your confidence drops, and your ability to accurately respond to social cues diminishes, lowering your self-esteem.

However, most fears and doubts are nothing more than memories being recalled from the past. The moment you realize this, the fear circuits in your brain begin to quiet down.[36] Once they are quieted, you can focus on new ways to overcome obstacles that stand between you and your desired goal, and this optimistic attitude will stimulate the M-Drive, releasing more dopamine to keep you focused on the prize. Anxiety is reduced, your reactions to stress are decreased, and you gain more control over your emotions. As researchers at the University of Pittsburgh demonstrated, when you practice the mindfulness exercises described in this book, you can actually shrink the size of the amygdala, the small, almond-sized structure in your brain that registers fear.[37]

In the past, little was known about how to stimulate

the motivation circuits in your brain. We now know that the more attention you give to building confidence, enthusiasm, and social empathy using the NeuroWisdom exercises in this book, the more energy you'll have to pursue the goals you desire:

- Self-confidence will increase your desire to seek more goals and rewards.[38]
- Enthusiasm and optimism will enhance motivation, performance, and persistence when carrying out work-related tasks.[39]
- Learning how to regulate your moods will improve your chances of attaining difficult, long-term goals.[40]
- Developing a sense of compassion for others (using the mindfulness exercises in chapter 11) will stimulate the motivation-and-reward circuit in your brain.[41]
- Cooperating with others will increase group motivation and decision-making skills.[42]

Motivation Is Only the First Pillar of Wealth—It Alone Is not Enough

Our strongest emotion is our biological desire to acquire as much of *everything* as we possibly can.[43] If it's new, we want it. If it's different, we become curious about it. If it's pleasurable, we crave it. And if someone else gets it first, we will experience a momentary pang of grief. Without this instinctual drive, we can slip into depression or despair.[44] This is true not only for people, but for every organism with a brain, and with each failure to succeed—to acquire more of everything—the less motivated the brain becomes. And that is the neurological definition of depression.

The M-Drive gets things going, but it's driven by the desire to seek immediate gratification. It's impulsive, and as we mentioned earlier, impulsivity leads to poor decision making. Here's the problem: pleasure is essential for neurological growth, development, and health, but if you only focus on self-centered pleasures, you will not experience a long-lasting sense of well-being.[45] That requires the *sharing* of your inner and outer wealth with others. Researchers at the University of California, Berkeley, have demonstrated that the more pleasure you experience through acts of fairness and generosity, the more you will feel deep, lifelong satisfaction.[46] So think very deeply about the following question over the next few days:

What do I *really* desire?

Say the question out loud—emphasizing the word "really"—and jot down on a sheet of paper the first few desires that come to mind. On each succeeding day you may notice that your answer changes, and in our research we have found that after four to seven days, your desires take on qualities that have deeper meaning and purpose for you, often shifting from outer, material gains to inner values that also benefit others. These global desires and goals may take years or decades to achieve, but the research shows that this is what will bring the greatest satisfaction to your life.

CHAPTER SUMMARY

1. The M-Drive is governed primarily by the nucleus accumbens, a tiny structure located in the deepest and most ancient part of our brain. It instinctually drives you to seek objects, friends, and experiences that give you immediate pleasure. Money is one the most powerful visual images that motivates the brain to take action. The *m* in M-Drive stands for "motivation," "money" (and what it can bring us), and the desire to acquire "more" of anything we view as extrinsically and intrinsically valuable.

2. When we are biologically motivated by new, different, and interesting stimuli, dopamine is released from the nucleus accumbens and travels to the decision-making area of the frontal lobe. When this happens, consciousness increases, pleasant memories are evoked, and the promise of a future reward keeps the M-Drive going.

3. If too much dopamine is released, we may exhibit impulsive and addictive behaviors. If too little dopamine is released, we'll lose interest in pursuing goals and experience boredom or depression.

4. Three things can stop the M-Drive from motivating us to move toward our goals, desires and dreams: (1) physical pain, (2) unpleasant emotional experiences and memories, and (3) ruminating on negative feelings and thoughts. Each one triggers a fear reaction, turning on primitive reactions to freeze, fight, or run away when we perceive a threat—either

real or imaginary—and turning off any motivation to achieve a specific goal.

5. The M-Drive is driven by pleasure, but pleasure is a momentary experience. Deeper levels of happiness and satisfaction are governed by higher brain functions involving self-awareness, social awareness, and the development of a values system that benefits other people and the communities in which we live.

CHAPTER 5.

Turning On the M-Drive: Nine Strategies to Stimulate Motivation and Desire

When it comes to motivation, it's important to keep in mind that you have two distinct forms of desire: bottom-up and top-down. Bottom-up processes begin in the most ancient parts of the brain with the urges to be cared for, to be fed, and to feel safe and secure, internally and externally. As the brain develops after birth, curiosity becomes another governing force. Children desire *new* objects to play with, *new* experiences to explore, and *new* people to engage with, and they continue to learn new skills to help them acquire more experiences, toys, and friends.

As the frontal lobe grows, the ability to imagine greater rewards increases. This is the top-down process of desire, where positive fantasies become a powerful motivational force. For example, when children see a television commercial for a toy they may impulsively run to a parent, crying out, "I *need* that toy; I have to have it *now*!" These demands are the direct result of a child's thoughts stimulating the motivation-and-reward circuit in the brain. Large quantities of dopamine are being released, and if the child's desire is not met, a temper tantrum can easily occur.

Bottom-up desires will always take precedence, but as you grow older top-down desires begin to dominate your life. This is where creating wealth begins on a conscious level, but there's a problem: children's imaginations often create an urgency that outstrip their ability to acquire the desired object. Children therefore need to develop patience when pursuing long-term goals, and they must maintain interest in their pursuit, believing that they will be able to master the skills needed to reach their desired goals.[1] Successful people don't just hope to succeed; they *expect* to succeed, no matter what, and they will take as much time as is needed to create a plan to achieve their desired goals.

The Neuroscience of Motivation and Success

The M-Drive runs on pleasure and immediate gratification. It doesn't have a way to push a pause button—an ability that slowly emerges with the development of the frontal lobes[2]—nor can it clearly distinguish when it has had too much of a good thing. Here's a dramatic example of how pleasure can compromise the brain's ability to patiently find wise ways to reach desired goals: when rats have probes embedded into their motivation-and-reward circuit, causing them to constantly press a lever that has been designed to stimulate it, they'll keep pressing the lever until they actually die because the intense pleasure causes their brain to ignore life-threatening cues. Pleasure keeps the M-Drive stimulated, but too much immediate pleasure undermines the self-control circuits in the brain.[3]

Humans have the same neural capacity to overdose on pleasure. Give a bagful of Halloween candy to a young child, and she is likely to overeat for days. Or try to pull your teenaged son away from a computer game; a power struggle will usually occur. After all, a child is more inclined—more motivated—to seek immediate gratification than to study for a school test. If these impulses persist, addictive behaviors may take hold in adolescence and adulthood. Focusing on pleasure and ignoring reason (regulated by the frontal lobe) overstimulates a child's M-Drive, effectively derailing the brain's ability from pursuing other activities that would lead to long-term satisfaction.[4]

When children learn how to regulate their doses of pleasure at an early age, they'll work harder on long-term goals. Research studies show that such children exhibit specific qualities that predict future success: they are able to maintain intense interest and curiosity in new experiences, and more important, they *believe* they will succeed.[5] The strong belief that one's efforts will be rewarded stimulates growth of very powerful neural circuits that control many top-down desires.[6]

Researchers have also discovered that the *expectation* of a future reward stimulates motivation in the present moment.[7] It's one of the keys that will keep you working when you have to perform unpleasant tasks. Expectation builds confidence, and when combined with a high degree of interest, your neurological ability to achieve long-term goals is enhanced.[8]

The Marshmallow Experiment: Patience Versus Pleasure

In a famous series of tests known as the Stanford Marshmallow Experiment,[9] preschool children were placed in the situation where a researcher placed a marshmallow, cookie, or a pretzel in front of them. The researcher then announced that he would leave the room and return after 15 minutes. The children were given a choice: they could eat the treat immediately or they could wait until the researcher returned, whereupon they would receive a second treat or reward. Some children would immediately gobble up a treat, others would squirm and struggle, sometimes picking up the treat and then putting it back on the plate, and a few had the capacity to sit there calmly and wait, knowing that they would double their reward by being patient.

Over the next four decades, these children were followed as they matured into adults. Those who delayed the neurological urge for immediate gratification performed better in school and were more socially competent. In their findings, the researchers emphasized that if you want to be successful in life, you must be able to "postpone immediate gratification and persist in goal-directed behavior for the sake of later outcomes."[10] This turned out to be especially relevant for developing healthy eating behaviors—the children who could patiently wait for a future reward had greater control over their weight and eating behaviors 30 years later.[11]

Can patience and self-control be learned? The research says yes, but you must reinforce your decision-making skills (the second Pillar of Wealth described in the next two chapters) and develop your awareness skills (the fourth Pillar of Wealth).[12] This includes the practice of mindfulness—deeply reflecting on your short- and long-term goals and desires—a strategy that has been shown to strengthen the self-control circuits in your brain.[13]

Temporarily postponing immediate pleasure strengthens those parts of your brain that give you more conscious control over your life.[14] But you must reward yourself, as you strive for larger goals, with a constant stream of small

HOW TO DELAY THE I-WANT-IT-NOW URGE

1. Hide your reward. This will enhance the "pause" circuits in your brain.
2. Distract your craving by engaging in a fun mental activity.
3. When you crave something, look at a picture of it. Research shows that this can satisfy the brain's desire.
4. Visualize giving yourself an *imaginary* reward. Savor the experience as if it were real. Your craving will immediately lessen.
5. Imagine yourself resisting temptation. Repeated mental rehearsing increases self-control.

A review study in *Science* (1989: Vol. 244) found that these strategies also help children develop patience and self-control.

rewards to satisfy the pleasure centers of the ancient part of your brain. And one more thing: your goal and your expected reward must be realistic and attainable. If not, the M-Drive will shut down.[15]

The following exercises have been designed to boost your motivation at work. As you read through this chapter and the rest of this book, we strongly recommend that you spend just a couple of minutes to briefly experience the usefulness of each one of these exercises. Do them as you read about them, and do them in the order they appear. Then select your favorite exercises, experiment with them for a week, and share them with your colleagues at work.

Create a Pleasure Board

When your brain knows that small, pleasure-based rewards will be received on a regular basis, especially when performing boring or unpleasant tasks, you'll experience increased motivation. With this exercise you can actually strengthen a very important part of your frontal lobe that gives you the power to resist pleasurable distractions.[16]

Take a sheet of paper and make a list of the most pleasurable experiences you've had throughout your life. Include food, personal relationships, physical activities, mental pursuits, vacations, and the most positive work experiences you can recall. Now relax and gaze at your list, immersing yourself in the pleasant memories that are evoked. Within a minute your two, you'll notice that your stress levels begin to drop. You'll feel more pleasure and a deeper sense of relaxation. You'll also feel more energy. That is the power of your creative imagination, and you can use it to increase your motivation for the next hour of work.

Post your Pleasure Board near your workstation and continue to add new items to it. Then, whenever you feel tired or irritable, spend a few minutes doing one of the simpler activities on your list. But keep the rewards small, because large rewards can turn off the M-Drive. In a review of sixty studies, researchers at the Whitman School of Management at Syracuse University showed that small rewards will enhance your creativity.[17] Regularly engaging in brief activities that you find interesting, pleasurable, and meaningful will help you to learn faster and increase your productivity at work.[18]

Because stress decreases motivation, why not take advantage of such pleasure breaks to decrease it? Sometimes a single yawn or stretch will suffice to keep you motivated, or you might need a three-minute power nap. That's why it's important to keep a mindfulness clock on your work computer or cell phone, a reminder to check in on your body throughout your workday to eliminate neurological fatigue.

Create a Curiosity Board

Curiosity not only stimulates the M-Drive, it also enhances your ability to learn new skills.[19] Make a list of all the activities, events, and topics that pique your curiosity. Write down experiences that have strongly interested you in the past and notice, while you write, how your mood improves and your anticipatory excitement increases. Voila! You have your Curiosity Board.

Continue to look at your Curiosity Board and mindfully observe the different thoughts and feelings that float into your consciousness. Ask yourself: "Which of these activities might I like to include in my life on a regular basis?" Circle them and ask yourself: "What new experiences—what novel activities—would I like to try in the future?" Listen to your intuition and write down everything that comes to mind. Again, gaze at your completed Curiosity Board and pay attention to any insights you may have.

This is one of the simplest ways to stimulate the M-Drive, and maintaining a high state of curiosity is one of the best ways to maintain a healthy brain because when curiosity wanes, clinical depression sets in.[20] In a multi-university study conducted in 2015, curiosity was the number one quality that boosted a person's sense of well-being.[21] Curiosity has also been shown to strengthen the learning and memory circuits in your brain.[22]

Many of our students have used the Curiosity Board and the Pleasure Board to offset daily work stress, and some have used these strategies to refine their long-term goals and career choices. When you take a personal inventory of everything that has stimulated your curiosity and brought you pleasure in the past, you'll find that your list is quite long, and as you study your list, you'll also notice that different interests are associated with different types of desires and goals. For example, if you want to increase your income, think about the jobs that feel most interesting *and* challenging. Or, if you want to find a suitable mate or build a new friendship, think about the people in your past who interested you the most and brought you the greatest satisfaction, and seek out those qualities in the new people you meet. But remain open to new experiences, new goals, and new relationships, because the M-Drive thrives on novelty.[23]

How to Use a Vision Board and Fantasies

Top-down desires often begin as fantasies. For decades, motivational speakers and entrepreneurs have encouraged people to create a personal Vision Board in the belief that dreaming big can lead to remarkable success. The formula is simple: cut out pictures from magazines symbolizing the lifestyle you want to achieve, mount them on a sheet of cardboard, and post your Vision Board where you can see it every day.

The principle makes sense: if you can't imagine yourself being successful—or worse, if you imagine yourself being a failure—you won't be motivated to take action. But there's a problem: when you picture an idealized vision of your future—if, for example, you imagine yourself being super rich—the mental images you form actually turn off the M-Drive![24] As Gabrielle Oettingen, a leading investigator in the study of visualization and goal achievement, explains: "Positive fantasies predict poor achievement... because they do not generate energy to pursue the desired future."[25] Her extensive research also shows that wishful thinking will "often lead to poor decisions."[26]

To illustrate how success visualizations work, try this mental experiment: Imagine that you've just been given a check for ten million dollars. Think about all the things you can buy and do. Visualize living in your dream house, driving your dream car, or taking your dream vacation.

Imagine that you are surrounded by your favorite family members and friends and notice how these fantasies affect your mood. Do you feel happy and contented? Probably! But do you feel like jumping up and rushing off to work? Probably not! If you are like most of the people who were given this visualization exercise, you'll notice that your motivation has declined. Your fantasies created a neurological "mirror" of success, and your brain responds to those fantasies as though they are real, and then it shifts into a state of relaxation. Positive fantasies won't motivate your brain, but research strongly suggests that recalling happy memories will improve your mood and help you to feel calmer and more relaxed.[27] On the other hand, visualizing something that will bring you pleasure in the future can motivate your brain to begin the complex decision-making process of making that fantasy a reality.

Visualize Goals and Obstacles

As Oettingen's research demonstrates, visualizing your wish or desire is the first step toward achieving it.[28] But you have to select your goal carefully, and you have to do something else: you must visualize both the inner and outer obstacles that could hold you back from reaching your objective. Without this essential step—called mental contrasting—you'll often fail to achieve your desired goal.[29] Mental contrasting actually energizes your frontal lobe in a way that motivates your brain to take action.[30] It also turns your desire into an expectation, and thus increases your willingness to work hard.[31] Oettingen recommends that you follow these steps, in the order listed below:[32]

1. First, clear your mind by deeply relaxing.
2. Identify a specific goal, wish, or desire that is important and meaningful. It can be challenging, but it must be feasible. Summarize your desired intention in a three-to-six-word sentence, and write it down.
3. Visualize yourself working toward that goal and then visualize the outcome of achieving that goal, imagining all of the benefits it will bring to your life.
4. Now identify all the internal obstacles that could interfere with your desire and write them down. Stay relaxed as you do this step, visualizing each obstacle in your imagination.
5. Think about different ways to get past each obstacle on your list by completing this sentence: "If this problem occurs, I will _____." Visualize yourself overcoming the obstacle.
6. Create a step-by-step action plan that will get you past the obstacles. Chart a specific time period that will lead to accomplishing your goal. Say the plan out loud and visualize yourself carrying out the first steps. Keep repeating these steps until it becomes second nature.

Oettingen calls her strategy WOOP, which stands for "Wish Outcome Obstacle Plan." You can apply this process to small or large goals, and you can repeat the WOOP process as many times a day as you'd like. Practice this mental contrasting exercise with a trusted friend or colleague and continue to ask yourself these questions:

Is this goal or desire really meaningful? Is the obstacle I imagine even real? Is the action I am taking effective?

Give WOOP a try right now. Visualize a simple goal you'd like to achieve today (your wish). Imagine the benefits you'll receive by achieving it (your outcome). Visualize any feeling, thought, or external circumstance that might hinder you (your obstacles) from reaching your goal. Visualize what steps you can immediately take to overcome that obstacle (your plan). Now take action!

Ask the Right Questions

John C. Norcross, Distinguished Fellow at the University of Scranton, also emphasizes the importance of visualizing your goals in order to fully psych yourself up to take action. He recommends that you ask yourself these questions:[33]

1. "What do I really want to achieve or change?" Norcross recommends that you take as long as necessary to answer this, even if it takes days or weeks.

2. "Am I ready to make the changes needed to pursue a new goal or behavior?" If not, find a smaller goal you feel ready to tackle. A series of small goal achievements will give you the confidence to tackle larger goals.

3. "Do I have the skills to achieve my goal?" If not, ask yourself, "Am I willing and able to get the knowledge and training I will need?"

4. "What will motivate me to take action?" You must have a clearly defined plan, with a clearly defined benefit.

5. "Is my desire stronger than my resistance?" If not, take steps to undermine the resistance. Think about the consequences of not changing or reaching your goal.

6. "Do I feel emotionally excited by my goal?" An intellectual desire is not enough to become motivated.

7. "Is my desire really about *me*?" You are less likely to change, or achieve your goals, if you are only trying to please someone else.

8. "Do I have a measurement tool to track my progress?" Charting your progress helps you to stay focused on your goal, and every positive step stimulates the motivation circuits in your brain.

BONUS EXERCISE: PSYCH YOURSELF UP BY AVOIDING "SHOULDS"

Each morning, before going to work, take 60 seconds to reflect on this question: "What would I really *like* to accomplish today?" Focus on the word "like," not on what you *have* to do or *should* do, which deactivates the M-Drive. The more you can visualize what you would like to do, the more you will want to do it. Try this exercise for seven days, and try it while working. Set your mindfulness clock to ring hourly and ask yourself: "What would I really like to accomplish in the following hour?" You'll immediately feel less resistance and greater energy. A 2012 study conducted at the University of Massachusetts found that focusing on "wants" rather than "shoulds" predicted increased life satisfaction as well. (Perceiving Value in Obligations and Goals: Wanting to Do What Should Be Done. Berg MB, Janoff-Bulman R, Cotter J. Pers Soc Psychol Bull. 2001 Aug 27; 8: 982-995)

Try out Norcross's questions. Close your eyes and visualize a goal—big or small—that you really want to achieve, and run through the questions above. When you've finished, ask yourself: "Am I really willing to commit myself to pursuing this goal?" If yes, begin to write out a long-term strategy and schedule it into your appointment book.

When using Oettingen's or Norcross's strategies, it's important to select a clearly defined goal. As decades of research have shown, it's the first step for getting what you really want.[34]

Tie Your Values to Your Dreams

There are many proven strategies that will motivate you to take action, and it begins by identifying what you really value. If your work goals do not align with your personal values, your motivation will be compromised, you'll experience less satisfaction, and you'll increase your risk of emotional burnout.[35]

In chapter 3, we introduced you to the inner values exercise, which is one of the most important strategies for ensuring lifelong happiness and success. We are often asked to define what we mean by "value." But the beauty of this exercise is that we *don't* define it or offer you a list of values to choose from. When someone else tells you what values you should embrace, the exercise becomes directed outward, not inward. But if you ponder the question, remaining in a deeply relaxed state of mindfulness, listening to and trusting your intuition—your inner wisdom—remarkable discoveries can be made.

Try this exercise. Write down five goals and desires you'd

like to achieve this year. Next, write down five big dreams: your ideal income, your ideal job, your ideal relationship, your ideal lifestyle, and so on. This is the Vision Board we talked about earlier.

Read the following steps described in this paragraph, and then close your eyes to practice these two relaxation techniques: Yawn a few times, becoming aware of your emotional and mental state. Then begin to stretch in superslow motion as you become aware of the tiny aches and pleasures in different parts of your body. Before reading the next paragraph, close your eyes for 60 seconds as you carry out these instructions.

Pay attention to the first word that comes to mind when you think about this question: "What is my deepest, innermost value?" Write that word down on a sheet of paper and repeat it several times to yourself, noticing how that concept makes you feel. Then close your eyes again, yawn a few more times, and ask yourself the same question several more times. Write down each new word that comes to mind. Listen deeply to your intuition, that small whisper that is generated by the awareness circuits in your brain. Repeat each word several times, paying close attention to how it affects your mental state and mood.

Gaze at the list of value words you've written and circle the ones that feel the most relevant and meaningful. In several recent studies, Herbert Benson's team at Massachusetts General Hospital discovered that the repetition of personally meaningful words immediately lowers psychological distress, and when continually practiced over many months, will turn on 1200 stress-reducing genes, creating permanent beneficial biological changes.[36]

Inner values can change from day to day, with certain words remaining meaningful for months or even years at a time. But different situations evoke different values. If you ask yourself, "What is my deepest relationship value?" you'll come up with certain words. If you ask yourself, "What is my deepest work-related value?" other qualities will come to mind. Our research has found that if you mindfully reflect on all of these categories—personal, relational, and work-related—you'll be able to identify which goals have the greatest meaning for you.

Write down your work and relationship values. You should have between 6–10 words. If you again relax and gaze at your list of values, ask your intuition this question: "Which goals on my list reflect my deepest core values?" Often you'll discover a new goal that you hadn't thought about, and that goal may point you in a more meaningful and purposeful direction.

Values-based goals are the most effective way to motivate the action centers in your brain,[37] but if they become too rigid—or turned into "shoulds"—they can generate inner turmoil and conflicts with others at work.[38] And if your values conflict with each other, or with your goals, they'll disrupt the functioning of many neural circuits.[39]

Dream Big, Plan Small, and Recognize Your Skills

To achieve big dreams requires a multitude of skills, so you must ask yourself, "Do I really have the time, resources, and perseverance to acquire those skills?" If not, you'll quickly exhaust the limited bursts of energy provided by the M-Drive. Here's a strategy that you can use to optimize the motivational circuits of your brain. We call it the "Skills and Strengths Board."

Here's how you create a Skills and Strengths Board: take out a sheet of paper and write down every skill you have, every strength, talent, ability, and area of expertise that comes to mind. What have you been really good at in the past? Math? Science? Art? Writing? Speaking? Teaching? Designing? Decision making? Leadership? Marketing? Selling? Managing? Communication? Networking? Research? Academics? Problem solving? Parenting? Organizing?

Now close your eyes and deeply relax for 20 seconds before opening them and mindfully gazing at your list. Ask your intuition to identify three other skills you have and write them down.

Close your eyes again and ask yourself "What strengths, qualities, and talents do other people say I have?" What would your best friend tell you? What would your colleagues at work comment on? What have previous teachers, trainers, and employers complimented you on? Put all of these qualities onto your board and ask your intuition, your inner voice, for three more qualities that capture your inner talents and add them to your list.

Two things will happen as you study your list. First you'll feel a sense of well-being as old worries and fears subside. This is a well-documented strategy for increasing your sense of self-worth and self-esteem. Second, by seeing all of your talents and strengths in front of you, you'll begin to see which avenues of work would be the easiest to pursue. Remember, your M-Drive is designed to seek out paths of least resistance, and when you use your accumulated skills, strengths, and talents, you can go after bigger dreams and goals. But you must also develop the discipline to persevere. As psychologist Andrea Duckworth, at the University of Pennsylvania, reports, "The achievement of difficult goals entails not only talent but also the sustained and focused application of talent over time."[40]

There's one more step to this exercise. Because we are often blind to some of our best talents, make a commitment to call up or e-mail some of your friends and colleagues. Ask them what they think your greatest strengths are. You'll be surprised at the qualities they identify that you may have overlooked. Post your Skills and Strengths Board where you can see it on a daily basis.

Create a Passion Board

Being deeply aware of your strengths will help you overcome the worries and doubts that naturally occur when we dream big. But your skills are not enough to keep you motivated over long periods of time. You have to *enjoy* your work, and you must feel *passionate* about your desire, and

---

BONUS EXERCISE: MAKE A "FUTURE ACCOMPLISHMENTS" BOARD

Warren Buffett uses this strategy to help people prioritize personal goals. Create a list of the top 25 accomplishments you would like to complete over the next few years of your life, and then pick the 5 most important ones. Buffett warns people to "avoid at all costs" taking on too many goals.

as the research shows, cultivating work passion increases job satisfaction.[41]

However, there are two kinds of passion: harmonious and obsessive. Obsessive passions cause too much dopamine to be released in the brain, which weakens decision-making skills while increasing risky behavior.[42] Harmonious passions are different, and are marked by a person's ability to integrate their values with goals without becoming overly emotional as they work toward completing specific goals. While harmonious passion enhances psychological well-being, obsessive passion interferes with goal attainment and often leads to burnout.[43] When harmonious passions are brought into the workplace, relationships with colleagues improve and work creativity increases.[44]

Research conducted at Stanford University shows that maintaining passion for a long-term goal is one of the best ways to achieve psychological well-being.[45] In other words, the more you can identify a meaningful goal that you feel passionate about, the happier you'll be. But how do you find that deep passion? One way is to make a list of everything you have been passionate about in the past. By creating a Passion Board, you'll see which interests and desires have strongly motivated you.

Take a sheet of paper and ask yourself, "What activities did I feel most passionate about prior to the age of 10?" Write down as many things as you can recall. Continue with each decade: What were your passions between 11–20? 21–30? 31–40? And so on. When you have finished, look at your list and circle those passions that would bring you pleasure today.

Now close your eyes and relax. Think about the next

10 years of your life and ask your intuition: "What kind of work would I feel passionate about pursuing?" If you have difficulty imagining a passionate future, think about the question we asked you in the beginning of this book. What would you do if you were the wealthiest person in the world? Immerse yourself in the fantasy, and then ask yourself these questions:

- What would I feel passionate about doing?
- What would I really like to buy?
- Who would I really like to help?
- What social or spiritual issues do I feel passionate about?
- What would I really like to change about the world?

Now ask yourself, "What can I do this week to take a tiny step toward that ultimate purpose and goal?" You see, it doesn't matter whether you are the richest or poorest person in the world. When you identify passionate interests, you'll be able to select future goals that keep you motivated for years. Passion, combined with perseverance, is the foundation for long-term happiness and success.[46]

One of our Executive MBA students—we'll call him Victor—raised this issue in class: "I want to double my income, but I'm not sure what to do and I haven't felt very motivated for the past year." Victor was a very successful entrepreneur, and his company already provided him with a million-dollar annual salary. Most people would be happy with that amount of income, and we know from the research that motivation can decline when you are highly successful. I asked him why he wanted to double it. "To provide for my children," he said. "Aren't they already taken care of?" I asked. "Well, yes," he replied.

That was his problem. He hadn't come up with a strong enough incentive that would motivate his brain. So I asked him, "What would you do if you were as wealthy as Bill Gates or Warren Buffett? What would you *really* like to do, if you had unlimited resources and the power it brings?"

Suddenly a look of surprise spread across Victor's face. "You know what I really would like to do?" he said. "I've always dreamed of going back to my hometown in India to build a library. You see, in my community, nobody had money to buy books and there was no place to go to read them. But I believe that books are essential if you want to get out of poverty. I was lucky. My parents moved to a town with a library, and that was what helped me to become successful."

Educating the poor was his passion. It motivated him to devote extra time to creating a plan and finding the necessary resources to fulfill his dream.

Boost Your Pleasure at the End of Each Day

Desires are like food dangled in front of a starving animal, and we satiate that hunger the best we can. Each time we succeed—each time we accomplish a tiny goal—the brain gets a jolt of dopamine, which motivates us to engage in more pleasure-based work. But if we fail to move closer to our goal, the M-Drive shuts down. To stop this from happening, we need to have a detailed action plan that guarantees success. We also need to feed our hungry brains with plenty of small rewards along the way. Work is inherently stressful and pleasure is the neurological antidote for stress.[47]

Even the anticipation of pleasure will motivate the brain to work harder,[48] and as long as we maintain the belief that our desires are reachable, the motivation circuits stay active. So if you want to stay motivated long enough to achieve your goals, fill each of your days with an assortment of experiences that make you smile, laugh, and relax.

The best way to do this is to take a one-to-three-minute pleasure break every hour during work. Turn on some music and dance. Go hug someone. Give yourself a head massage. Yawn, stretch, or meditate for 60 seconds. Focus on your values. All of these activities stimulate the M-Drive, and you'll immediately experience a boost of energy and an increase in the quality and quantity of your work.[49]

One of the best ways to boost your brain power *and* your self-esteem is to do this brief exercise in the evening: write down all the small pleasures and tiny successes you accomplished that day. This reinforces, in your memory circuits, that you are successful in the world. The result: a reduction in stress chemicals that interfere with sleep, a boost of neurological self-esteem that lowers anxiety, and more resilience when it comes to facing daily problems.[50] You'll wake up in the morning feeling refreshed, and the optimism you've embedded in your brain will propel the M-Drive into action.[51]

A Final Note: Talk to Your M-Drive and Listen to Your Intuition

The M-Drive, which is primarily controlled by the nucleus accumbens, is more than just a motivation machine. As the most recent research shows, it literally has a mind of its own, playing a key role in identifying which thoughts, feelings, and desires should be acted on, and which should be ignored. It even suppresses ineffective actions that hinder you in achieving your goals.[52]

We'd like you to think of the M-Drive as a neurological assistant that helps you evaluate your fantasies, desires, and fears. Because of the many ways that the language-based centers in your frontal lobe are connected to your emotional and motivational centers, you can actually have a "conversation" with different parts of your brain.[53] Talk to your M-Drive and listen to what it has to say. A pleasure-based lifestyle can be of tremendous value to you, particularly when you use it to also serve the people you care most about at the same time. It's a gift that should not be ignored. Nurture yourself as you strive for bigger and bigger goals, and maybe—just maybe—you'll change the world, making it a better place to live.

And don't forget to listen deeply to your intuition, the subtle forms of awareness within you that don't rely on words. These are the nonjudgmental inner voices that unconsciously shape your life, and they are filled with wisdom and practical advice. Intuition *predicts* effective action and problem solving; if ignored, the most recent brain research shows that you'll be more vulnerable to mental and physical disease.[54]

CHAPTER SUMMARY

- Bottom-up desires include objects and experiences that are survival oriented: food, safety, caring, friendship, health, etc. Dopamine is released from the M-Drive (the nucleus accumbens) which helps you to consciously devise strategies to achieve desired goals. Top-down desires (yearning for an ideal relationship or a particular job, desiring a new computer, wanting to lose weight, planning a celebration, etc.) begin in the imagination centers of your frontal lobe. These thoughts have the ability to stimulate the same motivation circuits governed by bottom-up desires, goals, and needs.

- Motivation is driven by the anticipation of pleasure or a future reward. When engaged in difficult tasks and long-term goals, regular pleasure breaks keep the motivation circuits active in your brain.

- The ability to delay immediate gratification improves academic- and work-related performance. However, you must also maintain a strong belief and expectation that you will achieve your goals.

- Combining pleasure, curiosity, patience, and perseverance with your skills and values is an evidence-based formula for continued success.

SUMMARY OF EXERCISES
TO INCREASE MOTIVATION

1. Pleasure is the fuel of the M-Drive. Create a Pleasure Board that identifies simple activities that you can do once every hour at work. This helps you relax while

releasing dopamine, making you work harder and more efficiently.

2. Curiosity is another engine of motivation. Create a Curiosity Board to help you identify goals that will hold your interest for long periods of time.

3. Practice Gabrielle Oettingen's WOOP strategy: Visualize your wish, desire, or goal. Visualize the expected outcome and the benefits of reaching your goal. Visualize obstacles that might interfere with your goal. Plan strategies that will enable you to overcome obstacles and visualize yourself taking action.

4. When selecting a goal, ask yourself the questions recommended by John Norcross, described in this chapter.

5. When creating a Vision Board, tie your values to your dreams, and then practice the inner values exercise daily to make sure your goals and daily priorities remain aligned with your core values.

6. Create your own Skills and Strengths Board to identify which long-term goals will be the easiest for you to achieve.

7. Cultivating work passion increases job satisfaction. Create a Passion Board to identify which of your goals and activities can generate more prolonged interest and deep satisfaction for you.

8. In the evening, briefly list all the pleasures and successes you had during the day. If you take a few moments to mindfully savor your daily accomplishments, you'll sleep better and feel more motivation in the morning.

9. Feeling tired, anxious, or stressed out? Have a "conversation" with your M-Drive and intuition. Don't depend solely on logic or outside advice.

CHAPTER 6.

Decision Making—The Second Pillar of Wealth: Turning Desires into Conscious Goals

Whatever you truly desire in life—be it money, happiness, love, or world peace—you won't get it if you're not motivated enough to work for it. The M-Drive gets you out of bed, but it only gives a brief boost of energy to point you in the direction of your desires. Then what? What gives you the ability to actually *acquire* what you want?

The answer lies in one of the most remarkable parts of the brain—your frontal lobe. It sits on top of the circuits of the M-Drive, taking up a third of the brain, and it gives you the power to choose what you want to do, to decide how you're going to do it, and to identify any problems you might encounter along the way.

108

The frontal lobe has a vast network connecting it to many other parts of the brain, giving it the power to influence other key structures through thoughts, feelings, and imaginative fantasies. At birth, the frontal lobe is

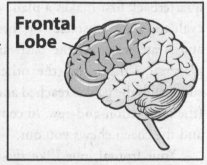

Figure 11. The frontal lobe.

extraordinarily disorganized, taking nearly thirty years to fully develop, continually forming new neural connections and dismantling old ones. This chaotic neuroplasticity accounts for the enormous creativity that lies dormant in the human brain.[1]

The Chief Executive In Your Brain

Your frontal lobe is the CEO of your life, shaping nearly every behavior that constitutes your personality.[2] It directs the voluntary movement of your body as you strive to achieve goals, it contains many speech and language centers, and it regulates your feelings, emotions, and the rules of social convention. It plans, organizes, and weighs the risks and ethics of your behavior. It is also the most vulnerable part of your brain, easily compromised by emotional stress and susceptible to many neurological illnesses.

Your frontal lobe, specifically the prefrontal cortex, controls nearly all of your conscious thoughts and decisions.[3] To use a football analogy, it is the quarterback of your brain, the player who, when handed the ball, must decide what action to take to reach the goal line. The quarterback first makes a plan, surveying the playing field, evaluating any obstacles or threats, pulling up memories and strategies from the past, and coordinating the other players on the team (the other parts of your brain). If successful, the goal is reached and the cheerleaders celebrate (the motivation-and-reward center); if not, the crowd boos and the coach chews you out.

Your frontal lobe, like the quarterback, is constantly weighing dozens of possible strategies, and this requires intense concentration and the ability to filter out distracting feelings and irrelevant thoughts. But there's a curious dilemma, because the decision-making processes in your brain are constantly being influenced by three competing "voices": An optimistic but impulsive demand to achieve one's goal no matter what (the cheerleaders in our football analogy), a more critical voice (the booing crowd) that

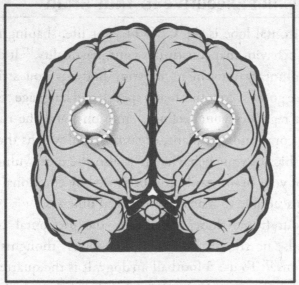

Figure 12. Consciousness, working memory,
and the dorsolateral prefrontal cortex.

tells you to wait or quit, and a mediating voice (your inner coach) that encourages you to persevere, serving up new strategies and game plans to help you succeed.

Taken together, all three voices—the inner speech of human consciousness—help you to regulate your mood and instill confidence. These positive and negative voices are constantly chattering in your frontal lobe and even though you are mostly unaware of them, they are essential for self-monitoring and maintaining peak cognitive performance.[4] Effective decision making—the second Pillar of Wealth— is driven by your conscious ability to integrate these three different types of inner speech.

The Birth of Consciousness

The M-Drive wakes you up, and the dopamine that is released from it increases your awareness of the environment and your needs. Then other areas in the frontal lobe become engaged, helping you to evaluate the importance of what you desire. As the prefrontal areas become more active, consciousness increases, giving you more voluntary control over your actions and decision-making skills.[5]

Consciousness is the workhorse of the M-Drive, helping you to stay focused on your goal. The process takes place in a tiny area situated just above your eyes, as illustrated by the two circles in figure 12. It's called the dorsolateral prefrontal cortex, and it only holds a tiny bit of information (also known as "working memory") about what's happening in the present moment. When you concentrate on a task, this is the part of your brain that is most active, turning off other areas in the frontal lobe that could distract you from completing a specific task.

Concentrated awareness is essential for goal achievement, but it also interrupts your ability to access other functions associated with creativity, imagination, and social awareness—skills that are essential for experiencing deeper levels of satisfaction.

The Optimist and the Pessimist In Your Brain

Here's another aspect of everyday consciousness that is important to understand: each half of your frontal lobe evaluates the world in a different way. One side tends to focus on positive decision making while the other side worries about possible problems and mistakes.[6] Together, your frontal lobe produces an endless stream of positive and negative thoughts that can greatly influence your actions and mood. But thanks to the limitations of consciousness—where you can only respond to a few chunks of information in any given moment—you have a choice. You can either focus on the negativity generated by your right prefrontal cortex, or you can optimistically immerse yourself in creating strategies that will bring you closer to your desired goal (processes that are largely shaped by your left prefrontal cortex).[7]

People who exhibit consistent optimism are happier and more productive, whereas people who exhibit greater pessimism tend to be more anxious, irritable, and depressed.[8] Optimists *expect* that their goals will be

THE LIMITATIONS OF EVERYDAY CONSCIOUSNESS

No matter how hard we try, it's impossible to be aware of everything that is happening in and around us in any single moment. Consciousness, as we normally experience it, is comprised of four to seven tiny pieces of information that are briefly pulled into the working memory circuits of the frontal lobe. Everything else is ignored. It helps you to focus, but it only gives you a limited perspective of yourself and the world. Here's an example of how limited your memory is. Look at the following sequence of 11 numbers:

8 — 0 — 0 — 5 — 5 — 4 — 5 — 6 — 5 — 7

Now immediately close your eyes and try to recall the numbers. Less than one in a hundred can do this because your brain is trying to process 11 chunks of information. But phone companies discovered that the brain can group numbers together into small chunks. By doing this, memory is actually expanded. Here's the same sequence of numbers above grouped together into three chunks: 800–554–5657. Most people can recall this sequence, but your frontal lobe will only retain that information for a few seconds before another series of chunks is brought to your awareness. That's how everyday consciousness works, but if you want to delve more deeply into a problem, you'll have to learn how to access deeper levels of awareness, creativity, and imagination. We'll explore those strategies in chapter 8.

reached and they *believe* that the future can be changed, overcoming any obstacle that might stand in their way.[9] Pessimists tend to believe that negative events from the past will repeat themselves in the future, but optimists tend to stay in the present moment, giving them a greater ability to analyze problems and resolve them.[10] Neurologically, optimists use their positive beliefs to turn off the anxiety centers in the brain.[11]

Optimists use the promise of future rewards to motivate them, but the pessimist uses irrational fears to avoid potential problems and imagined difficulties.[12] Optimists also demonstrate a greater ability to generate vivid mental images of their future desires,[13] which is why we emphasize the use of Oettingen's visualization strategy (WOOP) that we described in the previous chapter. For example, researchers discovered that if you were to spend just five minutes a day imagining your best possible self, your optimism would begin to increase, starting the very first day![14] When you take a few minutes to imagine the best possible future you can create for yourself, your positive mood will increase.[15]

Positive imagery can reduce a negative state of mind, whereas negative images will maintain or enhance a negative mood.[16] In fact, positive mental imagery, when compared to other forms of verbal processing, has a greater impact on reducing anxiety.[17] Negative imagery will only amplify it.[18] This raises an interesting question: can you arbitrarily create an optimistic attitude by manipulating your own thoughts? Researchers at the University of Toledo say you can,[19] and you can even undo negative memories from childhood by rescripting the event and imagining a different outcome or solution.[20]

According to Martin Seligman, the founder of positive psychology, you have to embed optimism in your brain "through the power of 'nonnegative' thinking."[21] This means that you will need to consciously identify, and then root out, the negative beliefs that have been unconsciously stored away in your long-term memory. Then, when you pull yourself into the present moment using the mindfulness exercises in this book, the negative voices generated by your right frontal lobe will lose their power.

Over time you can transform a helpless and pessimistic outlook into a realistic and lasting optimism, one that will dramatically reduce anxiety, depression, and self-doubt.[22] It will substantially increase your income, and if you teach optimism to your employees and colleagues at work, everyone's performance will be enhanced.[23] Positivity also makes you more neurologically sensitive to other people's needs.[24]

When you maintain a positive attitude, your incentive to work harder increases.[25] Work becomes more pleasurable, and the dopamine that is released not only enhances your ability to plan more effective strategies and make wiser decisions, it actually expands your consciousness by stimulating more areas in your frontal lobe.[26] As researchers at University College London found, this release of dopamine has a profound effect on our entire belief system by "reducing negative expectations regarding the future."[27] There's even evidence to suggest that optimism coupled with pleasure-filled activities increases our creative skills.[28]

Optimism is essential for happiness and success, and it will even increase your life span by several years. [29] Thus, it was no surprise that when researchers followed pessimists for 30 years, those individuals had a shorter life span and poorer mental functioning.[30] Here's the bottom line: everyone has the propensity to view any situation in a positive or negative way, and consciousness gives us the power to imagine future successes or failures. The object is to create the right balance between the two sides of your frontal lobe by briefly assessing potential problems and then emphasizing potential strategies to overcome obstacles as you chart a path toward success. The exercises in the next chapter will show you how to turn a worrisome or pessimistic attitude into permanent optimism and confidence.

Procrastination and Perfectionism

Two other forms of inner speech can undermine your ability to take action: procrastination and perfectionism. For most people, procrastination is a hindrance, reflecting layers of self-doubt and low self-esteem.[31] When you procrastinate, you are unconsciously saying to yourself that you are afraid of failure, causing you to avoid making a decision or taking action.[32] In the right side of your frontal lobe a voice constantly whispers, "I'm just not sure…There's too many steps…Maybe I forgot something…What if it fails?"

Instead of moving you forward toward your goal, procrastination holds you back, or makes you freeze or run. Most procrastination is based on an irrational belief that something may go wrong. But there are also healthy forms of procrastination.[33] It's your right frontal lobe telling you to look before you leap, giving you time to assess a difficult situation and gather more information before deciding on a specific action. If you find yourself procrastinating or excessively worrying about what to do, here's a writing exercise you can use to overcome this common problem. Writing shifts activity from the right side of the frontal lobe—where worry, doubt, procrastination, and pessimism are generated—to the left frontal areas involved with optimistic decision making.[34] We'd like you to do the following exercise now, before you read the next section:

STEP ONE: Write down a few goals, desires, or plans that have caused you, or could cause you, to hesitate before taking action. Pick one of them and write down, as briefly as possible, what you are concerned about. Then list all the reasons—rational and irrational—why you shouldn't take action. The more things you write down, the easier it will be to organize your thoughts and strategies, thus interrupting the forms of procrastination that disrupt the normal functioning of your frontal lobe.[35]

STEP TWO: Research shows that a combination of relaxation and mindfulness also reduces procrastination,[36] so put yourself into a deeply relaxed state and mindfully gaze at your list. Keep yawning and stretching, and when worrisome thoughts intrude, write them down. In less than five minutes your mind will become calmer and more attentive, the ideal state to do the next step.

STEP THREE: Ask your intuition for an answer to this question: "What is the best way for me to proceed with the issue I am struggling with?" Use your imagination and write down three things that will help you make a wise decision. Do you need more information? Gather it! Do you need a second opinion? Get it! Then take action.

Teachers and business psychologists have found that if you develop good time-management and organizational skills, the negative effects of unhealthy procrastination will decrease.[37] Self-imposed deadlines can also help you control procrastination and improve work performance,[38] but be careful of becoming too rigid. This can lead to another form of destructive inner speech: perfectionism.

For some people, no matter what they do or accomplish, a small voice whispers that it's not good enough; you could have done better. Perfectionists often set their goals, standards, and ideals so high that they are bound to fail. This, in turn, triggers a cacophony of inner criticism that undermines self-esteem, increasing one's risk of suffering from anxiety, depression, and other behavioral and emotional disorders.[39] Perfectionism, instead of being a beacon of excellence, becomes a form of self-sabotage leading to burnout at work, at school, and in sports.[40] Evidence strongly suggests that it disrupts the normal functioning of the brain.[41]

If you feel that perfectionism is undermining your confidence or self-esteem, ask yourself these questions and write your answers down:

- In what ways does my perfectionism interfere with my work or life?
- Are my standards too high or unrealistic? If so, how can I reframe them?
- What would be the benefits of lowering my expectations?
- What strategies can I use to lessen my perfectionism?

Finally, practice "imperfection" by following these

tips from Rene Brown, a research psychologist at the University of Houston: Substitute optimism and positive self-talk when you find yourself being overly critical of your accomplishments. Practice mindfulness and cultivate self-compassion. Seek meaningful work. Increase your time spent at play. Laugh and be grateful. Trust your intuition. Embrace your authenticity. And celebrate your wins.[42]

Become a Planner, Not Just a Dreamer

Making plans—clearly specifying what, when, where, and how you will accomplish a particular task or objective—will strengthen the decision-making circuits in your frontal lobe and increase your chances of achieving realistic goals.[43] According to Todd Rogers at Harvard, writing down your plan—including strategies to overcome potential obstacles—will increase your commitment to achieve your goals, and it will also reduce your tendency to get distracted or procrastinate.[44]

Making a backup plan may also lead to overall better results, especially when your goal is subject to unforeseen obstacles that are beyond your personal control. Then, when problems arise, try using if/then strategies that have been proven to help you achieve difficult goals.[45] Visualizing if/then scenarios affect the emotional centers of the brain by interrupting feelings of anxiety, uncertainty, and fear.[46]

Psychologist Heidi Grant recommends bringing if/then planning into the workplace because it improves performance and increases your chances of reaching your goal by 300%. If/then plans work, she says, because they "are built into our neurological wiring." This kind of thinking helps "people decide exactly when, where, and how they will be able to fulfill their goals," providing powerful triggers for taking action.[47] She recommends using these three styles of if/then thinking to undermine negative attitudes and behaviors:

1. Replacing: "If I start to engage in an unproductive behavior (procrastinating, worrying, stressing out, etc.), then I will _____."
    (Choose an activity that will interrupt it (relax, focus on your values, exercise, seek advice from a colleague, etc.)
2. Ignoring: "If I feel the urge to _____, then I'll ignore it." This form of thought suppression has been proven to be very effective.
3. Negating: "If I slip into a bad habit (overworking, overeating, etc.), then I'll choose to interrupt it." By consciously making this type of commitment, you are more likely to remain on track.

Turn Off Your Decision-Making Processes at Night

Your brain is designed to solve problems for only brief periods of time, and then it needs to rest. Workaholics, unfortunately, do not mentally disengage from their work. Instead, they bring it home with them. This is a form of work-related rumination that undermines self-reliance, self-confidence, and the brain's ability to solve difficult problems, and it ultimately leads to increased health risks, fatigue, sleep disorders, and work burnout.[48]

Our advice: put your work to rest when you come home. Reflect on what you accomplished that day, and if you find yourself still ruminating about work-related problems, write them down on a pad of paper and leave them on your nightstand. You'll find it easier to fall asleep, knowing that your brain will be solving those problems throughout the night. In fact, research shows that sleeping on a problem will give you greater insights and improve your performance the next day![49]

CHAPTER SUMMARY

- Motivation begins in your brain's M-Drive when events in the world capture your interest. Dopamine is released from the nucleus accumbens, which then stimulates a basic form of consciousness in the frontal lobe.
- The right side of your frontal lobe (the "pessimist") evaluates potential negative outcomes and tends to worry about the future, while the left side (the "optimist") maintains a more positive perspective as it devises strategies to acquire the object of desire. Chronic worry leads to indecision and a variety of emotional problems, releasing stress neurochemicals that decrease motivation and impair conscious decision making.
- Inner speech is constantly generated in both sides of your frontal lobe. Learning how to recognize the positive and negative self-talk helps you develop the capacity to access a third intuitive voice that can bring greater awareness and insight to your problem-solving process.
- Procrastination and perfectionism are two forms of inner speech that can undermine decision making

and achieving goals. Healthy procrastination reflects a careful analysis of complex situations where the outcome is uncertain. Unhealthy procrastination, on the other hand, often reflects chronic worry or negative thinking, low self-esteem, poor time-management skills, irrational fears of failure, and a lack of optimism. Healthy perfectionism encourages excellence and high standards, whereas unhealthy perfectionism undermines your confidence and sense of self-worth. Obsessive procrastination and perfectionism interferes with learning, memory, task performance, and achievement.

- Become a planner. Write down the goals you want to accomplish each day and allot the time needed on your calendar. But remember: your brain needs clear, simple goals and strategies in order to succeed at anything. When faced with a difficult problem, visualize if/then scenarios to find new solutions.

- Spending five minutes a day imagining your very best self will increase your optimism, confidence, and self-esteem. Then, at the end of the day, celebrate your daily accomplishments. Write down any lingering problems or worries, and then let your brain work on solutions while you sleep.

CHAPTER 7.

Sharpening Your Decision-Making Skills: Six Strategies to Increase Optimism and Performance

In order to turn your dreams into reality, you must turn your desires into goals that are clearly defined, carefully planned, and conscientiously monitored as you take action. These processes are carried out by specific circuits in the frontal lobe that control key executive functions: evaluating, planning, implementing, monitoring, and making adjustments to overcome problems.[1]

1. **Evaluating.** First your frontal lobe weighs the advantages and disadvantages of the situation. Is the goal achievable? Is it valuable? Will the

outcome be meaningful? What skills will be needed in the process of pursuing that goal?

2. **Planning.** Your frontal lobe begins to map out strategies to achieve the desired goal, and it directs your consciousness to ask self-reflective questions like these: Where exactly do I want to end up? Where am I today? How do I get to where I want to go? Where and when do I begin? How will I proceed? What resources will I need? Who will help me in my pursuit?

3. **Implementing.** Once a basic strategy is worked out and organized, your frontal lobe unconsciously coordinates your body to take action. As you begin to execute your plan, the frontal lobe encourages you to stay consciously focused and to persevere.

4. **Monitoring and Adjusting.** As you take action, your frontal lobe measures your progress and devises alternative strategies, altering the plan as needed to overcome obstacles.

Normally we move through these decision-making stages habitually, with little self-awareness. But if you train yourself to *mindfully* observe these processes throughout the day, you'll enhance the neurological functioning of these executive skills.[2] You'll be less likely to be knocked off balance by anxiety and negative thinking.[3] Your stress levels at work will drop, increasing productivity.[4]

Write Your Way to Success

Many people overlook one of the most important strategies for goal setting, planning, and achievement: putting those goals in writing. Gail Matthews at Dominican University compared four groups of people, a total of 267 participants (ages 23–72) from six different countries. The volunteers included bankers, students, artists, attorneys, healthcare professionals, educators, and a variety of business people and entrepreneurs. Those in group one were simply asked to think about their goals. In group two, participants wrote down their goals. Those in group three also wrote down a plan of action. The participants in group four wrote down their goals and strategies, and then shared them with a friend. Those who were in group five not only shared their written plan with an accountability partner, they also provided weekly progress reports.

After four weeks, this was the result: those who wrote down their goals increased their success ratio by 50% compared to those who only thought about them. Those who also gave weekly progress reports to a friend or colleague boosted their success ratio to 75%.[5] Here are some examples of the goals pursued in Matthews's study: completing a specific project (writing a chapter in a book, selling a house, learning a new skill, managing a problem at work, etc.), increasing personal income, enhancing performance and productivity, and reducing work-related stress.

So write down a specific goal you want to accomplish in the next month. Then create an action plan and a timeline, listing the strategies you'll use to achieve that goal. E-mail your plan to a friend or colleague, with a commitment to give them weekly progress reports.

The Daily Commitment Sheet

For every goal you achieve, large or small, the brain rewards itself with a pleasurable shot of dopamine, motivating you to accomplish more goals. But some people make the mistake of only focusing on big, long-term goals, ignoring the tiny accomplishments that occur each day. Others fail to realize that large goals are comprised of a series of smaller goals or steps. By taking the time to savor the dozens of successes you experience each day, you strengthen the motivation circuits in your brain.

If you feel you have trouble reaching your goals, the Daily Commitment Sheet will help. It incorporates 11 evidence-based strategies to keep you optimistically focused on your goals and your daily progress. Our Executive MBA students have found it very useful, helping them to focus on the most important goal they want to accomplish on a given day.

Write down the following words: "goal," "value," "obstacle," "counter-strategy," "affirmation," "accomplishments," and "gratitude." Later, we want you to print out enough copies to practice the following exercise for 8–12 weeks, the average time it will take your brain to turn this goal-achievement strategy into a healthy habit.[6] If you immerse yourself in the pleasurable aspects of this exercise (or any of the exercises in this book), you will change your neurological behavior and develop better work habits in just a couple of weeks.[7] Let's do a practice round.

THE DAILY COMMITMENT SHEET

TODAY'S GOAL:

TODAY'S WORK VALUE:
Visualize your goal, the desired outcome, potential obstacles or sabotage behaviors, and a plan to overcome them.

OBSTACLE:

COUNTER-STRATEGY:

AFFIRMATION:
"I breathe in _____; I breathe out _____."

TODAY'S ACCOMPLISHMENTS:

GRATITUDE LIST:

Relax—Intuit—Savor Your Successes—Repeat

STEP ONE: Identify a simple goal. Close your eyes and spend a few moments relaxing your mind and body. Ask your intuition: "What goal do I want to accomplish in the next 24 hours?" You'll often hear several ideas, but if you mindfully observe them, one goal will stand out as the most important or meaningful. Write that goal down in as few words as possible. But keep it simple; it should be something you know you can accomplish with relative ease. This is how you train your frontal lobe to focus and persist.

STEP TWO: Identify a core value or power word. Close your eyes again and relax. Ask yourself: "What inner value will help me achieve this goal?" Think of a word that you intuitively feel will guide you during the day (for example: "calm," "focused," "optimistic," "confidence," "clarity," etc.). A mindfulness clock can be very useful to remind you of your values several times an hour.

STEP THREE: Identify obstacles and problems. Visualize your goal and imagine yourself carrying out the tasks involved to achieve it. Then spend a few moments envisioning the accomplishment of your goal. Next, visualize one obstacle (an inner problem, a poor habit or behavior, an outer circumstance, etc.) that could interfere with reaching your goal and write it down on your Daily Commitment Sheet. This form of mental contrasting—comparing your desire with potential problems—will simultaneously energize you and reduce stress, thereby deepening your commitment to your goal.[8]

STEP FOUR: Create a solution. As you visualize this obstacle or problem, close your eyes and deeply relax. Then ask your intuition to provide you with a simple strategy to overcome it. Write it down and then close your eyes again, visualizing yourself using that strategy to get past the problem and back on track.

STEP FIVE: Use affirmations while working. When you repeat value words or self-affirming statements, you'll not only reduce stress, you'll strengthen the decision-making circuits in your brain.[9] In chapter 3 we introduced you to the popular affirmation "I breathe in _____; I breathe out _____," placing positive and negative value words into the blanks (for example: "I breathe in peace; I breathe out stress"), but you can create any affirmation using any quality or value that you want to bring into your life. In a study conducted at Carnegie Mellon University, students who wrote down values that were important to them were able to solve more problems under stress than those who did not.[10] Here are some examples of what the students wrote: *I'm strong, I'm independent, I'm creative, I'm kind, I'm talented, I can persevere, I will succeed, I am loved.* Extensive research shows that affirming personal values increases self-clarity and affirming positive qualities about yourself enhances self-esteem.[11] Self-affirmations also improve social interactions with others.[12]

STEP SIX: Acknowledge daily accomplishments. The research behind this helped to establish the field of positive psychology.[13] At the end of the day, instead of focusing on what you didn't accomplish (what most people do), reflect only on those things you did well that day and list at least three of them on your Daily Commitment Sheet. Close your eyes, right now, and visualize some of the small successes you've already achieved today and notice how these memories make you feel.

STEP SEVEN: Keep a gratitude list. Reflecting on things and people you feel grateful for has a powerful effect on your mood, well-being, and your brain,[14] and when you mindfully reflect on your core values and accomplishments, you simultaneously increase your happiness and success.[15] Take a few minutes right now and write down three things for which you feel grateful.

As you work with the Daily Commitment Sheet over the next few weeks, remember these four principles: stay *relaxed* as you work toward achieving your goals; use your *intuition* to access deeper levels of creativity and problem solving; *savor* every small success throughout the day; and, *repeat* these steps until they form new neural circuits of enhanced performance.

The C.R.A.P. Board

When it comes to achieving goals, your biggest enemy is stress. Even brief periods of anxiety, frustration, or ruminating on negative thoughts will interfere with the healthy functioning of neurons in your frontal lobe. Stress, as illustrated in figure 13, actually causes the dendrites—the neural receptors that gather information from other neurons—in your frontal lobe to dramatically shrink, thereby interfering with every dimension of the decision-making process. But if you interrupt stress through frequent relaxation breaks—even taking just a few yawns

Figure 13. The effects of stress on neurons in the prefrontal cortex.

or stretching slowly a couple of times each hour—the dendrites recover and grow back.[16]

Research also shows that a few minutes of mindful focusing—sitting quietly and reflecting on your current goal and task—increases your ability to concentrate and remain attentive.[17] Thus, the neurological secret to success is to consciously alternate between brief periods of concentrated work—20–60 minutes maximum—and brief periods of relaxation and mindfulness.

You can even train your brain to remain mindfully relaxed when you are in the middle of a conflict or a highly stressful task, and the following exercise will show you how. It's called the C.R.A.P. Board—a variation of a well-documented cognitive therapy strategy—and it's one of the most fun and useful strategies we've developed. When we posted it on Facebook it went viral, reaching over a quarter million people. It's also one of the fastest ways to stop your brain from ruminating on problems, fears, and weaknesses.

C.R.A.P. stands for "Conflicts," "Resistances," "Anxieties," and any other "Problem" you think you have, and when you write these things down your brain begins to dissociate from the words on the page. Writing down your "crap" actually turns off the negative emotional circuits that shut down the decision-making processes in your frontal lobe. Grab a pen and a large sheet of paper, and write "C.R.A.P. Board" at the top. As quickly as possible, without thinking too deeply about it, write down every worry, fear, weakness, and fault you have. Are you lazy, cranky, easily distracted, or judgmental of others? Do you waste time, procrastinate, or carelessly complete your tasks? Are you lonely or insecure?

When you can't think of any more negative qualities, close your eyes and relax for a few moments to clear your mind. Then ask yourself these questions and add them to your C.R.A.P. Board: What bad habits do you have? What behaviors would you like to change? What beliefs do you have that interfere with you being successful or feeling happy? Make this exercise a game, trying to put down as many things as possible. You should notice that a tinge of boredom will occur the longer you write—that's the brain disconnecting from the emotional memories associated with your words—but if you start to feel anxious, just stop and spend a few minutes relaxing. Yawn, slowly stretch, or stroke your arms and the palms of your hands. These

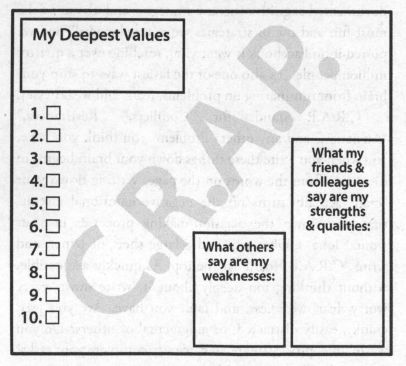

Figure 14. The C.R.A.P. Board.

pleasurable sensations, when combined with making a list of negative traits, will have a powerful soothing effect, one that actually weakens the neural circuits of negative memories.

Now ask your intuition what else you should add to your C.R.A.P. Board as you remain mindfully observant of the subtle feelings and thoughts floating through your consciousness. Write them down and then continue to mindfully gaze at your list. Just look at the words without judging them, and ask yourself: Are these negative thoughts *really* true? Are they happening right now, or are they just memories from the past? Cross off the items that don't have an impact on your present life and then circle the top 10 faults or concerns that you believe are holding you back in your life.

Now, take a new sheet of paper, and using the template pictured in figure 14, divide it into four sections: a small box in the upper left hand corner for core values, the blank area in the middle to list your C.R.A.P., and two more boxes at the lower right for the weaknesses and strengths that other people say you have. Mindfully observe your feelings and thoughts as you complete the following steps:

STEP ONE: Close your eyes and ask yourself: "What are my deepest inner values?" Write down, in the upper left box, three core values—words that have deep meaning and purpose in your life (for example: "love," "integrity," "family," "peace," etc.).

STEP TWO: Write down the top 10 weaknesses, faults, or problems that interfere with your happiness and success. As you list each one, take a slow deep breath and consciously relax your body and mind.

STEP THREE: Think about your friends, family, and colleagues. What faults and weaknesses would they say you have? Write them down in one of the two remaining boxes, and then close your eyes and relax. Remember: you are learning how to consciously interrupt the negative emotions associated with each item you have listed on your C.R.A.P. Board.

STEP FOUR: In the remaining box, again think about your family, friends, and colleagues and write down all of the positive qualities and strengths that they would say you have. This list is very important because when your mind is ruminating on negativity, it blocks out all of the positive qualities that are also part of your personality.

When you have completed your C.R.A.P. Board, place it in front of you and gaze at it, relaxing as deeply as you possibly can. Don't judge anything you see; just observe it as you would any another object in the room. You should immediately notice a gradual reduction in the intensity of your negative thoughts and feelings.

We recommend that you put your C.R.A.P. Board on a wall where you can see it regularly while at work. Don't throw it away! If you do, your unconscious mind will start to ruminate on all that negativity. When your "C.R.A.P." is on a sheet of paper, your brain knows that your problems have been recognized, and are waiting to be dealt with when you have the time and desire to do so. Your paper becomes like a second hard drive on a computer, freeing up your memory to focus on your desires, goals, and dreams.

Writing down negative thoughts and feelings throughout the workday is one of the easiest ways to remain positive and productive.

Calculate your Positivity Ratio

The C.R.A.P. Board exercise interrupts your brain's tendency to ruminate on negative feelings and thoughts,[18] but it's equally important to increase your awareness of positive thoughts and feelings. As Barbara Fredrickson, Distinguished Professor of Psychology at the University of North Carolina, says, positivity "comes in many forms and flavors":

> Think of the times you feel connected to others and loved; when you feel playful, creative, or silly; when you feel blessed and at one with your surroundings; when your soul is stirred by the sheer beauty of existence; or when you feel energized and excited by a new idea or hobby. Positivity reigns whenever positive emotions— like love, joy, gratitude, serenity, interest, and inspiration—touch and open your heart.[19]

Fredrickson also identified one of the most important factors for predicting success in both personal and business relationships. It's called the "positivity ratio," and it's a comparison of the number of positive thoughts and negative thoughts you generate while working and conversing with others. In general, if you habitually express fewer than three positive thoughts or behaviors for each negative one, you can damage your relationships at home and at work. This finding confirms Marcial Losada's research with corporate teams, showing that when the positivity ratio falls below 3:1 in a company, bankruptcy is more likely to result.[20] In addition, John Gottman's research with marital couples shows that low positivity ratios predict impending divorce.[21]

Fredrickson, Losada, and Gottman realized that if you want your relationships to flourish, you will need to consistently generate five to seven positive messages for

---

HOW LONG CAN YOU GO WITHOUT HAVING A NEGATIVE THOUGHT?

Do you think you could go through a single day without having some degree of worry, doubt, or disappointment? We did several online surveys, and only 3 out of 50 people got past one hour! Some people made it through 3–5 hours, the average was 20 minutes, but only 2 people reported making it through the entire day. Here are some of the comments made by our participants:

LC: *I failed miserably; only stayed positive for 20 minutes! But I'm committed to fail better tomorrow!*

GM: *I made it through an hour, but I really had to concentrate to control my thoughts!*

VS: *I went several hours by writing the negative thoughts down; it made them insignificant! The more I thought of positive things, the less negativity I had.*

LS: *I did it for a whole day! It's great…made me feel like everything is going to be ok.*

EXTRA CREDIT: When you catch yourself being negative, generate three positive thoughts or recall three positive memories. This helps to strengthen the optimism circuits in your frontal lobe.

each negative utterance you make. For example, saying, "I'm disappointed," to another person (or to yourself) counts as an expression of negativity, as does a frown or a gesture of anger or contempt. People with low positivity ratios are likely to be diagnosed with depression.[22]

Here's one of the easiest ways to calculate your positivity ratio, but it takes three days to do. On day one, write down every negative thought and feeling you have— anything that irritates or frustrates you, any small or large disappointments, annoyances, suspicions, moments of anger or depression, feelings of shame or embarrassment, negative thoughts you have about other people, feelings of disgust, instances in which you blamed yourself or others, felt anxious or nervous, worried about something, or felt guilt, etc. Don't be surprised if you find yourself having a dozen or more negative thoughts in the first hour of this exercise.

Do the same exercise on day two, writing down your negative feelings and thoughts. You'll probably have far fewer items on your list because of the increased awareness generated by day one.

On day three, write down all of the positive thoughts and feelings you have. The more you observe your positivity, the more items you'll be able to list. Examples: things that made you smile or laugh, experiences that made you feel interested or curious, thoughts of gratitude or appreciation, pleasurable feelings and thoughts, activities that made you feel happy or joyful, moments of serenity or peacefulness, feelings of confidence or contentment, etc.

Compare the number of positive feelings and thoughts you had on day three with the number of negative thoughts and feelings from day two. That's your positivity ratio, but if your number is low, don't despair (that's just adding more negativity to the list!). Look at it as a potential indicator of your degree of optimism. Some people, for example, can have a very high negativity ratio, but they do not overly react to their negative thoughts. Still, the research is convincing: the pursuit of positivity will bring you greater happiness, mental health, and success.[23]

Take Control of Your Inner Speech

Everyday consciousness, as we discussed in the previous chapter, involves a continual stream of inner dialogue called inner speech. It gives voice to your interior experience of the world around you,[24] and as researchers at the University of Toronto found, "the inner voice helps us to exert self-control by enhancing our ability to restrain our impulses."[25]

Inner speech begins in the first few years of life, and it never stops, even when you think your mind is quiet.[26] It plays a specific role in orienting you toward other people in the world,[27] and it also helps to regulate self-awareness.[28]

When you pay close attention to your inner speech, you'll discover that each emotional state—anger, fear, depression, joy, contentment, etc.—has its own personality. Some of these subtle voices are critical, others are supportive, and a few have the ability to give you wise counsel. The self-critical voices stimulate error-detection circuits, whereas a self-reassuring voice will stimulate the neural circuits involved with compassion and empathy.[29] They all serve a purpose, and when you learn how to mindfully observe them, they become your neural board of advisors.

Here's an exercise that will help you to identify these inner voices and distinguish the useful ones from the disruptive ones. First, you need to be very relaxed, so take a few moments to yawn and slowly stretch. The more relaxed you are, the easier it will be for you to hear your inner speech. Close your eyes and remain silent for as long as you can. Soon you'll notice fragmentary thoughts drifting in and out of consciousness. Take a slow relaxing breath after each thought, let it float away as if it were a cloud in the sky, and pay attention to the next thought. You might hear voices of criticism or support or confusion, like these: "This is boring." "I really like this." "Am I doing this right?" "I need to get back to work." The longer you observe these thoughts and voices, the more intense the experience becomes. Your job is to simply observe, without judgment, so that you can learn how your inner speech influences your actions and mood. As eight randomized controlled studies have shown, this mindfulness exercise is one of the fastest ways to reduce stress, anxiety, irritability, and depression.[30] Observing your inner speech helps you manage strong emotional reactions, and it gives you the power to modify inappropriate behavior.[31] You can even have conversations with these inner personas, debating and negotiating with them.

You can also manipulate negative inner speech by deliberately substituting positive speech. For example, if you notice that your inner voices are worrying, you can tell yourself this: I can do it! I will succeed! I am confident that I will find a solution. Research shows that if you are feeling anxious, worried, or highly stressed, positive inner speech can help you to feel calmer.[32] Positive self-talk also improves work performance, weeding out the critical voices that cause you to worry or procrastinate.[33]

When inner speech turns chronically negative, it can cause eating disorders, insomnia, agoraphobia, compulsive gambling, sexual dysfunction, low self-esteem, and depression. But if you continually interrupt the negative voices with positive speech, you'll improve attentiveness, autonomy, confidence, and work performance.[34] Sara White, at the University of California, San Francisco, recommends the following strategies for turning negative inner speech into positive self-talk. Doing so will help enhance your performance, satisfaction, and professional success.[35]

- Keep a written record of your inner speech
- Confront your inner critic with a positive voice and rewrite self-limiting scripts
- Look for the gift and opportunity in every obstacle you meet
- Focus on your accomplishments, not your setbacks
- Review, reinforce, and practice your new self-talk

As you practice mindfulness—noticing the flow of inner thoughts, feelings, and sensations, you'll discover a new level of awareness: the voice of intuition. It gives you a bigger picture of yourself and the world. If you remain mindfully alert, a sudden insight may burst into your consciousness. This kind of intuitional awareness is often difficult to put into words, but it *feels* true, and it's driven by areas of the brain that extend far beyond the decision-making centers in the frontal lobe.[36] Intuition is your inner voice of wisdom and you can directly ask it for advice.

> ## THE BEST ANTI-ANXIETY DRUG IS...
>
> Pleasure! Mental anxiety is a thought process generated in your right frontal lobe, but it also stimulates the fear circuits in deeper regions of the brain. Fortunately, pleasant experiences and memories reduce the fight-or-flight response by sending signals to the brain that everything is safe and going well.
>
> Make a list of activities that give you a sense of pleasure and that take less than 60 seconds to do. This is your anti-anxiety arsenal, and it's faster than any pill or therapeutic intervention!

"Stop It!"

Many years ago, the comedian Bob Newhart created a television skit in which he played a psychotherapist. No matter what the patient's problem was—worry, fear, anger, depression, procrastination, etc.—he had a two-word solution. He'd lean forward and shout, "Stop it!" It's called thought suppression, and it's a highly effective strategy for interrupting minor negative thoughts, feelings, and behavior. The technique is simple: tune into the unwanted thought or feeling and tell that inner voice to stop it. You'll be surprised how often it works, and the latest research suggests that it may even enhance your sense of well-being over time.[37]

But if the negativity remains, research shows that mindfully observing it is a more effective way to weaken its influence on your life.[38] Or you can merely focus on your breathing for a minute or two. This has a powerful effect on eliminating intrusive thoughts and keeping your mind focused on your goal.[39]

However, if you suffer from chronic anxiety or depression, thought suppression can make matters worse, disrupting the decision-making processes in your frontal lobe.[40]

CHAPTER SUMMARY

- Decision making involves the conscious use of four essential decision-making processes controlled by your frontal lobe. First, you need to realistically *evaluate* your ability to achieve a specific goal. Second, you must create a comprehensive *plan* to follow. Third, you must take action, *implementing* your plan. Finally, you need to *monitor* and measure your progress, making *adjustments* and modifications to your plan to overcome problems and obstacles.

- Writing down your goal increases your chances of success by 50%. Sharing your written plan, combined with weekly progress reports to a friend or colleague, increases the likelihood of success by 75%.

SUMMARY OF EXERCISES
TO IMPROVE DECISION MAKING

1. For each important goal, create a written action plan and a timeline, listing the strategies you'll use to achieve that goal. Send your plan to a friend or colleague who will act as your accountability partner. Provide weekly progress reports until your goal is achieved.

2. Use a Daily Commitment Sheet for 8–12 weeks to

train your brain to stay focused on specific goals and successes. Our Executive MBA students found this to be one of the most helpful tools for getting through busy days.

- Each morning, write down a goal you know you can achieve, and then write down a value word that will deepen the meaning and purpose of your goal. Visualize yourself achieving the goal, and visualize any obstacle or sabotage behavior that could interfere with your plan.
- Write down the obstacle along with a counter-strategy that will help solve the problem. Then visualize yourself overcoming the problem.
- Create an affirmation: "I breathe in [a quality I desire]; I breathe out [a quality I want to rid myself of]." Repeat this throughout the day.
- At the end of the day write down what you accomplished, the things you did well, and the things and people you feel grateful for.

3. When you find yourself ruminating on negative thoughts and feelings, jot them down on a sheet of paper (your C.R.A.P. Board). When you relax and mindfully gaze at your list, the emotional centers of the brain become less reactive, and this negative ruminating will lessen.

4. Push your positivity ratio as high as possible. Each time you notice a negative thought or feeling, reflect on several positive memories and personal strengths. Test yourself: see if you can go a single day without having a negative thought (few people can do this).

5. Train yourself to mindfully observe your inner

speech—the positive and negative voices that control many of the decision-making processes in the frontal lobe. Control them through mindful awareness and by substituting positive self-talk for negative ruminating. And, when in conflict, have an imaginary conversation with the different personas.

6. When you notice minor negative thoughts and feelings, you can deliberately interrupt them by saying "Stop it!" or consciously ignoring them. If the negativity continues, or if you find yourself anxiously ruminating on your problems, take a few minutes to focus on your natural breathing and then mindfully observe the negativity as you remain deeply relaxed. Then focus on your values.

Remember: the human brain evaluates the world and your actions using an instinctual pleasure/pain system. Any time you experience anything pleasurable, or recall a pleasant memory, or visualize yourself successfully reaching a goal, the fear centers quiet down and the negative speech generated in your right frontal lobe decreases. So use your mindfulness clock to remind yourself, once or twice an hour, to do something pleasurable.

CHAPTER 8.

Creativity—The Third Pillar of Wealth: Imagination, Daydreaming, and Intuition

Although the study of the brain dates back to ancient Egypt, it wasn't until the 1800s that scientists began to understand how neurons influenced a person's thoughts, emotions, and behavior. Only within the last decade have scientists turned their attention to intuition and sudden moments of insight—key neurological processes associated with human creativity. We now know that creative imagination is essential for learning, enhancing personal development, and maintaining a healthy brain.

To understand the distinction between decision making (Pillar #2) and creativity (Pillar #3), it's important to clarify the difference between consciousness and awareness.

145

Quite often the terms are used interchangeably, but for the purposes of this book, we define awareness as the bigger picture, one that includes different forms of conscious behavior. For example, you may be barely conscious of the contents of your dreams, but when you wake up, you are often *aware* of the fact that you were dreaming.

The images below exemplify this. Figure 15 shows the location of the motivation-and-reward circuit—the

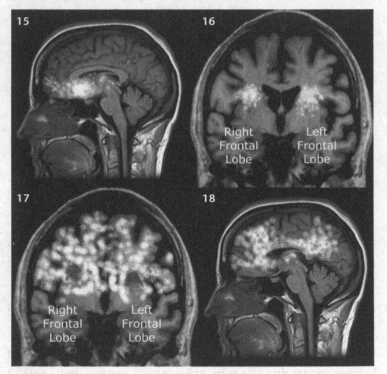

Figure 15. Awareness begins when the nucleus accumbens (the M-Drive) releases dopamine that travels into the frontal lobe.

Figure 16. Conscious decision making activates a very small area in the front part of your frontal lobe. Other brain areas become less active.

Figure 17. When you relax, the decision-making areas turn off as other frontal-lobe areas activate. Daydreaming, fantasies, and awareness increase.

Figure 18. Creative imagination involves many areas of the frontal and parietal lobes, including the insula and anterior cingulate.

M-Drive—and how the release of dopamine spreads into the lower portions of the frontal lobe to initiate conscious decision-making processes. Figure 16 shows the small areas in the frontal lobe that activate when you are consciously focusing on a goal or task. Figures 17 and 18 (front and side views of the neocortex) show much larger increases in activity throughout your brain when your mind slips into semiconscious states of imagination, daydreaming, and creative problem solving.

Consciousness (figure 16) is primarily a language-driven process, whereas awareness (figures 17 and 18) is more of a wordless "felt" sense, an experience of what is happening in the present moment. Your brain is aware of many things going on around you and inside of you, but consciousness is more limited, a frontal-lobe activity that selectively ignores any detail that could distract you from performing a particular task or pursuing a specific goal. Here's an example: as you focus on reading these words, you are probably not aware of what you are sitting on. But the moment you shift your conscious attention to the feelings of your body pressing against the chair, your ability to focus on these words rapidly fades. If you then shift your attention to your feet or the background noises occurring in the present moment, you'll become less cognizant of the chair.

This exemplifies the four to seven chunks of working memory information we discussed in chapter 6—our neurological definition of consciousness. With practice, you can expand your consciousness to become more aware of what your brain is constantly processing (figures 16 and 17, above). Try it right now: see if you can simultaneously be aware of these words, the chair you are sitting on, your feet, and the background noises in the room. It's not difficult to do, but you'd probably have a hard time describing to someone else what you actually did in your mind. Instead of focusing your attention on just one or two things (called convergent thinking), you allow your mind to become aware of as many different thoughts, feelings, and sensations as possible. You neither select, judge, nor focus on anything in particular. This is our formal definition of mindfulness. Psychologists and neuroscientists call it open monitoring, or divergent thinking, a unique state of mind that has been shown to generate new creative ideas.[1]

Creative Imagination

Many animals and insects also have varying degrees of consciousness that allow them to make decisions and take voluntary action in the world.[2] For example, bees can analyze a problem, predict future outcomes, and avoid making decisions that would interfere with achieving specific goals.[3] Even mollusks and squid exhibit limited degrees of awareness and consciousness.[4]

Most neurobiologists agree that some degree of awareness exists in almost every living organism, and as brains evolve, consciousness slowly emerges, giving some animals greater abilities to learn new behaviors that will help them thrive in a competitive world. As the human brain matures, humans become more aware of their own cognitive and emotional processes, and that is what we are calling consciousness, a neurological state of mind that is dependent on—and mostly limited to—small areas in the frontal lobe (figure 15, above). You can have awareness without consciousness, but you cannot have consciousness without awareness.

Consciousness keeps you focused on the present moment, but awareness gives you the ability to tap into your imagination and creativity, processes that involve some of the newest evolutionary structures in your brain.[5] Whimsical reveries, autobiographical memories, elaborate visions about the future, imaginary social interactions, and vague feelings are all mixed together in a dreamlike state of awareness that often defies description.[6]

Creativity is a form of spontaneous cognition, or mind wandering, and it's the default state that your brain goes into when you are mentally and physically passive. Your focus softens and your mind turns inward. It is, in essence, a semiconscious form of dreaming.[7] You can enter this state of exceptional awareness by deliberately interrupting the normal decision-making processes you use when working. It's neurologically similar to what a musician does when he or she improvises.[8] The more you open yourself to new experiences, with the willingness to suspend old belief systems, the more you will stimulate the creativity circuits in your brain.[9]

Daydreaming and Creative Problem Solving

Physically, your brain is constantly changing as billions of neurons slowly rearrange their connections in a vast soup of neurochemical and neuroelectrical activity. Different electrolytes migrate through the envelope of each neuron, telling it when to rest or take action, and as the activity changes so do your thoughts and feelings. Throughout your day, different patterns of brain activity occur that generate different states of mind.

But what happens when you encounter an unusually difficult problem, one you can't solve with your current knowledge? Initially, your decision-making processes begin to slow down as your prefrontal cortex gets tired. When this occurs, the creativity circuits (figure 17) in your brain begin to light up.[10] Your mind begins to daydream and your prefrontal cortex refreshes itself so that the rest of your brain can engage in creative problem solving.[11] You are literally thinking outside the box of everyday consciousness and decision making.

This is when you are most likely to have sudden insights that allow you to see a problem in a new way. During these "aha" moments—as neuroscientists refer to them—there is a rapid shift of neural activity throughout the brain.[12] The rational mind is interrupted and your sense of self is altered as a different form of awareness emerges. You'll see problems differently and you'll intuitively find solutions in ways that often feel mysterious.[13] Most people unconsciously slip in and out of these daydreaming states hundreds of times a day, never realizing how useful they can be for consciously evaluating problems and making wiser decisions.

The Two Minds in Your Brain: Conceptual Creativity vs. Decision Making

Creativity, imagination, and daydreaming all share similar neural circuits that involve many parts of the brain. For example: your parietal lobes might generate fanciful images of people and places,[14] your visual cortex can construct otherworldly images,[15] and different areas of your frontal and temporal lobes can work together to produce improvisational masterpieces.[16]

But it's the *conceptual* creativity of abstract thinking that is truly remarkable, giving your frontal lobes the power to turn new ideas into original strategies that can greatly increase your income, happiness, and health. Conceptual creativity allows you to build new neurological circuits that bring long-term satisfaction and fulfillment.[17] What this means, in practical terms, is that everyone has two separate "minds" that are constantly struggling to achieve desired goals: your "creative mind" (Pillar #3) and your "decision-making mind" (Pillar #4). Your decision-making mind is the mind you associate with your thoughts, and is illustrated in figure 16, above. In this logical and rational process, you are recalling past memories and planning future events. You are concentrating on different tasks, fully aware of how your actions are affecting the outside world. You use your decision-making mind to notice how you feel, to talk with other people, and to evaluate your degree of success. These are conscious processes that you can manipulate at will.

Conceptual creativity, a part of your creative mind, is very different, and it appears to be actively engaged in an unconscious dialogue with the decision-making processes taking place in your prefrontal lobes.[18] It is governed by a vast network that can interact with many parts of the brain that are illustrated in figures 17 and 18, above. Conceptual creativity functions independently from external stimuli and it is filled with *self-generated thoughts*, a unique and often mysterious cognitive process that integrates spontaneous perceptions with feelings, memories, fantasies, and aspirations.

These creative thoughts and concepts are formed without any conscious effort, and they often seem meaningless, which explains why most people don't recognize the potential value of their inner creativity. But if you take the time to mindfully observe this strange landscape of your inner, conceptually creative mind, you'll often find novel solutions that can resolve some of the most difficult problems in your life. But there's a hitch: many neuroscientists believe that these creative thoughts can disrupt normal decision making, causing serious distress and unhappiness. [19] We believe, based on the research presented in this book, that the mindfulness and NeuroWisdom exercises you are learning will teach you how to tap into the healthy side of conceptual creativity.

Creativity is a Double-Edged Sword

Mind wandering and daydreaming also play crucial roles in planning and innovative problem solving.[20] But creativity also has a dark side: after 40 years of investigation, psychologists and neuroscientists agree that too much can make you crazy.[21] Creative fantasies are like a drug, and they can cause the M-Drive to release so much dopamine that your conscious mind becomes delusional.[22] In other words, you can become so immersed in your specific desire that you lose perspective, and even lose touch with reality. Greed is a perfect example—when monetary temptations are great enough, the M-Drive becomes overly active, interfering with the neural circuits governing social cooperation and ethical behavior.[23] Money becomes an addictive drug instead of a beneficial tool, so when it comes to creativity, moderation is the best choice. Too much and you'll be governed by the primitive impulses of pleasure and greed; too little, and your ability to change will be impaired.

Concentrate, and Then Take a Creativity Break

Uncontrolled creativity can have detrimental effects on a person's mood, but controlled creativity appears to have many positive effects.[24] You can take control over your creative circuits by consciously shifting back and forth between periods of high work productivity and brief periods of intense imagination. The first and most important step is to relax. As researchers in the Department of Cognitive Science at Case Western University point out, a relaxed mental state (when you are not focused on any task, goal, or problem) "plays a central role in emotional self-awareness, social cognition, and ethical decision making. It is also strongly linked to creativity and openness to new ideas."[25]

When you are fully relaxed, the next step is to mindfully observe the way your thoughts and feelings constantly change. This increases your ability to gain intuitive insights into problems,[26] and the more you practice mindful awareness the more you'll increase your creative performance.[27]

Mindfulness will also give you the ability to weed out

negative fantasies that undermine the healthy aspects of mind wandering and creative daydreaming.[28] Close your eyes and yawn about 10 times, noticing how each yawn changes your awareness. You'll notice afterwards that it becomes difficult to focus on anything specific, allowing you to become more aware of what is happening in the present moment.

Now allow your mind to wander wherever it wants to go. If you have trouble doing this, recall a time from childhood when you used to daydream, or imagine yourself falling asleep, entering that twilight state where fleeting images occur.

Next, bring yourself back into everyday consciousness and deliberately think about a problem you've been

THE NEUROSCIENCE OF LEARNING

Want to change a behavior or develop a new skill? It doesn't matter if you are a person or a snail, for as Nobel Laureate Eric Kandel discovered, all you need is "repeated training interspersed with periods of rest."

Repeated exposure to any new activity or thought process (even if for just a few days) will form neural habits that will last for weeks. Select a new behavior you'd like to develop (staying focused, remaining optimistic, etc.) and commit to four days of conscientious practice, 20 minutes per day. After each round of practice, close your eyes, yawn a few times, and slowly stretch. In his book, *In Search of Memory*, Kandel explains how the learning circuits in your brain need those periods of relaxation "to establish long-term memory." However, if you don't keep practicing the new skill, the learned behavior will fade away.

struggling with. Notice how your mind analytically studies the problem, and then deliberately shifts back into a restful state of daydreaming. Going back and forth like this allows you to grasp these subtly different states of mind. In the resting state, thoughts are fragmentary, images are fleeting, and feelings are constantly changing.

Once again, think about that problem you've been struggling with. Reimmerse yourself in that dreamlike state of relaxation and ask your intuition for an insight. Internally watch and listen to your intuition. The longer you remain calm and observant, the more likely it is you'll discover something new. Most insights will occur in the first five minutes of this exercise, and the research shows that it leads to better decision making when you resume work.[29]

A Presummary Quiz!

Creativity is one of the most important tools we have, but it's one of the least studied areas in business, psychology, and neuroscience. This is due in part to the fact that creative problem solving is a largely unconscious process that relies on your view of the world and subliminal perceptions of your inner reality. In contrast, conscious decision making is heavily dependent on language, conceptual reasoning, and paying attention only to those details related to carrying out specific tasks and achieving desired goals.

Learning is significantly dependent on the creativity circuits in your brain, but the process is unique for each person. We want you to take a moment, right now, and try this little experiment before you read the following summary. Get some paper and a pen, and write down the most important insights you gained from this chapter. First, close your eyes and deeply relax, letting your mind wander and daydream for a minute or two. Then use your imagination and intuition to answer these questions:

1. What, for you, were the most interesting points made in this chapter?
2. How might you use this information to lower stress and increase your performance level at work?
3. Can you visualize the areas in the brain that control decision making and creativity?

Answering these questions *intuitively* will increase the value of the material you just read, and since you're not going to be tested on it, your brain is free to choose the most useful information and reject the rest. This strategy helps you to embed important information into your long-term memory.[30]

The next time you encounter a difficult problem, or fumble while pursuing a desired goal, put yourself into a deep state of relaxed mindfulness and ask yourself these questions: "What am I missing? What have I overlooked? What can I do differently?" Self-reflective questions such as these will enhance your cognitive skills and increase future chances of success.[31] And don't forget to ask your intuition, which is the creative problem-solving mechanism that operates outside of the everyday decision-making strategies you normally use!

CHAPTER SUMMARY

1. Consciousness is the limited part of your awareness in which you pay attention to details as you perform a particular task. When the decision-making circuits in the frontal lobe tire, your brain briefly defaults to a dreamlike resting state enabling neural activity to increase throughout your brain as logic and reason give way to spontaneous imagination. This enhances the brain's natural creative problem-solving process, which can bring surprising moments of insight, clarity, and intuitive inspiration.

2. You can deliberately enter a state of enhanced awareness by relaxing and mindfully observing the constant flow of your fragmentary thoughts, feelings, images, and sensations.

3. By shifting back and forth between conscious decision making and creative imagination, you improve the cognitive functioning of your brain in ways that allow you to make better decisions.

CHAPTER 9.

Thinking Outside the Box: Nine Strategies to Increase Creativity at Work

Tapping into creativity is one of the easiest things to do, because the brain does it all the time! It happens when you get tired at work, when you get distracted and your attention wavers, and when you relax. When your mind begins to wander, thoughts become fragmentary, and fantasies often kick in as the imagination circuits in your brain are stimulated. Even if you aren't aware of it, this creative process happens many times each hour, giving your frontal lobe a chance to recharge itself with the neurochemicals needed for concentration and decision making.

Sadly, many children are raised in school environments where teachers criticize them when their attention wanders away from classroom material. We now know that the brain needs these brief daydreaming breaks to turn new information into long-term memories. Educators can deepen the learning experience of their students by requiring them to take frequent relaxation breaks in the classroom and applying the key principles of brain-based experiential learning described in chapter 2:

- Visualizing goals, obstacles, and solutions
- Training the mind to remain highly focused for brief periods
- Practicing mindful awareness of feelings, sensations, and thoughts
- Integrating intuitive thinking with logic and reason
- Using a values word or phrase to increase motivation
- Integrating pleasurable activities into the classroom and work environment
- Maintaining unwavering optimism and interrupting negative rumination

Novelty, Playfulness, and Creativity

The same principles hold true at home, work or school: if you don't take time to relax, play, and daydream once or twice an hour, productivity decreases. When you do, your intuitive creativity can give you a competitive edge, particularly in the workplace. Take, for example, the unique environment created at Google called the Google Garage: a playground-like space cluttered with unusual items, computers, and idea boards. When the Google Garage was first created, they accidently put too many people in the room, literally elbow to elbow, and the employees had no choice but to interact with each other. Something amazing happened: creative innovation soared, social cooperation increased, and a number of new products were devised.[1] This illuminates several key principles of creativity: when you bring together people from different backgrounds, and then ask them to think outside the box, new discoveries are made. Teams function better and work satisfaction increases when you create aesthetically pleasing environments that encourage empathy and imagination.[2]

Ask Your Inner Genius

When you do something new and seek out novel experiences, you stimulate the motivational centers of the brain. So if you want to be creative, be curious. Interrupt your routine and brainstorm with other people. Look at the world through different perspectives. Be wild, daring, and even silly—like a child—because it enriches your problem-solving skills.[3] For example, let's say you're struggling with a work-related project. Imagine yourself having a conversation with Steve Jobs or Warren Buffett, or anyone whose expertise you admire. What might they say to you? What would Einstein or Bugs Bunny suggest? When you bring this type of playfulness into the creative process, it actually improves cognition—and the neural circuits governing the social brain.[4]

To consciously enter a creative state, begin by using any of the relaxation exercises described in this book:

yawning, superslow stretching, gently stroking your hands and arms, even taking a 60-second power nap. This interrupts the narrow-minded focus involved in everyday decision making.

Once you are deeply relaxed, mind wandering begins. But you'll need to practice mindfulness if you want to become aware of these fast-moving forms of cognition just outside your conscious decision-making activities. Just follow your imagination wherever it wants to go, without controlling or censoring it. Observe your inner experience and immerse yourself in the sensations. Do this for 3–10 minutes, and when you return to work, you'll immediately feel more energized, focused, and productive, even if you weren't able to notice any specific feeling or thought. You'll also notice that most of the stress from the previous hour of work will have vanished.

When your mind is wandering and daydreaming, you can actively engage it in dialogue. For example, you can ask your intuition—a specific neural process that takes place when you are mindfully relaxed—for a new solution or insight. Try this simple exercise. First, close your eyes and visualize a small problem or obstacle you are currently wrestling with. Then allow your mind to wander for one or two minutes (use the timer on your phone or mindfulness clock). When you hear the tone, directly ask a question of your intuition, shift into your internal listening mode, and then mindfully observe the subtle thoughts or feelings that emerge. Write them down. Then close your eyes again and ask for another suggestion. Write down whatever comes to you, and when you have done this three or four times, mindfully gaze at the items on your list. Often you'll gain greater insight into your situation, and the insight will often surprise you. You might be worried about money or closing a sale, and that inner voice of wisdom might whisper: "You don't really have a problem; you just like to worry!" Look for those kinds of thoughts, but if nothing comes to you, resume work and repeat this exercise several hours later. You'll feel more relaxed, and the unconscious processes in your brain will continue to work on the problem. As Einstein purportedly said, "We cannot solve problems using the same kind of thinking we used when we created them."[5]

Create an Insight Board

You can also train yourself to become more cognizant of your inner creativity and the ways it can change your life. Take out a sheet of paper and think about the previous times you've had sudden bursts of insight—those "aha" moments that solved a problem or made your life feel more meaningful and purposeful. Write them down, and when you can't think of any more, close your eyes and deeply relax, letting your imagination and intuition take over.

Think about the experiences you've had that changed your outlook and beliefs, and write them down. Visualize past teachers, therapists, or mentors who enlightened you, or illuminated a side of yourself you had not recognized. Add them to your list and savor each memory. Think about the people who opened your heart, or taught you how to feel more connected to yourself and others. If you have had spiritual epiphanies, put them on your Insight Board.

Writing will slow your thinking down, and as you go

back and forth between the writing task and remembering experiences that changed your life, you'll increase your ability to recognize the smaller insights that happen on a daily basis. Close your eyes again and take 60 seconds to yawn and slowly stretch. Then ask your intuition to respond to each of the topics below, and briefly add those experiences to your list. If nothing comes to mind, move on to the next category:

- Books, movies, plays, music, etc., that deeply affected you or changed your life
- Friends, lovers, and family members who profoundly influenced you in positive ways
- Experiences that changed your view of yourself
- Events or activities that changed your view of the world
- Exceptional experiences that changed your relationship to money and work
- Realizations that profoundly changed your beliefs
- Anything else that you would consider enlightening or life-transforming

Once more, gaze at the items on your Insight Board and immerse yourself in the feelings they evoke. Here is an example of how one of our students responded to this exercise:

> I realized that my life has been filled with many amazing moments, and I realized that I usually just recall the difficult times I've had. I immediately felt better about my whole life, my past and my present, and I felt more optimistic about the future. These feelings stayed with me for weeks!

We highly recommend you do this experiment with a friend or colleague, sharing your memories with each other. You'll find that the dialogue will trigger other insights you have forgotten about. An important tip to remember: when describing these events, don't just talk *about* them; talk *from* them in a way that resonates with the original experience.

Research shows that when you savor the memories of prior insights and "aha" moments, you're priming your brain to have more.[6]

Be Unpredictable

Mihaly Csikszentmihalyi is the Distinguished Professor of Psychology and Management at Claremont Graduate University, and one of the world's leading researchers on creativity and optimal performance. His suggestion: be unquenchably curious, and surprise yourself every day.[7] His research found that creative people never lose their sense of awe and wonder about the world, nor do they allow themselves to be trapped by repetitive daily routines. They maintain a childlike curiosity about everything, exploring areas of interest that are far removed from their work.

Csikszentmihalyi recommends that you constantly look for things that are different and unusual. For example, when looking at a familiar object—a tree, a plate, a person's face—ask yourself penetrating questions: What is its *essence*? How is this experience *unique*? He also recommends that you try to surprise another person every day. Do or say something unexpected. Break a predictable routine. Or just send them a note of appreciation.

Do the same thing daily with your own life. Surprise

yourself. Eat something you've never tried before. Walk backwards down the street. Sing in the office. Csikszentmihalyi adds that it is important to keep a daily creativity diary if you want to deepen this essential quality that leads to happiness and success.

He also recommends that you engage in *divergent thinking*—open-ended, nonlinear, irrational thought—when seeking solutions for problems. Convergent thinking is what you do when you're making daily decisions; you usually select one of just a few solutions or ideas. Divergent thinking is less organized and less rational—you are literally thinking outside the box of everyday consciousness. Here's how you do it. Pick a problem—personal, emotional, social, or busness-related—and write it down. Now, thinking as fast as you can, come up with as many possible solutions as you can, even crazy ones (which is how your creative brain actually thinks). When you have 10–20 items, look at your list. One of these ideas will often stand out as a simple way to address your problem.

Also, when a colleague asks you a question, try not giving them a typical response. Instead, say something different, unexpected, or even humorous. Take risks with your thinking and engage in brainstorming sessions, making as many original suggestions as you can dream up. This process enhances cognitive and emotional functioning,[8] and it helps you integrate the spontaneous productions of daydreaming with the decision-making processes in your frontal lobe.[9]

Clear Your Mind with a Single Sound

Sometimes it's difficult to suspend the chatter of everyday consciousness. Here's a very simple sound meditation that not only interrupts inner speech, but also lowers neural activity throughout the brain.[10] First you'll enter a state of inner silence and peacefulness. The experience can be profound, because everything you are consciously aware of begins to fade away—your thoughts, your feelings, even your sense of yourself and the world surrounding you. But as your awareness returns, it becomes very easy to intuitively engage in creative problem solving.

The exercise involves the repetition of "om," a word often used in different Eastern spiritual practices. When researchers conducted a brain-scan study on the om meditation, they decided to test whether other sounds had the same effect. They asked the meditators to make an *s* sound, which eliminated the vibration sensations in the body and face. We really don't know why the *m* part of the sound is so important for eliciting this decrease in neural activity, only that the *s* sound didn't affect the brain. When you rapidly change the neural activity in your brain, it appears to prime the brain to have more insights and "aha" experiences. But you have to have the *intention*—the conscious desire—to discover something new,[11] and the *willingness* to be spontaneous.[12]

For this exercise, all you have to do is to sit upright in a chair and close your eyes. First, take 60 seconds to yawn, slowly stretch, and become as relaxed as you possibly can. Next, take a very slow, deep breath in through your mouth, and as you slowly exhale, make the sound of

"Oooommmm," drawing it out as long as you comfortably can. The *o* sound will come out first, and as you slowly close your mouth, the *m* sound will cause your lips to vibrate. When the sound fades away, take another slow, deep breath through your mouth.

As you begin the om meditation, pay close attention to every nuance of the experience: the resonant sound, the sensations in your chest, throat, and face, and the tonal qualities as you say the om sound in different ways. Then allow the sounds and sensations to take you into a deeper, trance-like state. Go as long as you like, and when your intuition tells you to stop, sit quietly for a few more minutes observing your feelings and thoughts. Then ask yourself any of the following questions:

- What insights or self-discoveries have I just had?
- What would be a new way of addressing a current problem, obstacle, or issue?
- Which of my inner values would I like to focus on for the next hour?

Now take out a pen and a sheet of paper, and write down a question that you would like to gain a new perspective on. Repeat the om meditation, and once again lose yourself in the sounds and sensations. After a few minutes (go as long as you wish), open your eyes and look at the question on your paper. Begin to spontaneously write for the next few minutes. Be creative and use your imagination, trying to remain in this altered state of consciousness throughout the process.

At work, try taking a two-minute om meditation

during your relaxation break. Then return to work. You'll be surprised at how much energy and focus it will bring you. That's the benefit of consciously going back and forth between decision making, inner silence, and creative play.

CHAPTER SUMMARY

1. Relaxing slows down everyday consciousness and decision-making processes, making it easier to access the creative-problem-solving circuits that extend throughout the brain.
2. When you mindfully observe how your mind wanders and daydreams, you gain greater access to your intuition and imagination.
3. When you train yourself to think outside the box, you'll solve more problems with greater ease.
4. Encourage playful, innovative, and spontaneous conversations with others. It enhances teamwork cooperation and work productivity.
5. Dialogue with imaginary experts and ask your "inner wisdom" for advice.
6. Create an Insight Board, listing past insights and transformative experiences. Savor those memories whenever you feel frustrated or emotionally stuck.
7. Keep a daily Surprise Journal. Each day, do something new, different, and unusual—for yourself and for someone else. Look at familiar objects and people as if you were seeing them for the very first time. Be curious about everything and maintain a childlike sense of awe and wonder toward your work and life.

8. When solving problems, be prolific. Write down as many possible solutions—even silly ones—as you can think of. Brainstorm with your colleagues and push the boundaries of your imagination.

9. Try saying "Oooommmm" for a few minutes to clear your mind. Then mindfully ponder any problem, obstacle, or issue you are curious about or struggling with.

Remember: the most recent neuroscientific research finds that mindfulness is the most reliable way to enhance creativity and originality.[13] When your frontal lobe goes into a resting state, other parts of your brain become highly active. This, in turn, interrupts habitual ways of thinking while simultaneously making you more productive, creative, and self-aware.[14]

CHAPTER 10.

Awareness—The Fourth Pillar of Wealth: Fairness, Empathy, and Generosity

Awareness begins when you are born and continues to grow until the day you die. An infant, living in the present moment, takes in the world and creates subtle distinctions between itself and others. But there isn't much consciousness involved in the first year of life, and this limits a young child's ability to recall autobiographical memories or reflect on decisions they make.[1]

The frontal lobe is just beginning to make connections with the other parts of the brain, and an infant's actions are mainly governed by the core emotions of fear, sadness, pleasure, curiosity, and the desire to be cared for. In the second year of life, instinctual desires slowly give birth to a rudimentary form of consciousness that allows children to seek out simple goals.[2] "I want _____" becomes the first conscious effort of young children as they struggle to turn vague fantasies into clear goals that can be verbally articulated to themselves and to others.

A young child's *conscious* awareness is directed toward the fulfillment of immediate desires and emotional needs. As language is acquired and motor coordination increases, instinctual awareness shifts from impulsivity (Pillar #1) to conscious decision making (Pillar #2). Awareness of the present moment becomes automatic—and mostly unconscious—as a repertoire of memories, social desires, and creative fantasies fill a child's mind. Then it's off to school to learn more skills, where the imagination is often put on hold.

Rules are imposed, playfulness is limited, and social exchanges are monitored, causing the impulsive child to feel frustrated. This is not the fault of teachers or parents. The problem is in the child's brain, because the circuits governing self-awareness and social awareness won't be fully functional for many decades. Divorce rates reflect this neurological weakness: they are the highest for those under the age of 30. Young adults may be fully conscious of their inner needs and desires, but they are barely aware of the feelings and desires of others.

Selfishness rules the lives of most adolescents. They can be highly motivated by competitive activities, but they are mostly out to win, not share. These narcissistic tendencies are not unhealthy; they simply reflect the underdevelopment of two of the slowest developing structures of the human brain: the insula and anterior cingulate.[3] These structures help to connect the goal-seeking desires of the frontal lobe with the emotional centers buried deep within the brain.[4] When fully developed, this unique human circuit will turn children's natural greediness and self-centeredness into caring, generosity, and fairness.[5] The insula and anterior cingulate are the heart of the social brain, allowing you to feel compassion when someone else is suffering, and guilt when you emotionally hurt another person.[6]

Morality is also governed by the social brain, along with the ability to grasp the complex dynamics of interpersonal relationships, which explains why young adults are far more likely to run afoul of the law or end up in divorce court.[7] Virtues like kindness, compassion, generosity, or the ability to forgive others can remain underdeveloped for decades, and this raises an important question: can you consciously strengthen the neural connections responsible for social awareness? The answer is yes! As far as we can tell from the accumulated research in psychology and neuroscience, contemplative practices like mindfulness are at the top of the list. Mindfulness makes you more self-aware and socially aware—the final Pillar of Wealth that leads to lifelong happiness and success.

Social Mindfulness

Mindfulness, as most people think about it, is a solitary process, helping you to become calm, focused, and self-reflective. You close your eyes, screening out the world around you as you tune into the inner chatter of your mind. As you become more observant, the activity in your brain begins to change, altering your consciousness and

more consciously aware of the present moment, they learn how to manage stress at an early age.[10]

In a randomized controlled study, 99 elementary school children (in the fourth and fifth grades) were divided into two groups: a mindfulness program and a traditional social-responsibility program.[11] The students in the mindfulness program spent 40–50 minutes once a week doing traditional self-awareness exercises like focusing on one's breathing, listening to a single resonant sound, smelling and tasting different foods, and learning how to think optimistically. But they were also introduced to social mindfulness, learning how to perform acts of kindness toward others and practicing gratitude for the people in their lives. After 12 weeks the mindfulness group, when compared to those who had studied only traditional social responsibility, showed greater improvement in empathy, perspective-taking, emotional control, and optimism. They became more social, showed less aggression toward others, and were more accepted by their peers.

Social mindfulness is proving to be a powerful adjunct for many educational environments. When a five-week social mindfulness program was introduced to 409 students in a California public school (from kindergarten to sixth grade), the teachers reported improved classroom behavior. The students exhibited greater self-control in the presence of teachers and peers, they participated in more activities, and they showed greater care and respect for others.[12] In both children and adults, mindful awareness increases social sensitivity.[13]

Preparing for Social Mindfulness

In chapters 1 and 2, we introduced you to the basic principles of mindfulness, and in each chapter we had you apply mindful self-awareness to many of the experiential exercises in this book. Now we'd like to give you a more formal training to prepare you for the development of social mindfulness, in which you bring your self-awareness directly into the workplace, into conversations with others, and use it to make financial decisions that affect other people's welfare.

As you read this section, it's very important that you spend a few moments doing each of the following steps so that you can fully experience mindful awareness. Do these exercises with your eyes closed, because for most people, having their eyes open will neurologically pull them back into the ordinary consciousness governed by everyday decision making (Pillar #2).[14] Also, if you take a few moments to yawn, stretch, and consciously relax— as we taught you in chapter 3—you'll enter deeper states of awareness more quickly and with greater ease. Each of the following steps will actually change the way your brain functions. If you practice any of them daily, for several months, our neuro-imaging studies show that you will begin to change the *structure* of your brain, causing neurons to reconnect in different ways.[15]

STEP ONE: Mindful Concentration. The easiest way to begin is to turn your attention to your natural breathing. However, most people discover that, within moments, their mind quickly wanders away. That's okay, and it's perfectly natural; when you're awake, your brain is programmed to take action in the world. After all, watching your breathing certainly won't make you rich! So it's going to take a little time to train your brain to stay focused on your breath. When your mind does wander, all we want you to do is to become aware of where it goes—thoughts, images, future plans, or even the urge to sleep—and then gently bring your attention back to your breath. Soon you'll become aware of different bodily sensations, like aches and pains, or different feelings, like sadness, tiredness, irritability, or worry. Again just notice how they feel, without judging or reacting to them, and then switch your attention back to your breathing.

Let's give it a try. Close your eyes and see how easy or difficult it is to keep your attention on your breath. How long can you remain thought-free, and is it easy for you to be aware of the productions of your wandering mind? Here's a tip to help you stay in the present moment as you pay attention to your breath: immerse yourself in every detail of the breathing experience as if you were looking at it through a high-powered microscope. For example, notice the *sensations* of the air in your nostrils, and how the *temperature* of the air is different during the inhalation and exhalation. Place your hands on your chest and belly and notice how it rises and falls. Pay attention to the *sound* of your breathing. See if you can experience the *pleasure* of a single breath. It should be easier to keep your focus on your natural breathing.

STEP TWO: Mindful Awareness. This exercise will help you to increase your awareness of the present moment. Rather than focusing on your breathing, don't focus on anything in particular. When your mind wanders, don't focus on where it goes, just allow yourself to be aware of the constantly changing landscape of all the different sensations, thoughts, and feelings. Try this exercise and then compare it to mindful concentration.

STEP THREE: Awareness of Mindfulness. The third and most difficult step in this training exercise is to turn your attention onto your own awareness. This, you'll discover, is a wordless state of being, and you may feel like you are briefly zoning out, temporarily dissociating from reality. This is similar to step one, but instead of concentrating on your breath, you concentrate on the experience of pure awareness. Don't worry if you find this difficult. Even many advanced practitioners can't do this, and the few who do will often say that they can only remain in this state—where thoughts, feelings, and sensations literally cease—for a few seconds or minutes. Trust your intuition as you focus on the *sensation* of pure awareness. Each time you do so you'll have a different experience, but you'll find that it's almost impossible to describe with words. Try it: see if you can become conscious of the *experience* of awareness for just a few seconds as you remain free of all thoughts and distractions.

STEP FOUR: Mindful Intuition. It's time to apply mindfulness to a specific topic or problem, something you want to gain greater insight about. State your objective in a clear sentence—a verbal command or written directive— and then turn your awareness onto it. The object is to combine the previous three steps with your conscious intention, going back and forth: focusing on the issue or problem, watching where and how your mind wanders, bringing your attention back to the problem, shifting your attention to your breathing or on pure awareness—constantly observing the dreamlike process without judging any thought or feeling that comes to mind. Continue the process for as long as you like—anywhere from three minutes to an hour, if you wish. When you stop, ask your intuition—your awareness—for an insight. Write down any image or feeling that might suddenly pop into your consciousness.

Next, pick a topic that interests you, or select a specific problem (a conflict, an undesirable behavior, a health issue, the nature of money or self or consciousness or truth—*anything*) that concerns you, and just spend a few minutes becoming aware of the issue. Notice how it feels to just sit with a problem rather than working on it with your conscious, decision-making mind.

Here's how Mark Williams, John Teasdale, Zindel Segal, and Jon Kabat-Zinn—pioneers in mindfulness research—describe the process:

> The intention in mindfulness practice is not to forcibly control the mind but to perceive clearly its healthy and harmful patterns. It is to approach our minds and bodies with a sense of curiosity, openness, and acceptance so that we may see what is here to be discovered, and to be with it without so much struggling. In this way, little by little, we begin to release ourselves from the grip of our old habits of mind. We begin to know directly what we are doing as we are doing it.[16]

Don't just limit mindfulness to a silent, solitary process that you do in the confines of a quiet world; take it into the world, where it matters most.

Bringing Mindfulness into Your Daily Activities

The next stage in your development of self-awareness is to practice mindfulness throughout the day. Try practicing mindful walking, taking as long as 60 seconds to complete a single step as you notice the dozens of muscles involved. When 75 highly anxious and distressed people were randomly assigned to two groups—normal walking for 40 minutes, or slow mindful walking for 10 minutes—after four weeks only the mindfulness group had much lower stress levels.[17]

Try adding a minute of mindful eating during your meals, studying and savoring a single bite of food; you'll eat less and enjoy it more. Several dozen studies have shown that regular mindful eating will reduce your propensity to overeat and consume sweets.[18]

In chapter 11, we'll show you how to bring mindful awareness into your conversations with others. You'll experience increased intimacy in a matter of minutes, and if you and another person mindfully dialogue together, you'll solve problems more quickly and eliminate conflicts *before* they begin. Think about it: How often do you give your full awareness to your conversations with others? Often we just talk at each other as we try to organize the hundreds of thoughts we have every minute; no wonder we're so often misunderstood!

Using Mindfulness at Work

In traditional mindfulness programs, the student is taught to spend 10–40 minutes a day practicing the different forms of awareness described above. The practice is usually done alone, either before or after work, or sometimes during the lunch hour. But we have found—from teaching mindfulness to our Executive MBA students and to hundreds of people throughout corporate America—that most people won't take the time to do any lengthy awareness exercise during the workday. They're just too busy, and preoccupied with the endless deadlines they face. But they are willing to commit one minute once every hour or two, and that is all you need to do to stimulate the other three Pillars of Wealth: 60 seconds of any mindful activity done periodically throughout each day—a superslow stretch, recalling a pleasant memory, concentrating on a value word, taking a moment to consciously daydream—will increase your motivation, improve your decision making, and enhance your creative problem-solving skills.

Doing brief mindfulness exercises at work has the added advantage of helping you become mindfully aware of the way you work. You can use brief mindfulness breaks to eliminate stress that has unconsciously built up over the past hour, you can use it to refocus your energy and concentration on a task or deadline, or you can use it to tap into your intuition and creativity to solve an immediate problem. And when you bring mindfulness directly into your communication with others, you'll increase cooperation and collaboration.

After many years of teaching students how to engage

in brief mindfulness exercises during work, we continue to get feedback from our graduates on how much their lives continue to improve. They find it easier to deal with difficult people at work, they worry less, and they often find a surprising side benefit: their relationships at home become more caring and intimate.

Each year, as mindfulness grows in popularity, more articles appear in business journals and popular magazines describing how teachers, managers, and people from all walks of life are benefiting from awareness training. And everyone agrees: mindfulness increases your ability to build more inner *and* outer wealth.

Money: A Win-or-Lose Game?

In the 1950s, a young man made history playing games and drawing up mathematical equations to explain how people behave when making financial decisions. He concluded that when it comes to money, people are greedy and selfish. John Nash's research had such an effect on the world of business at the time that he received, in 1994, the Nobel Prize in Economics.[19]

Nash used game theory to measure how people compete with each other. His contributions helped to identify an underlying human propensity (also found throughout the animal kingdom) when it comes to getting what we want—people will use every clever and deceitful trick to achieve a greater reward for themselves.

Nash's model helped to explain many aspects of how financial transactions took place at that time. But over the last two decades, with the accumulation of thousands of published peer-reviewed studies, a startling discovery was made: Nash was wrong. It turns out that if you really want to build a successful business and make a lot of money, you can't afford to be selfish. Instead, you need to constantly exhibit genuine empathy, kindness, and fairness—even generosity—to everyone you interact with at work: employees, bosses, customers, even your competitors. You need to develop social awareness—orchestrated by the insula and anterior cingulate—and you also need to put the brakes on instinctual greed, the basic principle that governs the motivation-and-reward circuit of the M-Drive.[20]

Modern game theory is now part of a growing field called neuroeconomics—the study of what goes on in people's brains when they make decisions in social contexts.[21] The new research makes the very bold claim that if you take care of others first, giving the best advice and support you can, they will take care of you (emotionally and financially) at a later time.[22] In fact, many species of animals behave altruistically in order to gain future cooperation and rewards from others.[23] For example, different birds, mammals, and fish will solicit other species to help clean them or assist in seeking food. In exchange they will protect and feed their "helpers" instead of preying on them.[24]

If you don't exhibit altruistic behavior, other people will perceive you as being selfish or greedy, causing them to instinctually react with hostility. Remember altruistic punishment, the willingness to cause suffering to selfish people, even if it costs the punisher money to do so? That type of moral behavior is controlled by unique circuits in your social brain.[25]

23 TRAITS OF MORAL CHARACTER

Contemporary research in positive psychology identifies these character traits as associated with happiness, well-being, and success: compassion, kindness, fairness, open-mindedness, forgiveness, appreciation, gratitude, leadership, social sensitivity, social responsibility, bravery, persistence, integrity, vitality, creativity, curiosity, love of learning, wisdom, hope, humor, humility, prudence, and spirituality.

But Nash did have a point, and as we explained earlier, selfishness is the default position of a young person's brain. For example, when no one is looking, most people leave less money at the "honor bar" when they help themselves to cookies, coffee, and snacks. But if you hang a picture of staring eyes above the table, three times the amount of money will be left.[26] The reason: anonymity makes it feel safer to cheat, but even a picture of a face can make people feel guilty, reminding them of society's moral code.[27]

Most people unconsciously lean toward selfishness, especially when it relates to work and money. Psychologists at the University of Kansas tested this by bringing different people into an experimental situation.[28] They asked the person to assign two different tasks, one to themselves, and another to a participant who didn't really exist. One task was interesting, and offered a reward, but the other was boring and would not result in any benefit. Most of the people chose the beneficial task for themselves. Then the researchers added a wrinkle. They told another group of participants that they could flip a coin to help with the decision-making process. After all, that would make it fairer. The participants were sent into a room where no one could see them, but a camera recorded what they did. Half used the coin, and half did not. But of those who flipped the coin and lost, they still assigned themselves the positive task, even when the coin toss went against them. The only thing that changed the outcome was when a mirror was placed in front of the person making the assignment. Apparently, even seeing our own reflection makes us more conscious of being fair.

Does that mean we are all moral hypocrites? Perhaps, but becoming mindfully aware of other people's feelings has been proven to make people act more caring toward others. When researchers asked participants, before they assigned the disagreeable task, to first imagine how the other person would feel, the participants were more likely to assign the other person the positive task.[29] Social awareness increases empathy, compassion, and caring, and if you train yourself to become more socially mindful, the research shows that you'll simultaneously build both inner *and* outer wealth by maximizing those decision-making skills that affect the lives of other people as well as your own.[30]

In Nash's zero-sum game model, one person emerges victorious over the other. It doesn't matter if it's a game of tennis or a game of chance; you either win or you lose. Nash's research has also been used to understand why high-paying jobs increase self-centered aggressiveness in the workplace. In fact, the more ambitious you become in pursuing anything, the more you'll be prone to what is called "dispositional greed."[31] While greed has been hailed as a chief contributor to economic growth—and has been vilified as the main reason for the economic crises of

2007—it blurs the lines between ambition, insatiability, and addiction.[32] Greed makes you neurologically insensitive to other people.[33]

New research shows a different picture: greedy entrepreneurs end up with less customer and employee satisfaction. But when people perceive a colleague or a boss as having high moral character, specific circuits within the social brain are stimulated and people will be more likely to trust and cooperate with that person.[34] When you give something freely to others, it builds neurological trust in others, causing them to reciprocate—emotionally and financially.[35]

Money Games

It's a dilemma that every person faces: we have a neurological tendency toward selfishness and greed. Yet we resent others for exhibiting those tendencies. To understand this conflict of interest, researchers have conducted hundreds of psychological and neurological experiments using the Ultimatum Game to document how people respond when treated fairly or unfairly in a monetary exchange.

Two people are usually involved, and they must divide a sum of money between them. The first person (the proposer) suggests a specific split: any division they want, 50/50, or an unequal division. The second person (the responder) decides whether to accept or reject it. If accepted, both people take their share of money, but if the responder rejects the offer, neither person gets any money. End of game.

Let's assume that there are a hundred one-dollar bills

placed on a table in a room. Nash's game theory predicts that a person will accept any division of money, no matter how unfair the offer might be. If the proposer wants to take $99 and only leave $1 for the responder, the recipient should accept it because they will still come out with more money than they started with. Here's our question: What would you do if you were the responder in this experiment? Would you consent to the other person taking most of the money, or would you take offense, like most people would, and reject the offer? Another question: how much money would they have to promise you before you would accept the offer?

Before you play this game yourself, we want you to read each of the following five scenarios and then take a full minute to contemplate your response, paying close attention to your emotions and reactions as both the proposer and responder. In this way you'll learn how to develop mindful awareness concerning money transactions, and how they affect your relationships with others.

> **GAME #1: Free Money and Anonymity.** The researcher meets you outside of a small room, telling you that there are a hundred one-dollar bills on the table. "You may take as much as you like, and leave by the back door," the researcher says. Close your eyes and visualize the scene as clearly as possible. Imagine yourself walking into the room and gazing at the money on the table. How much do you feel like taking? What kinds of thoughts go through your mind as you decide, and how much do you take? Write down

your responses on a sheet of paper so that you can proceed to the next game and compare them later.

GAME #2: Anonymous Sharing. Again there's a room with a hundred dollars on the table, but this time the researcher says, "You can take as much money as you like, but if you want to do so, you can leave some money on the table for another person who will come into the room after you." Does this scenario change the way you feel or think? Do you take it all, or leave some or all of it behind? Close your eyes and pay attention to how your mind grapples with this situation. Write down the amount you decided to take, and the reasons why. Take a deep breath and relax before playing game #3.

GAME #3: Unilateral Decision Making. In this scenario, you and another person are sent into the room with a hundred dollars on the table. You are given permission to take as much as you want and leave the rest to the other person, who has no control over how much you take. Close your eyes, visualize the scene, pay attention to your feelings. Write down the amount of money you keep for yourself and the reasons that governed your decision.

GAME #4: Initiating the Ultimatum Game. You're in the room with another person, and you are free to take as many of the dollar bills as you want, leaving the remainder to the respondent.

However, they can veto the split if they choose to do so, and neither of you will get any money. Two questions: how much do you think you can take without the other person rejecting the offer, and how much do you prefer to offer the other person? Write down your responses, and your underlying logic.

GAME #5: Responding to the Ultimatum Game. The tables are turned and you are the respondent. The other person offers to take $90, leaving you $10. Do you accept the offer or do you reject it, guaranteeing that neither you nor the proposer will get anything? Close your eyes and notice how the unfair offer makes you feel, then write down your answer and the reason that governed your decision. If you chose to reject the $10, what's the least amount of money the proposer would need to offer for you to accept the deal? Again, close your eyes and think deeply about the least amount of money you would be willing to accept. Write your answer down, along with the rationale you used to accept that specific split. Does the proposer *have* to equally divide the money for you not to punish them? If so, explain why. The writing process is designed to allow you to become more fully aware of how you deal with simple transactions and your moral beliefs concerning fairness.

Look back over your notes as you mindfully reflect on the different reactions you had to each of the five versions of the game before you played the game yourself as the responder. What did you learn about yourself when it comes to taking free money? How generous did you feel about leaving money behind for someone you've never met? How did you decide what percentage of money to take when another person was involved, and how did you feel when the person offered you an unequal share? Don't judge yourself if your actions differ from what you think is the correct moral decision. There isn't a correct moral decision here! After playing these games with hundreds of students, workers, entrepreneurs, and CEOs, researchers have discovered that there are many different reactions and responses that influence the decisions people make, and a lot of it depends on a person's perception of the other person's beliefs.

In Game #1, some people happily took all the money. Why not, the thinking went—it's free! Others wanted to take all of it but felt uncomfortable. "It just feels wrong," some would say. Others became suspicious of the researcher's motives and wouldn't take anything: *There must be a trick; I don't trust this game*, they thought. Or they believed it was part of their cultural upbringing—money isn't free; you must work for it—and this moral standard appeared to be imprinted on the social brain.[36]

In Game #2, most people left some money behind for the next person to enter the room, but many would pocket the majority of it. In the workshop games we have conducted with different classes and groups of people, those with a strong entrepreneurial spirit—who had a strong desire to make a lot of money—would often take all of the money, something that risk-takers and sociopaths are also prone to do.[37] When asked why, their responses rarely reflected awareness of the anonymous person. And then there were those who left all of the money on the table. "I don't need it," one person replied, making the assumption that the respondent might have a greater a need. Thus the financial decisions you make often reflect the social and monetary values you grew up with.

In Game #3, where people are face to face with the other person but that other person can't interfere with the decision, many act with greater fairness. However, they often take more than half. A few—usually those who were highly focused on being successful—take all of the money. Perhaps they didn't care, or were too self-absorbed, or perhaps they didn't think that the other person would suffer. As one participant said, "She (the respondent) didn't really lose anything; she just didn't gain anything," reflecting Nash's winner-take-all mentality.

Close your eyes and reflect on the feelings the first four games evoked, followed by how it felt when you played Game #5 yourself. What did you learn, and how long did it take you to decide what to do? The longer you spent pondering what decision to take in these games, the more time your social brain took to weigh the potential benefits and losses of making a moral judgment that would affect the lives of others.[38]

Before we examine how different people respond to the Ultimatum Game, let's take a brief look at one of the underlying principles governing business transactions, personal relationships, and morality: sharing.

The Biology of Resentment

Sharing appears to be a survival-based instinct, one that is learned from other people as to what will be fair and kind in the future. Both humans and primates, when treated unfairly, will discontinue or limit future interactions with the selfish person.[39] The same dynamic has been found in parrots. Normally, when left to themselves, dominant birds will not share their food with others. But when a team of French biologists paired the birds with people, something remarkable occurred when both the parrot and the human took turns opening a cup with two rewards. If the person was selfish and didn't share, the bird didn't share its reward either. But if the person shared the reward, the bird reciprocated.[40]

The same thing happens with children. They learn to share when they see that other people will share with them. Sharing gives a triple dose of dopamine to the brain: one for the pleasure of receiving a reward, a second boost for the pleasure of prosocial engagement, and a third reward that comes from the feeling that you are being cared for by others, a biological need that people, mammals, and birds all share.[41] Behaviors reflecting generosity and altruism are evident between different species of animals[42] and even between plants,[43] thereby facilitating cooperation throughout the world of living organisms. Why then is this evolutionary process so lacking in children and many adults? Evidence suggests that it's the result of the ultraslow development of the social brain, but evidence also suggests that you can speed up the process by deepening your awareness of the way you interact with others, especially around one of the most universally sought-after objects in the world: money.

Sharing and the Ultimatum Game

The Ultimatum Game is one of the most consistently used tools to measure the nature of human fairness. Look at the notes you made when you played Games #4 and #5 described above. When you were the proposer, what percentage of the $100 did you offer the other person? And when you were the respondent, what was the least amount of money you would accept without rejecting the proposer's offer? $10? $20? $30? $40? Or would you only agree if the proposer offered you half—$50?

Research showed that half of the proposers in the United States would offer $50 to the other person, 25% would offer $40, and the remaining 25% would offer between $10–30. The lower the offer, the greater the number of rejections, causing both players to walk away with nothing. When responders' brains were measured, unfair offers would stimulate a negative emotional reaction, triggered by the amygdala. There was also increased activity in the insula and anterior cingulate, which researchers interpret to mean that the person is unconsciously weighing the moral significance of the unfair decision and whether or not to react to their feelings of resentment by punishing the proposer, causing a financial loss for themselves.

In our workshops, there were many different responses and reactions, and it often took a responder a long time to decide if they would accept an unfair offer. Some people would reject any deal that was less than $50, and most rejected offers of $10 or less. But not everyone. "Money is money," these people often said. These individuals were often the ones who would keep all of the money for themselves in the first two games. We also found that very wealthy people would give all of the money to the other person.

We recommend that you play these money games with your friends and colleagues because it will deepen your understanding of how you unconsciously respond to complex moral and ethical issues associated with every financial proposition. It's actually a great party game, and you'll be amazed at how different people react and struggle with their choices. The research shows that the more you play the Ultimatum Game, the more your brain changes in ways that allow you to reduce your negative emotions when you feel like you've been treated unfairly.[44] You remain calmer and more rational, and are less likely to retaliate with anger that further undermines your ability to negotiate with such people.

Mindfulness allows you to remain socially engaged when interpersonal conflicts arise, and it gives you the upper hand when negotiating financial deals.[45] As one of our workshop participants said after mindfully reflecting on her reactions to these money games, "It made me aware of how much anxiety I have about money, especially when asking for a raise. Now I feel more confident when I'm being treated unfairly."

Highly anxious and depressed people are often filled with indecision when playing these money games. These same people often make poor and risky decisions when dealing with real-life money issues.[46] Mindfulness can help develop the empathy and cooperation circuits in your brain, and the research shows that when mutual sharing and fairness is brought to bear in financial situations, everyone wins.

The Million-Dollar Game

What would happen if, instead of playing these games with $100, there were ten million dollars on the table? Do you think this would change any of the decisions you previously made? Let's find out. Imagine each of the following scenarios, paying close attention to your emotional reactions and the logic you use to make your financial choice:

> **GAME #6: Free Money and Anonymity.** You walk into a room and see the money on the table, laid out in one-million-dollar bundles. You are told that you may take as many bundles as you want and leave, no questions asked. Do you feel comfortable taking all of it?

> **GAME #7: Anonymous Sharing.** The same amount of money is on the table. The researcher says: "You can take as much as you like, but if you want to do so, you can leave some money on the table for the next person who will come into the room." How much, if anything, do you leave behind?

> **GAME #8: Unilateral Decision Making.** The setup is the same as in Game #7, but this time the other person is in the room, facing you. How

much do you leave, and does it feel easier or harder to take the money?

GAME #9: Initiating the Ultimatum Game. Knowing that the other person can veto your decision of how to share the money, leaving neither of you with anything, how much do you take? But here's the challenging question: How much do you think you can take without the other person rejecting the offer? Nine million dollars? More? Less?

GAME #10: Responding to the Ultimatum Game. This time you are the person who must decide if you accept an unfair split or reject the offer. Imagine that the proposer is greedy. The person wants to take 90% of the money, leaving you with a million. Do you accept the offer, or do you reject it, if rejecting it means that you will not get anything? Think of all the things you could do with a million dollars, and deeply reflect on the feelings you have about the greedy proposer. Imagine that the proposer is extraordinarily greedy, offering you only 1% of the money. Do you punish that person for being unfair, or do you accept the $100,000?

Nearly everyone who played this million-dollar game had a different reaction compared to the $100 scenarios. Researchers created a computerized Ultimatum Game to find out if the same outcomes occurred. They scanned the participants' brains and discovered that the decision-making processes in the frontal lobe disconnected from the main structures in the social brain.[47] The result: greediness increased, and nearly everyone was willing to accept more unfair proposals. As another study demonstrated, the higher you raise the stakes, the more often proposers take larger percentages and responders accept lower offers.[48]

When we changed the stakes in our workshops, people were surprised at their increased anxiety and ambivalence. In Game #6 where you are free to take the ten million dollars, many people froze. Some could not bear to take the whole amount, but most of the wealthy and highly successful participants barely hesitated: "Of course I'd take it." In Games #2 and #3, most people left at least a million dollars for the other person, but a few didn't. When asked why, they often made comments like this: "I know how to put that money to better use." One woman was a philanthropist, and she also took as much as possible in every game, reasoning that the money would help millions of suffering children in the world. Another wealthy philanthropist did the opposite: he took nothing from any of the games: "I have no particular need for more money, so the other people are free to use it in any way they wish."

Respondents, however, would usually accept a very low percentage of what was left for them if the money being offered was significant. But they would still feel highly resentful toward that person, increasing the possibility that the respondent might find other ways to disparage the proposer's character, if given the chance. Interestingly, several wealthy respondents actually rejected even slightly unfair splits (the proposer would take six million dollars, leaving four million for the other person). They demanded that others be fair—even when they made unfair proposals themselves.

The neurological struggle between greed, fairness, and generosity even plays out on a global scale. For example, diplomats and political negotiators often exhibit high degrees of selfishness for their own countries while demanding high degrees of fairness and equality from foreign diplomats.[49] Sadly, neurological greed often wins: within most cultures and societies, fairness declines when more money is involved, and fairness also declines when there is more distance from other people and cultures.[50]

Billanthropy

In our opening chapter, we asked you to consider this question: *If you had to choose between being either the happiest person in the world or the wealthiest, which would you select?* At first nearly everyone in our survey chose happiness—until we asked them to reflect on what they could do with their wealth. When they realized what they would be able to accomplish, 90% changed their decision, choosing to be the wealthiest person in the world.

What would you do with all that money? We invite you to play one more game. Assume that you've worked hard and accumulated a billion dollars. One day, two men looking remarkably like Warren Buffett and Bill Gates show up at your door and ask you to play the Ultimatum Game for billionaires. They want you to join their billionaires' club, but you have to give up a substantial amount of your wealth to fund a philanthropic project of your own choosing. Will you write a check for $10 million, $100 million, or $250 million, which is a quarter of your savings? Would you give more? How much money do you think you'd be comfortable giving away to people who are not members of your family? Take a moment and deeply reflect on what you choose to do in this imaginary game. Consider this: if you offer less than half your wealth, you cannot join the club! If you had $50 billion, would you give away 50%?

There are no academic studies analyzing the personality of billionaires or brain scans showing how billionaires respond to different financial situations; only anecdotal stories and gossip. But there is a Billionaire Game that is very real, and the proposers are Bill Gates and Warren Buffett. In 2010 they created "The Giving Pledge," asking billionaires to contribute a minimum of half their wealth to philanthropic causes that would help address society's most pressing problems. After five years, only 141 billionaires out of 1800 had signed the public pledge, which is less than 10% of the wealthiest people in the world. Buffett found that there were so many people reluctant to commit that he quipped, on a *60 Minutes* special, "Maybe I should write a book on how to get by on $500 million. Because apparently there's a lot of people that don't really know how to do it!"[51]

It is astonishing how large sums of money can interfere with a person's ability to be generous. Perhaps if we became more aware of our relationship to money, we might be able to overcome the remnants of childhood selfishness and adolescent greed. Current neuroeconomic research shows the fabric of a healthy economy and society is based on fairness and generosity, qualities that appear to be rooted in the rapid evolutionary development of most species on this planet.[52] Cooperative fairness may even be embedded in our genes, waiting to be expressed once our social brain matures.[53]

Philanthropy is an American tradition, and the more people share their monetary wealth, the more democracy will spread throughout the world. As historian Oliver Zunz observes, philanthropy has "given Americans...a stronger voice in defining the common good."[54]

CHAPTER SUMMARY

1. Awareness begins at birth, when you become conscious of your personal desires. However, young children have little awareness of other people's feelings or needs.

2. The insula and anterior cingulate are located just below the surface of the neocortex. These deeper structures—part of what is often referred to as the "social brain"—develop slowly, taking three to four decades to mature. They help you become more aware of how your behavior affects others.

3. The social brain creates a balance between the self-centered desires of the decision-making frontal lobe and your emotional reactivity, which is generated by circuits located in the deeper regions of the brain.

4. Mindfulness can be used to increase both your self-awareness and your social awareness, and this will build stronger circuits between your cognitive and emotional centers, thereby increasing levels of empathy, trust, cooperation, and moral character.

These qualities are associated with increased activity in the insula and anterior cingulate.

5. Contemporary neuroeconomic research has shown that the older models promoting selfish competition are obsolete and less financially rewarding when compared to newer models emphasizing fairness and generosity. This is because people will resent and instinctually punish those who are greedy and unfair to them.

6. Money games can also increase your self-awareness and social awareness. When you become mindfully aware of how your monetary choices affect others, you can consciously exercise greater fairness and compassion for others in the workplace as well as at home. This is the foundation of what we call social mindfulness, where you consciously turn your attention to the needs, feelings, and desires of other people.

CHAPTER 11.

Developing Your Social Brain: 12 Strategies to Deepen Communication, Empathy, Kindness, Forgiveness, and Gratitude

Throughout this book we have shown you how to use mindfulness to strengthen your motivational drive and decision-making skills. It's one of the easiest and most effective ways to access your imagination, creativity, and intuition when it comes to solving difficult problems. You can use it to identify unconscious stumbling blocks and to intuit more meaningful and purposeful directions in which to take your life. Simply put, mindfulness enhances self-awareness.

In the previous chapter, we showed you how to use mindfulness to become more socially aware of how your behaviors and actions affect others, guiding you through a series of money games to help you recognize two neurobiological impulses: the instinctual selfishness and greed that dominate the first two decades of life, and the instinctual desire to punish people who treat others unfairly.

Now we want to introduce you to specific strategies that will rapidly increase social awareness. They have been shown to cause substantial neural changes in your social brain, and they will change your behavior in ways that will cause others to trust you more and treat you with greater respect. We hope that you will make a lifetime commitment to the practice of social mindfulness, bringing the following strategies and principles directly into the workplace and teaching them to others.

Observing Others Mindfully

Preparing to be socially mindful is simple: just before you meet and engage with another person, you spend a couple of minutes practicing any or all of the following strategies:

STEP ONE: Yawn and slowly stretch to relax your mind and body, bringing yourself into the present moment. Look for any lingering negative thoughts or feelings and release them.

STEP TWO: Find a single word that reflects a deep relationship or communication value, one that you feel could improve the quality of your interaction. Repeat the word several times, noticing how it affects your attitude.

STEP THREE: Recall a pleasant memory of someone you love or respect, visualize the person's face, and savor the feelings that the memory evokes. Notice how the image makes you smile. When others see this "Mona Lisa" expression, it stimulates their social brain, causing them to relax and feel more trusting.

STEP FOUR: Take a moment to visualize having a positive interaction with the person you are about to meet.

To get you get started on developing your own social awareness, here is your homework assignment for the following week: Commit to spending five minutes each day being socially mindful with different people—those you know well and those you might casually meet. Write down the names of people you'd like to mindfully engage with over the next seven days. Pick a family member for one day, a friend or a neighbor for another day, then someone from work. Also, think about the strangers and casual acquaintances you are likely to meet during the week and add them to your list: the bank teller, the server at a restaurant—anyone who you are likely to converse with for a couple of minutes. When you have finished your list, visualize as many of them as possible and imagine yourself having a meaningful exchange with them. Each day this week on your calander, remind yourself to be socially mindful with one of these people and notice how you feel afterwards.

After you have mindfully engaged with someone, take a few minutes to reflect on these questions: What did you become aware of that you hadn't noticed before? Did you feel more relaxed? Did you feel more empathy, kindness, or compassion toward that person? Did the other person respond to you with greater interest, or in any other way that was different than usual? You'll probably experience all of these subtle benefits, and each time you do this exercise, you'll deepen your social awareness and sensitivity.

Here's what's interesting: you don't have to tell anyone what you are doing; they usually won't be conscious of your increased attentiveness, but their brain will be aware that your behavior has subtly changed. If you continue to practice social mindfulness with your colleagues and family members, they will often comment—weeks or even months later—that you appear to be different—more relaxed, more peaceful, or happier. Neurologically, they will be more attracted to you.

When our executive MBA students brought social mindfulness into their conversations with their colleagues at work (it was one of their homework assignments), many were surprised by the changes that occurred:

> At first I was skeptical of using any of these strategies at the office because I didn't want to interrupt my work. Turns out it wasn't impractical at all. I stayed much more relaxed during our meetings and I didn't feel as tired at the end of the day as I usually do. I even slept better.

> Doing this exercise in my managerial position has made me a better leader. It made me think back on what I said and how I could have conveyed information more eloquently. My team is working better and there seems to be less conflict.

I'm amazed that yawning makes me feel so much more comfortable before speaking to others in public.

I have the tendency to shut down when I am stressed and I then avoid interaction with others at work. By relaxing and using value words to stay grounded, I can make eye contact more easily and that made having conversations easier.

I began to show more gratitude for my staff. I could see that they were more willing to do things when I asked.

I can't stand my boss, but when I used mindfulness, I stopped getting my buttons pushed as much. A while back I was thinking of quitting, but now I wonder: maybe I can talk to her about a better way to delegate work to me and my team.

I'm a person that typically pushes through the workweek with a warrior's mentality. I address the problem, not the person, and it's stressful. I found out I can be just as effective if I stayed relaxed, and when I visualized my peers and staff members at work, I was able to step into their shoes and experience an issue from their point of view. Since doing this exercise I have become more positive and upbeat at home as well as at the office.

Social mindfulness has been shown to increase moral and ethical responsibility toward others in both children and adults.[1] When you closely watch a person's face, their gestures, and their tone of voice, your brain will begin to

align with theirs—a process we call "neural resonance"—
and this allows you to experience, as best as possible, what
the other person is feeling and thinking.[2]

If you really want to understand another person and
have them understand you, you must remain relaxed,
observant, and nonjudgmental. Otherwise the other person
may resonate to *your* inner stress, causing their brain to
assume a defensive stance, compromising *their* ability to
trust and empathize with you. In normal conversations,
most people become so absorbed in their own thoughts,
feelings, and words that they break their social connection
with the listener.

Train Your Brain to Connect with Others

To increase your ability to resonate and empathize with
someone else, begin by using your imagination: Think
about someone you will soon engage with and walk yourself
through these steps:

1. Relax and reflect on your personal, relational,
   and communication-related values.
2. Visualize the person's face.
3. Recall a pleasant memory from a previous exchange and notice how it makes you feel.
4. Think about their positive qualities and feel
   those qualities inside yourself.
5. Think about their weaknesses and allow yourself
   to briefly experience them.

During important conversations, particularly when

the person in question is speaking, imagine you are them. Mentally visualize yourself in their situation and put in as much detail as possible, as if you were actually them. According to researchers at the University of Chicago, this form of mental simulation allows your brain to build a better understanding of the other person.[3] As Antonio Damasio, at the University of Southern California, writes: when you put yourself "into the shoes of another person, imagining someone's personal, emotional experience as if it were one's own," you will trigger "the neural mechanism for true empathy."[4] This, in turn, will cause the other person to be more empathetic toward you.[5]

Dealing with Difficult People

The real challenge occurs when you must interact with an angry person or someone you don't like. But if you take a moment to imagine how they might be suffering, you'll feel more compassion. And if you can maintain that feeling when actually engaging with that person, their defensiveness—as well as your own—may lessen.

Use your imagination to visualize someone you have trouble communicating with. Put yourself in their shoes and imagine how they see the world. What do you think they really desire? Now ask yourself, "How might I help them achieve their goals?" Notice how this makes you feel. Then, when you know you must engage in a difficult conversation, run through this imagination game in your mind using as many of the steps described above in the previous two sections.

If you have trouble with this exercise, practice the

loving-kindness meditation described later in this chapter. But remember: avoid anger at all costs. Researchers throughout the world concur that negative social feedback often generates aggressive feelings and behavior, causing nearly all of the circuits in your social brain to malfunction.[6] And when you look back on unpleasant exchanges that hurt you, try to interrupt your natural propensity to ruminate on angry thoughts, since that too will disrupt the healthy functioning of your brain.[7]

WHAT DID YOU *MEAN* TO SAY?

The average speech rate throughout the world is 150–200 words per minute. The average amount of time a person speaks before stopping and listening to a response is 2–3 minutes—300–600 words. But the listener's brain can only absorb about 1/20th–1/40th of what the person said, meaning that they are likely to respond to something that was less important.

The 10–10 Game

Research shows that a relaxed demeanor, gentle eye contact, and a half smile, when combined with slow speech and a warm tone of voice, builds trust and increases comprehension in the listener's brain.[8] But here's the problem: When was the last time you *consciously* relaxed or *consciously* maintained a gentle gaze when talking to someone? Have you ever consciously spoken a little slower, or consciously increased the warmth in your voice? In our NeuroLeadership class, all of our students had difficulty doing this, and most had trouble maintaining eye contact for more than a few seconds at a time. Instead they—as do many people, especially during work—spoke rapidly with little awareness of the other person. And nearly everyone used too many words when they spoke. This turns out to be one of the least effective ways to convey important information.

The first thing to remember is that a listener's brain can only recall about 4–7 words with accuracy. When researchers at the University of Missouri tested young and old adults, they found that even a single sentence composed of 10 words was difficult to recall accurately.[9] If you have something important to say, say it briefly and slowly, with as few words as possible! This makes your message more powerful, and the brevity eliminates irrelevant information. When you don't stay on point—or when you try to verbalize the endless inner dialogues that occur when your mind wanders—you make it neurologically impossible for the listener to pay attention to and understand what you are really trying to say.[10]

Irrelevant speech also interferes with judgment and learning.[11] Scientists at the Air Force Research Laboratory in Ohio found that when two people talk at the same time, it degrades each person's ability to pick up important verbal cues.[12] In fact, any background conversation—as when you're sitting in a restaurant or a cubicle in a crowded office—will interfere with your brain's ability to perform mental tasks.[13] Even hearing traffic noise in the background is enough to impair a person's ability to learn.[14] Our advice: if the conversation is important, find the quietest place possible so that you can fully concentrate on each other and on every word you hear.

The more slowly you speak, the more the listener's comprehension will increase,[15] while at the same time relaxing both the speaker's and listener's bodies.[16] The result: less stress and greater understanding. But as we mentioned earlier, people have a hard time slowing down and speaking briefly. To solve this problem, we guide all of our students and workshop participants through a highly unusual and entertaining game. It trains your brain to speak more efficiently and effectively, and you only have to practice the game three times with three different people to improve your speaking clarity.

Here's what you do. Find a partner—a friend, a colleague, even one of your kids—and sit down facing each other. Bring your chairs close together, with knees almost touching, so that you can closely observe the other person's face. You both hold up your fists in front of you, and then you raise one finger for each word you speak. When you run out of fingers, you must fall silent, even if you

THE SUPERSLOW SPEAKING GAME

Counting your words on your fingers slows down your rate of speech. But some people, when playing the 10-10 game, will still talk rapidly. In our workshops, we have participants experience what it's like to put two-second pauses between each word. Try it now: Say—whatever—you—want—for—the—next—minute—or—two. Then try it with a friend. This game will make you more aware of what words sound like. In the silence between each word, you may at first hear your inner speech, then your mind goes silent. When you return to normal speaking, you'll automatically speak a little slower and be more mindful of what you say and how fast you talk.

are halfway through a sentence! Then your partner speaks, raising one finger with each word and stopping when the 10-word limit is reached. As you both talk, listen closely to the tone of your voices and pay attention to your partner's subtle facial expressions.

The exercise forces you to slow down, and the finger counting ensures that you speak briefly. Your brain will soon adjust to the exercise and select better words that convey more meaning than the way you normally converse.

When we explain this strategy to our students—and to the many professionals we train in corporate settings—many people seemed shocked! "It's not possible," they say, "I have to explain everything for them to understand me!" But that's the problem: you *think* that more words will help the other person comprehend the depth of the situation, but it ignores the fundamental rule of consciousness: the listener's brain can only absorb about 10 words, and then it needs time—silence—to integrate them in a meaningful way.

It takes about three or four minutes playing the 10-10 game—10 words, 10 fingers—to realize how profoundly intimate your conversations will become. Often it starts out awkwardly, so that's what you say to your partner. "This feels weird," you might say. And the other person might respond, "I know just how you feel." But if you stay deeply relaxed and trust your intuition as you allow a spontaneous conversation to emerge, you'll often find yourself talking about deep feelings and problems. After 10 minutes of practice, you'll feel much closer to your partner, even if you are paired up with a stranger, which is what we have people do in workshops. It is not unusual to see tears running down some of the participants' faces.

When you play this game with children, they love it. They don't feel overwhelmed by your words. Because they feel that you are really listening to them, they will speak more openly about difficult issues.

The research is clear: rapid speaking can cause people to distrust you, whereas slower speaking will deepen their respect.[17] A slow voice has a calming effect on someone who is feeling anxious, whereas a loud, fast voice can stimulate anger or fear.[18] And if you are speaking to someone with any form of language disability, it is essential to talk slowly, articulating one word at a time.[19] Slowness and brevity—it's a recipe that enhances social empathy with everyone.

The "20-Second Rule"

The 10-10 game is a training exercise—an experiment in mindful communication. It teaches you to be aware of what you really want to say and it helps you to become more aware of your listener as you speak. But when it comes to important conversations or dealing with conflicts—at work or home—brevity is essential for reaching mutually satisfying solutions. When time is of the essence, or when conversations get bogged down, we recommend that you ask the other person or the team to adhere to a 20-second rule: all parties agree to speak no longer than 20 seconds, and then listen to the 20-second responses. The time limit allows you to speak about three sentences, more than enough time to make clear points that can be followed and fully understood by others.

We also suggest that you count your fingers to yourself to help you build an intuitive sense of how to speak briefly. The goal is to eliminate rambling and the propensity to get caught up in emotions that could interfere with empathetic communication. The 20-second rule helps groups solve problems and conflicts in a quarter of the time it normally takes speaking the way most people talk at each other. Also, if you are feeling anxious during a meeting, you can count your words on fingers under the table. It will help you to remain calm and be confident that you are communicating with greater clarity.

In business, time is money, so brevity is valuable. In fact, some executives ask that important questions and statements be written down on an index card so that the most important information can be conveyed as briefly as possible. It's also a great brain-training exercise—writing down an important thought makes it easier to formulate your message in a meaningful, concise, and accurate way.

Mindfulness in the Board Room

Social mindfulness is essential when you are in a business meeting or working with teammates to achieve communal goals. As we mentioned earlier, any form of anger or hostility will derail the social brain and undermine cooperative efforts with others. Even saying "I don't like that idea" can cause interpersonal distress, but if you carefully phrase your response, you can turn a minor negative into a positive and socially enhancing exchange. For example, you might say, "Here's another idea we might consider. Let's talk about the best strategy to move forward with."

This will take practice, because you must first become aware of the brain's natural inclination to respond negatively to ideas you don't agree with. This is where the practice of social mindfulness, as described in the exercises above, can help, especially when it comes to reframing unconscious negativity. Remember, even the slightest expression of irritability or frustration can generate interpersonal conflict, releasing a cascade of stress neurochemicals in both the speaker's and listener's brain within a few seconds.[20]

In any business interaction, demonstrating a genuine desire to be fair and kind will be a win-win scenario for everyone. Before a meeting begins, follow these strategies drawn from the literature on social mindfulness and effective communication:[21]

1. Make sure you are mentally relaxed and alert. Take at least 30 seconds to mindfully yawn and stretch as you bring your attention and awareness into the present moment.

2. Rehearse, in your mind, what you really want to convey. Imagine how the other person or people might respond, and tweak your "presentation" to achieve the most positive reaction.

3. Think about a core value you want to bring into the meeting. Write it on a card and keep it with you throughout the upcoming conversation.

4. *Mindfully* walk into the meeting room, slowing down and paying close attention to each step. When you enter the room, make eye contact with everyone, displaying the Mona Lisa smile described several pages ago (you can evoke it by

recalling any memory that brought you deep pleasure or satisfaction).

5. Open the conversation on a positive note, with a compliment or comment of appreciation.

6. Pay close attention to nonverbal cues: facial expressions, tone of voice, hand gestures, etc.

7. Slow your speech down to two thirds your normal rate and add warmth to your tone of voice. This neurologically improves listener comprehension and lowers stress.

8. Speak as briefly as possible—ideally 20 seconds or less, although this isn't always possible—and then listen to how each person in the meeting responds. This will tell you if they are following what you are saying.

9. Listen nondefensively, without judgment, to each person without interrupting. Avoid any negative language or facial expression, even if you feel provoked by anyone's words. If tension increases to the point where someone may feel anger, call for a brief time-out to relax, reflect on your core values, and rehearse in your mind how to resume the meeting in such a way as to quickly achieve the communal goals of the group.

10. After the meeting, take a few minutes to mindfully reflect on the interaction, asking your intuition—the creative problem-solving circuits that form part of your social brain—for insights. When you bring your inner wisdom into your decisions and social interactions, you are integrating all four of the Pillars of Wealth.

We want to emphasize the importance of bringing warmth into your tone of voice in every conversation. If you drop the pitch of your voice, you'll automatically talk more slowly, allowing the listener to better understand you. This strategy was originally developed and tested in 2011 at the Department of Communication Sciences and Disorders at the University of Houston to help oncologists present bad news to patients. When the doctors reduced their speaking rate and pitch, the listener perceived them "as more caring and sympathetic."[22] Organizational psychologists at the University of Amsterdam concur: a strong, harsh, or dominant voice will generate resentment and weaker performance in the workplace, whereas a warm, supportive voice will generate more satisfaction, commitment, and cooperation between members of a team.[23]

Kindness and Compassion

One of the most effective ways to increase social mindfulness and strengthen the neural connections of the social brain is to practice four specific types of self-reflective exercises: Loving-kindness meditation encourages you to project feelings of care and gratitude onto yourself and others, including people you have difficulty with. Compassion meditation teaches you how to remain calm and empathetic toward others when they are suffering. In gratitude meditation, you reflect on the people and experiences in your life that bring you joy and satisfaction. In acceptance meditation, you relinquish your attempts to change other people and the emotional states or circumstances that are out of your control. Nearly a hundred peer-reviewed experiments, conducted at universities around the world, have concluded that these contemplative practices, when practiced for a few minutes every day:

- Will increase positive emotions, improve inter-personal interactions and prosocial behavior, and deepen your understanding of others[24]
- Will decrease selfishness and increase empathy by stimulating specific structures in the social brain[25]
- Will reduce depression and symptoms related to past traumas by increasing self-compassion[26]
- Will reduce self-criticism[27]
- Can decrease symptoms relating to trauma and abuse[28]
- Will lower stress and improve immune function and cardiovascular health[29]
- Will help you to better handle social anxiety, marital conflict, anger, and coping with the suffering of others[30]
- Will alter neural circuits throughout the brain, enhancing attention, creativity, and conflict resolution[31]
- Will increase social connectedness and positive feelings toward others[32]
- And they will even stimulate the altruism circuits in your brain[33]

In fact, a single 20-minute session practicing any of these forms of meditation can decrease migraine pain and emotional tension,[34] and they may even add longevity to your life by lengthening the telomeres in your chromosomes.[35]

The following exercises have been proven to simultaneously enhance your health, your happiness, and your social interactions with others. That is why we consider them to be the most important strategies for creating inner and outer wealth. The more prosocial you become, the more successful you'll be.

Count Your Acts of Kindness

A team of Japanese university researchers found that college students could increase their sense of happiness "simply by counting one's own acts of kindness for one week." People became kinder and more grateful as a result of doing this exercise.[36] All you have to do is keep a list of any act of kindness you show to yourself or someone else, no matter how big or small (e.g. being helpful, giving a compliment, sharing, smiling, recycling, taking yourself on a "pleasure" walk, etc.).

Do this little experiment and watch what happens tomorrow. Take out a sheet of paper and write down every act of kindness you did yesterday. Don't be surprised if you can't think of anything. Make a commitment to consciously do one act of kindness tomorrow. Write down three or four things you might do, then close your eyes and use your imagination to carry out these acts of kindness. What compliment could you pay to someone who deserves it? What small gift of appreciation could you give to a colleague? What kind of help can you offer someone?

Also, try writing "kindness" on several pieces of paper

and placing them around your house and workspace. You can even use your mindfulness clock to pause for a moment and hold in your mind a kind thought for someone you work with. Each day you do this, you'll find yourself performing more acts of kindness. Continue until it becomes a habit.

Extra credit: in the evening, write down three things that went well for you that day. If you do this for a week, research not only shows that your happiness will increase but that, even if you stop keeping your journal, your self-esteem will continue to grow for the next three months, and will remain higher for many months to follow.[37]

Random Acts of Kindness

This exercise has become a popular game played by college students and corporate executives, and although few academic studies have been conducted on consciously increasing the number of daily acts of kindness you perform for others, teachers have increasingly been teaching children and teenagers this social game. The object is to do something kind for a fellow student, a colleague, or a complete stranger. For example, a person, when ordering a drink from a coffee shop, might pay the cashier to give the next person in line a free cup of coffee.

You can practice random acts of kindness anywhere—give a flower to a clerk where you're shopping, put a coin in an expired parking meter, send a warm e-mail to someone you haven't seen in a year, or tell a child how awesome she is (kids never get enough appreciation from adults!). Use your creative imagination and think outside the box.

Imagine yourself doing something kind for someone

you will see tomorrow. What could you do that would be different or surprising that shows your appreciation? With each act of kindness, you temporarily increase social awareness and generosity in the other person's brain—a phenomenon known as "pay-it-forward reciprocity."[38] A Duke University School of Medicine newsletter even suggests that patients, when their treatments are working, boost their happiness and optimism by performing acts of kindness.[39]

It makes sense that acts of kindness would cause other people to be kinder, but the evidence is unclear. When people were given gifts in a money game, it did not make them respond with greater fairness.[40] However, when children were told to perform three acts of kindness each week toward their peers (who did not know that the children had been given that assignment), after a month, those who consistently performed kind acts received greater peer acceptance.[41]

Another study showed that positive emotions and academic interest increased when college students practiced random acts of kindness, but the effects were temporary,[42] suggesting that if you want to permanently boost your happiness and peer respect, you'll need to practice kindness regularly. And remember, being unfair or unkind to others causes them to act unfairly and unkind toward others as well as toward you.[43]

Random acts of kindness are a form of generosity, and as researchers at Harvard University demonstrated, generous people are not only more cooperative, they also make faster and better decisions, especially when it relates to money.[44] Our suggestion: if you want to create more inner and outer wealth, practice random acts of generosity—they don't even have to be big ones.

Loving-Kindness Mediation: "May We Be Happy"

This highly documented meditation may be the most effective way to improve your social brain's level of functioning, and today it is taught in schools throughout the world—at the university level all the way down to kindergarten.[45]

You begin by sitting quietly, sending love to yourself by repeating any variation of the following phrase, either out loud or silently to yourself:

"May I be happy. May I be well.
May I be filled with peace."

Each time you say it, notice how it makes you feel, and keep repeating it until you are filled with a warm, caring attitude toward yourself. Visualize yourself as being loved and turn your attention to a person you really like and say the following phrase: "May *you* be happy, may *you* be well, may *you* be filled with peace." Visualize that person smiling and feeling contented, then refocus on yourself, repeating, "May I be happy, may I be well, may I be filled with peace."

When you become comfortable doing this—sending kindness to yourself and to someone you deeply care for—begin to send this blessing to other people, moving from those you know well to more casual acquaintances—distant family members, friends, neighbors, and other colleagues at work—as you repeat, "May *you* be happy, may *you* be well, may *you* be filled with peace." Visualize each person that comes to mind (each time you practice select a different person to visualize). You can visualize as many people as you want during your meditation, but if you start to lose interest or feel uncomfortable, bring your attention back to yourself and repeat, "May I be happy, may I be well, may I be filled with peace."

Now for the hard part: visualize someone you don't particularly like and say, "May *you* be happy, may *you* be well, may *you* be filled with peace." Then pick another person—someone who has offended you, a rude or selfish person, a politician whose beliefs you dislike—and say, "May *you* be happy, may *you* be well, may *you* be filled with peace." Don't be surprised if all kinds of negative feelings come up, especially anger and disgust. Just mindfully notice them without judgment, and then turn your attention back to yourself or someone you deeply love, visualizing them and repeating, "May I be happy, may I be well, may I be filled with peace."

Do *not* push yourself to do this too long; only do it enough that you feel your discomfort and release it. In the beginning, you might only feel comfortable doing this for five minutes, spending only a few seconds focusing on the difficult people in your life. If you've been seriously wounded by someone in your past—an abusive spouse, a sexual impropriety in childhood, or a traumatic event involving injury or the death of another—it's best to do this loving-kindness meditation with a friend or a therapist trained in mindfulness. When you feel ready, visualize a person who has deeply wounded you, allow yourself to feel the pain, and say to yourself, "May you be happy, may you be well, may you be filled with peace." Then immediately come back to loving yourself: "May I be happy, may I be well, may I be filled with peace." Keep going back and forth until your negative reactions recede. Also, don't criticize yourself for not being able to send a kind thought to someone you hate or who has hurt you. Just keep practicing and one day—it could be years—you'll find yourself able to relinquish your negative feelings and thoughts.

There's one more step in this meditation. Extend your love and kindness to the whole world, saying, "May everyone be happy, may everyone be well, may everyone be filled with peace." Or try the phrase, "May *we* be happy, may *we* be well, may *we* be filled with peace." Hold a vision in your mind of all the different people in the world, people of all cultures, all colors, all religions, and all political groups, and imagine, just for a moment, everyone getting along with each other and living together in peace.

Feel free to change the wording of this loving-kindness exercise to suit your personal or spiritual beliefs, and make a commitment to practice this exercise regularly.

What about Forgiveness?

Forgiveness has long been a virtue emphasized in religious and spiritual traditions, but little is known about the neuropsychological effects on people who extend forgiveness to those who have hurt them, or on those who receive forgiveness from others. Even minor transgressions against socially accepted rules of moral behavior disrupt the cognitive, social, and emotional circuits of the brain to such an extent as to make it very difficult for people to forgive others who have been dishonest, deceitful, selfish, verbally or physically hurtful, or unfair.[46] Even when the transgressor apologizes, the injured party will rarely show increased empathy or caring, but it may lower the neural propensity to remain hostile toward the offending person, thus promoting a degree of mutual forgiveness.[47] And when it comes to your own transgressions, it is wise to repent, which will sometimes—but not always—lower the other person's desire to punish you.[48] This suggests the following neuroscientific motto: be kind to others lest they be unkind toward you.

At Virginia Commonwealth University, researchers found that the ability to consciously replace unforgiving feelings with positive feelings affects the peripheral and central nervous systems, increasing your own feelings of well-being.[49] While unforgiveness may be damaging to your health, emotional forgiveness of others reduces anger and stress.[50]

How powerful is the act of forgiveness? In a series of studies conducted at the University of Kansas, researchers found that people who practiced forgiveness toward those who offended them saw an improvement in their mood, which spilled over onto a wide range of social situations. They became more cooperative with others and more charitable, and their personal relationships improved.[51] People who practice forgiveness report fewer mental and physical symptoms, their fatigue decreases, and the quality of their sleep improves.[52] Other research shows that if you practice forgiveness frequently, you'll experience more satisfaction with life and a deeper commitment toward those you care for and love.[53] A meta-analytic review of

175 studies and 26,000 subjects found that forgiveness can restore psychological balance, fortitude, and serenity.[54]

Forgiveness can even increase your financial wealth. When vice presidents and advisers at American Express were given a one-day forgiveness workshop, followed by four teleconference follow-ups over the following year, they generated an increase of 14–46% in gross sales. Those who didn't participate only improved their sales by 10%. Additionally, the participants' stress levels at work dropped by 25% and their positive emotions increased by 20%.[55] This study was conducted by Frederick Luskin, director of the Stanford Forgiveness Project. He also suggests that you embrace these principles to increase your sense of well being:[56]

- Forgiveness does not mean that you actually have to reconcile with the person who upset you. Rather, you seek the peace and understanding that comes from blaming people less.
- When memories of past offenses surface, engage in stress-reducing exercises to soothe your body's fight-or-flight response.
- Don't expect things from other people who choose not to be forgiving or kind to you.
- Don't mentally replay your hurt. Instead, seek new ways to get what you want from those who are willing to respect you. Learn how to embrace the love, beauty, and kindness that surrounds you.
- Change your grievance story and make the heroic choice to forgive.

Write Your Way to Forgiveness

Keeping a Forgiveness Journal has also been shown to increase one's ability to forgive. Here are some of the things you can write about: What do you think caused the person to offend or hurt you? What reasons did they have to behave that way? What personal needs were they trying to fulfill? What do you see as their weaknesses and frailties? These types of questions foster empathy by helping you to shift your focus away from your hurt feelings and toward seeing the other person's perspective and imperfections.

You can also ask yourself this question: What role, if any, might you have played that would have provoked or encouraged that person to behave irresponsibly? Finally, consider writing a letter to that person, expressing how you felt or your desire to forgive. Then put the letter away and read it at a later time, knowing that it is not necessary to send the letter or directly confront the offender.

Forgiving takes time, and the research shows that the longer you practice it the more benefits you'll receive.[57] However, even a few hours of writing in a Forgiveness Journal will help a person to start down the path of forgiveness.[58]

When Words Fail, Try a Hug

Sometimes, when someone offends you, kind and forgiving words, whether from yourself or from someone else, just aren't enough. So when you feel hurt or angry, why not try a hug? As researchers at the University of North Carolina discovered, receiving a warm hug from your partner or spouse lowers blood pressure and releases oxytocin—the caring-and-cuddle hormone in your body and brain.[59] A hug reduces stress and a kiss will boost serum proteins in your blood that contribute to your sense of happiness and well-being.[60]

Fill Your Day with Gratitude

We end this book with one of the simplest ways to simultaneously increase happiness and promote prosocial behavior in the workplace as well as at home—practice gratitude on a daily basis. In the mid-twentieth century, the famous psychologist Abraham Maslow proposed that one of the primary causes of personal suffering was taking your blessings for granted.[61] Today we know that gratitude stimulates key structures within the social brain.[62]

But what, exactly, is gratitude? Think back to a time when you were suffering or in trouble. Did anyone go out of their way to help you out, and do you remember how that act of kindness felt? Or imagine yourself being in a life-threatening situation and someone—even a stranger—stepping in to save your life. A fireman carries you out of a burning building. A friend consoles you as you go through a nasty divorce. A teacher spends an extra hour of her time showing you how to excel in math. An artist takes you under his wing and teaches you his craft. Or just think of a time when someone gave you an exceptional or needed gift. That is the feeling of gratitude—a deep sense of appreciation for another person. The more you reflect on the gifts you have received from others in the past, the more you appreciate life. A very large body of evidence, constituting hundreds of studies, indicates that both expressing and experiencing gratitude is *strongly* related to *all* aspects of well-being.[63]

- Keeping a diary of the things you feel grateful for will improve your optimism, enhance your social relationships, and increase your overall satisfaction with life.[64]
- Expressing gratitude will improve communication and relationship dynamics.[65]
- Worried about aging? Spend 15 minutes reflecting on things in the past that made you feel grateful. Your anxiety will subside.[66]
- Researchers at the Wharton School of Business at the University of Pennsylvania found that people who received brief written notes of gratitude are more likely to provide assistance to others. They also found that when managers expressed gratitude to their sales teams, the number of calls made increased.[67] Gratitude promotes prosocial behavior, but it must be *genuine*.
- Feeling tired at work? Immerse yourself in feelings of gratitude for a few minutes and you'll find yourself striving harder to achieve more goals.[68]
- Daily reflections on gratitude can even help you abstain from risky behaviors.[69]

How do you practice gratitude? The list is rather long: think about the people you trust and respect, think about the times you've been praised; recall those moments when you felt a sense of awe and wonder about the universe; visualize your friends and the people you love; savor the times when people went out of their way to help you and recall those times you helped someone out; think about some of the best gifts you've received and the best gifts you've given to others. And then visualize all the ways that you could do something for some else that would make them feel grateful for you. Even saying a heartfelt thank you will stimulate the gratitude circuits in your social brain.

Make yourself a promise to express gratitude to one person you meet tomorrow. Close your eyes and visualize the person, and then imagine yourself showing gratitude for them or for their work. Then, for the next seven days, make a commitment to write down three things you feel grateful for before going to sleep. Visualize the situation and savor it. Fill yourself with an appreciation of all the tiny, simple things in your day that brought you a sense of pleasure, and all of the pleasant exchanges you had with other people. Your sleep will be sounder and you'll feel more pleasure and energy the following day.[70]

The research is definitive: gratitude increases alertness, enthusiasm, determination, attentiveness, self-esteem, prosocial behavior, and life satisfaction.[71] In essence, you'll be stimulating and strengthening the neural circuits that govern all four Pillars of Wealth.

CHAPTER SUMMARY

- Practice social mindfulness by increasing your awareness of the many different aspects of interpersonal relationships: facial expressions, tone of voice, body language, and your emotional responses toward other people. Take a few minutes every day to become more socially mindful of your interactions with different people: at work, at home, and with people you casually meet when running errands.

- Before you meet someone, take a few moments to relax and reflect on your personal, relational, and communication-related values. Visualize the person's face and recall a pleasant memory about them.

- When conversing, increase your empathy by imagining how the other person is thinking and feeling, noticing how they view the world in a different way.

- When dealing with difficult people and situations, imagine how they might be suffering and how you might help them to achieve their goals. Avoid anger and do not ruminate on past negative experiences. Instead, mindfully reflect on ways to build mutual respect and trust.

- Learn how to speak more slowly and briefly by practicing the 10-10 game with three people. Count out each word you speak on your hands, and when you run out of words, stop talking and let the other person respond in 10 words or less. Have fun with this game. When dealing with complex or difficult issues, we suggest that all parties speak for 20 seconds or less, and then deeply listen to each person's response. You'll solve problems in a quarter of the time it normally takes.

- During important conversations, speak at two thirds your normal rate. Bring as much warmth as possible into your tone of voice. Others will perceive you as more kind, caring, and compassionate.

- Bring mindfulness into group meetings at work. Experiment with having everyone yawn and stretch for 30 seconds before beginning, and suggest that each person share one of their deepest values. Teach them the 10-10 game and explain the purpose of speaking for 20 seconds or less whenever possible (two or three sentences). Encourage everyone to speak positively and invite everyone to use their imagination, creativity, and intuition for solving problems.

- Once each day, surprise a different person with an unexpected act of kindness. Keep a Kindness Journal in which you write down what you did. Think about the things you feel grateful for and write them down as well.

- Add loving-kindness and forgiveness exercises to your daily practice of social mindfulness.

- Hug more people and laugh as much as possible. Humor and laughter—or even telling or listening to a good joke—simultaneously stimulates your social brain and the M-Drive, motivating you to engage more meaningfully with other people.[72]

EPILOGUE.

Putting it All Together

By Chris Manning

We sow a thought and reap an act;
We sow an act and reap a habit;
We sow a habit and reap a character;
We sow a character and reap a destiny.
—Ralph Waldo Emerson

Every person has a uniquely configured brain, which means that every person will sow their own thoughts, actions, habits, and character in unique and highly creative ways. Likewise, every reader will select and arrange the strategies in this book in a manner that intuitively reflects their deepest values and desires. In this closing chapter, I would like to share with you how I integrate these NeuroWisdom principles into my daily routines.

Like many of us, I was born into an emotionally troubled family. Early on, I learned that strangers were safer and more comfortable to be around than the confusing family dynamics in which I was raised. I was on my own, continually searching for a lifestyle and belief system that would overcome the feelings of depression and anxiety that haunted me in high school. Each step I took gave me new tools and greater confidence. I went to college. I served as a U.S. Army officer in the Vietnam War. I became a corporate banker, a venture capitalist, a chief financial officer, and an entrepreneur. All of these enhanced my self-esteem, but something was still missing. I wasn't happy.

I used to think that hard work, success, and money were the answer, but found myself becoming a workaholic and never taking enough time to enjoy the fruits of my labor. Then I thought that the addition of a marriage would be the answer to a fulfilling life. But I discovered I had married a fearful person who was married to her work, and after eighteen years of marriage that ended in divorce, I finally realized that I was living life according to other people's values.

Then I discovered meditation. By mindfully turning inward, I could finally connect to myself in a deeper, more satisfying way. Self-reflection became my new habit—my way of nurturing a healthy mind. In essence, I discovered myself by learning how to be true to *my* values and maintain *my* integrity, and to honor my inner truth. I decided to return to school to get a PhD in business management and finance that has enabled me to enjoy being a tenured professor at Loyola Marymount University for the past 30 years.

I wanted to pass on my business expertise, but I also wanted my students to learn how to live well and live life from their own personal truths. I didn't want them to just be successful or rich—that's rather easy to do if you follow sound business practices—I wanted them to *savor* their work and to bring higher values into the corporate world. I wanted my students to go beyond material success and to *flourish* in every area of their lives.

In 2007, I brought Mark Waldman into our Executive MBA program so that we could collaborate in creating a brand new learning experience. Our model was based on two core themes: using cutting-edge neuroscience to keep work stress low and performance high, and creating evidence-based strategies that would help students, managers, and corporate leaders to communicate more effectively and compassionately. Today our NeuroLeadership class has become an international model for creating a new work ethic, one that is *values-based* and *people-based* as well as emphasizing work effectiveness, and one that is anchored in mindfulness and self-reflection (which, by the way, is the heart of the Jesuit educational philosophy that our university was founded upon).

We teach our students how to start each day by taking just one minute to contemplate one's life. It's a practice that I have been doing for many decades, and one that I would like you to experiment with starting tomorrow morning. I want you to feel the inner joyful energy that is hidden in all of us, and I want you to get out of bed feeling excited about the positive things you can experience and accomplish during the day.

As you awake in the morning, "check in" with your

body and notice how you are really feeling. Don't judge anything, just become aware. Do you feel rested or tired? Anxious or calm? Then take a few minutes, as I do, to notice how good it feels just to lie in bed, cozy and warm between the sheets. Become aware of all the tiny pleasures you can feel. Next, take a slow deep breath and exhale, and notice how that makes you feel. Do you feel more awake and alive?

Now pay attention to how your mind begins to think about the day. Are you looking forward to work, or anticipating a difficult day? Be as aware as possible of your thoughts and feelings (both inside your own body and about the external world) and just "sit" with them, without judgment. Then turn your attention, as I do, to the things and people you value the most. Focus on setting *meaningful* goals for your day at work, and take a moment once each hour throughout the day to nurture your creativity, to reflect on your values, and to check in with your body to make sure you are relaxed and alert.

Whenever something unpleasant occurs at work, or if you find yourself struggling with something, just notice your thoughts and feelings, take another deep breath, and remind yourself how good the rest of you is feeling at that moment. There is always something pleasurable and positive happening inside you and around you (even if it is just looking forward to completing an unpleasant task), and all you have to do is become aware of it for just a few seconds. This fact—that there is always pleasure, no matter how much pain is occurring—is one of the biggest discoveries in my life, and when I remember this, my body relaxes and returns me to the inherent peacefulness that I've been nurturing for years.

It's a wonderful feeling to embrace the notion that you always have the power to improve things around and inside you, and this is how you can turn problems, challenges, and discomfort in your daily life into positive opportunities. There is always a part of your brain that can "light the fire" of inspiration and motivation, giving you a dose of dopamine to help you find true wealth—be it money, friendship, intimacy, or anything else you want.

If, after doing the above, you still find it difficult to get excited about the positive opportunities opening up for you, I recommend that you select the most pleasurable and interesting exercises you read about in this book. Immerse yourself in the experience of becoming *aware*. The point I'm trying to make is this: beneath all the worries, anxieties, fears, and negativity that haunt us, there is also a place of selfless wonder and joy. For me, it's the joy of just being alive, of surrendering myself to my own intuition and self-love, and of savoring the feeling of my connection with those I care most about.

Every day, from the moment I awaken, I repeat these simple rituals. And whenever I feel drained or frustrated, I turn my awareness inward, where I always discover something new. Life is never boring when I am open to each new sensation and experience: a new ache, a new pleasure, a new perspective on something, a pleasant memory, or the opportunity to create a new solution to any problem I face. I deliberately take time to notice the positives in everything, and this I have found is the best antidote for all those years of emotional suffering I endured as a child.

Each year, when Mark and I teach the Inner Values exercise to our EMBA students, I am amazed at the transformations that take place in 90% of our students. Without our telling them to do anything else, they find themselves entering levels of awareness they had never experienced before. I have learned that this is the perfect meditation for busy executives who have no more than a minute in a day to reflect on what is truly meaningful for them.

Enlightened Hedonism

Each morning, in addition to the Inner Values exercise, I do a variation of the warm-up exercises described in Chapter 3, focusing on what feels good and right and true for me. Then I pay attention to what I want to do for the rest of the day, visualizing the pleasure I'll feel when I've accomplished those goals. I bring mindfulness and awareness to what I eat and to how I exercise, and I savor the pleasures of each moment of my life. This is what I like to call *enlightened hedonism*. It's the best way to get that "dopamine fix" that is so essential for stimulating the motivation centers of the brain, the first pillar for building inner and outer wealth.

But what about the second Pillar of Wealth? How do you apply enlightened hedonism to conscious decision making? For me, it's very simple: I actually take pleasure seeing that everything in life has both a negative and positive aspect, and that there are many positive ways to react and respond to every problem I encounter. I mindfully and playfully observe my negative thinking, my worries, my fears, and my doubts. I don't take them seriously; after all, they are only thoughts warning me of potential potholes in the road to success and fulfillment. I notice them, I evaluate them, and then I turn them off—like a light switch—as I shift my attention to all the positive ways I can approach the obstacles that stand between me and my goal.

This is when I engage the third pillar, creativity. I avoid negative thought patterns by substituting positive feelings and innovative ideas. I can then take great pleasure in meeting new challenges, overcoming old obstacles, and anticipating future accomplishments.

When facing difficult issues I take advantage of the *power of focus* by turning big problems into a series of smaller obstacles and goals. Many people allow themselves to become overwhelmed by the "big problem." This assumes that there is one huge barrier stopping them from reaching their goal, and they never realize that big problems are really made up of many separate issues. By using the power of focus, you can break apart any big problem into its smaller components. Then you can use your creative intuition to resolve each small obstacle, beginning with the easiest ones and progressing toward the more complicated ones. Your brain will respond to each tiny success with a burst of dopamine to power your motivational drive and enhance your decision-making abilities. As your confidence builds, you'll be more likely to trust your intuition and creativity as you rapidly overcome the "big problem" you originally thought was standing in your way.

In my professional experience, this is the easiest and most effective way to approach any business challenge, but it's equally useful for dealing with social and emotional problems. A person who is feeling highly anxious or depressed can take out a sheet of paper and easily make a list of a dozen smaller issues that contribute to the feelings of being overwhelmed. When viewed this way, these smaller problems become manageable. They now can be viewed as opportunities to improve your life that can lead you to finding the best possible solutions.

As an enlightened hedonist, I love to split apart big challenges in my life and break them down into their inherent smaller components, where I can begin to use my intuition and deepening awareness (Pillar Four) to guide me toward greater accomplishments that are meaningful and deeply satisfying. As an enlightened hedonist, I take pleasure in trusting myself and bringing my core values into the classroom, the workplace, and my intimate relationships at home.

I also find it useful to make the important distinction between an "enlightened" person (hedonist or otherwise) and the "unenlightened" person. The "enlightened" person, when he or she suffers an injury or unpleasantness, will say "Ouch, that hurts!" and then immediately reflect— with calmness and clarity—on the cause of the problem and how to keep it from happening again. However, the "unenlightened" person might respond to the same problem or injury by saying "Ouch, what is wrong with me (or that other person)!" He or she will continue to ruminate on negative thoughts, neurologically undermining their ability to tap into the creative and optimistic problem-solving circuits of the brain.

Social Hedonism and Selflessness

You might be wondering, "Doesn't hedonism imply selfishness, and the immediate gratification of one's impulses? Doesn't hedonism imply putting oneself first and ignoring the needs of others?" Well, yes and no. I like to use the metaphor of what the flight attendant tells you to do in case of an airline emergency: Put on your own oxygen mask first before you attempt to assist the other passengers. Think about it: how can you truly be available to assist others if you don't take care of yourself? That's what I'm referring to as social hedonism and why we place so much emphasis on social awareness in our Four Pillars of Wealth model.

Neuroscience tells us that the brain needs constant pleasure to maintain motivation (that's personal hedonism), but success—in work or personal relationships—can never exclude the needs of others. Love is a two-way exchange, and so is every business endeavor. So for me, it's not enough to just take care of myself. Enlightened hedonism takes me beyond selfishness to enjoying *selflessness,* where my sense of pleasure demands of me that others achieve similar levels of happiness and success. It's not enough for me to just *wish* others well; I want to practice social mindfulness in a way where I can effectively help others achieve the goals they desire. This is what brings me the greatest joy: To integrate each of the Four Pillars of Wealth—motivation, decision making, creativity, and social awareness—in a way that brings happiness and success to others in the world, as well as to myself.

Acknowledgments

NeuroWisdom is the result of many years of research, development, and testing, and there are many people to thank, especially the students who have graduated from our Executive MBA program at Loyola Marymount University and who were enrolled in our NeuroLeadership class. You gave us exceptional feedback on which exercises and strategies to include in this book, but even more importantly, you brought these principles into the organizations you manage. Thank you!

We also want to extend our gratitude to the director of the EMBA program, Bill Lindsey, and to the EMBA faculty members and staff, who lent invaluable support to us for so many years. Our deep appreciation goes to our agent, Jim Levine, and to the wonderful people at Diversion Books. Your faith in our project and the wise advice and editorial direction helped us to realize our vision. We also want to acknowledge Andrew Newberg,

MD, whose neuroscientific research laid the foundation for the development of this book.

Finally, we send a big hug to John Assaraf, the NeuroGym community, and to the thousands of workshop participants who have traveled with us on our mutual journey to build inner and outer wealth. Thank you for sharing these brain-changing exercises with your friends and family and for promoting the practice of mindfulness in the workplace.

APPENDIX.

NeuroWisdom 101:

An Eight-Week Audio Training Program in Mindfulness, Positivity, and Stress-Reduction

In our NeuroLeadership class—part of the Executive MBA program at Loyola Marymount University—our students use this book to help them lower the enormous stress they are under as they complete an intensive graduate degree while simultaneously maintaining grueling work hours. They have little time to devote to anything beyond work and school, which is why we developed very brief mindfulness exercises that they could easily incorporate into their busy schedules. In class they are personally guided through some of the core exercises described in this book, and then they are given an audio training program, *NeuroWisdom 101,* to take home with them so that they can deepen their mindfulness practice throughout the school year. Our students, and the thousands of other people who have bought *NeuroWisdom 101,* have found this to be one of the most valuable programs for lowering anxiety, building confidence, and maintaining peak performance at work.

Being guided through an audio exercise is easier than guiding yourself through a written exercise, which is why we highly recommend that you augment this book with *NeuroWisdom 101,* which includes 58 experiential exercises designed to reduce stress, build positivity, and deepen self-reflective and social skills. Listen to one track each day, and then, with the help of a mindfulness clock (described in chapter 2), take 60-second breaks throughout the day to practice or reflect on the morning's exercise. You'll find many new strategies not featured in this book that will help you turn negative thinking into unwavering optimism, boost your sense of pleasure and well-being, and give you the tools to create a personalized daily practice that has been proven to specifically strengthen neural circuits that are vulnerable to age-related problems.

The eight-week program can be downloaded as a series of mp3s onto your computer or phone, or you can order the CD package by going to **www.NeuroWisdom.com**. It comes with a 90-page workbook and a money-back guarantee, and if you would like Mark Waldman to keynote at your event and guide your audience or team through these brain-enhancing techniques, send an e-mail to **MarkWaldman@sbcglobal.net** or visit his website at **www.MarkRobertWaldman.com**, where you can get a free copy of his ebook *10 Mind-Blowing Discoveries About the Human Brain* and check out his NeuroCoach Training and Certification program.

Endnotes

Chapter 1: What Do You *Really* Want?

[1]   We have used a variety of semi-formal and informal surveys. Using two different Facebook communities, 627 people (men and women from around the world, from different cultural and socio-economic backgrounds) responded to the question, "If you were given a choice between happiness and wealth, and you could only have one of these, which would you select?" Ninety-two percent selected happiness. In workshops and classroom settings, approximately 90–95% of the 2000+ students and participants consistently chose happiness over wealth.

[2]   The relation of economic status to subjective well-being in developing countries: a meta-analysis. Howell RT, Howell CJ. Psychol Bull. 2008 Jul;134(4):536-60.

[3]   How Your Bank Balance Buys Happiness: The Importance of "Cash on Hand" to Life Satisfaction. Ruberton PM, Gladstone J, Lyubomirsky S. Emotion. 2016 Apr 11.

[4]   The pursuit of happiness can be lonely. Mauss IB, Savino NS, Anderson CL, Weisbuch M, Tamir M, Laudenslager ML. Emotion. 2012 Oct;12(5):908-12.

[5]   Can seeking happiness make people unhappy? Paradoxical effects of valuing happiness. Mauss IB, Tamir M, Anderson CL, Savino NS. Emotion. 2011 Aug;11(4):807-15.

[6]   The Effects of Activating the Money Concept on Perseverance

247

and the Preference for Delayed Gratification in Children. Trzcińska A, Sekścińska K. Front Psychol. 2016 Apr 27;7:609.

[7] Whole Life Satisfaction Concepts of Happiness. Feldman F. Theoria. 2008 Sep 74:3:219-238.

[8] Hamilton, Carol. Why did Jefferson change "property" to the "pursuit of happiness"? http://historynewsnetwork.org/article/46460.

[9] Lay Definitions of Happiness across Nations: The Primacy of Inner Harmony and Relational Connectedness. Delle Fave A, Brdar I, Wissing MP, Araujo U, Castro Solano A, Freire T, Hernández-Pozo Mdel R, Jose P, Martos T, Nafstad HE, Nakamura J, Singh K, Soosai-Nathan L. Front Psychol. 2016 Jan 26;7:30.

[10] The role of the orbitofrontal cortex in the pursuit of happiness and more specific rewards. Burke KA, Franz TM, Miller DN, Schoenbaum G. Nature. 2008 Jul 17;454(7202):340-4.

[11] Circuits regulating pleasure and happiness: the evolution of reward-seeking and misery-fleeing behavioral mechanisms in vertebrates. Loonen AJ, Ivanova SA. Front Neurosci. 2015 Oct 23;9:394.

[12] Towards a functional neuroanatomy of pleasure and happiness. Kringelbach ML, Berridge KC. Trends Cogn Sci. 2009 Nov;13(11):479-87. doi: 10.1016/j.tics.2009.08.006.

[13] A reassessment of the relationship between GDP and life satisfaction. Proto E, Rustichini A. PLoS One. 2013 Nov 27;8(11):e79358.

[14] The Easterlin paradox revisited. Frank RH. Emotion. 2012 Dec;12(6):1188-91.

[15] General social surveys, 1972-2010: cumulative codebook. Smith TW, Marsden P, Hout M, Kim J. National Opinion Research Center, 2011.

[16] The new stylized facts about income and subjective well-being. Sacks DW, Stevenson B, Wolfers J. Emotion. 2012 Dec;12(6):1181-7.

[17] What Makes a Successful Retirement? Finke M. Research Magazine. Feb 2014.

[18] Frank RH. "Does Income Matter?" In Luigino B and Pier L (eds). *Economics of Happiness.* Oxford University Press, 2005.

[19] Layard R. "Rethinking Public Economics: The Implications of

Rivalry and Habit." In Luigino B and Pier L (eds). Economics of Happiness. Oxford University Press, 2005 p.148.

[20] Wealth and happiness across the world: material prosperity predicts life evaluation, whereas psychosocial prosperity predicts positive feeling. Diener E, Ng W, Harter J, Arora R. J Pers Soc Psychol. 2010 Jul;99(1):52-61.

[21] The relation of economic status to subjective well-being in developing countries: a meta-analysis. Howell RT, Howell CJ. Psychol Bull. 2008 Jul;134(4):536-60.

[22] World Happiness Report, 2015, edited by Helliwell J, Layard R, Sachs J. Published by the United Nations: http://worldhappiness. report/.

[23] Subjective well-being, health, and ageing. Steptoe A, Deaton A, Stone AA. Lancet. 2015 Feb 14;385(9968):640-8.

[24] Wealth and the inflated self: class, entitlement, and narcissism. Piff PK. Pers Soc Psychol Bull. 2014 Jan;40(1):34-43.

[25] Zeroing in on the dark side of the American Dream: a closer look at the negative consequences of the goal for financial success. Nickerson C, Schwarz N, Diener E, Kahneman D. Psychol Sci. 2003 Nov;14(6):531-6.

[26] The effect of amount and tangibility of endowment and certainty of recipients on selfishness in a modified dictator game. Chang SC, Lin LY, Horng RY, Wang YD. Psychol Rep. 2014 Jun;114(3):720-39.

[27] Narcissistic CEOs and executive compensation. O'Reilly CA, Doerr B, Caldwell DF, Chatman JA. Leadership Quarterly. 2013 Sep;25(2).

[28] Wealth and the inflated self: class, entitlement, and narcissism. Piff PK. Pers Soc Psychol Bull. 2014 Jan;40(1):34-43.

[29] Unpacking the hedonic paradox: a dynamic analysis of the relationships between financial capital, social capital and life satisfaction. Gleibs IH, Morton TA, Rabinovich A, Haslam SA, Helliwell JF. Br J Soc Psychol. 2013 Mar;52(1):25-43.

[30] To do, to have, or to share? Valuing experiences over material possessions depends on the involvement of others. Caprariello PA, Reis HT. J Pers Soc Psychol. 2013 Feb;104(2):199-215.

[31] The relationship between materialism and personal well-being: A meta-analysis. Dittmar H, Bond R, Hurst M, Kasser T. J Pers Soc Psychol. 2014 Nov;107(5):879-924.

[32] Neural components of altruistic punishment. Du E, Chang SW. Front Neurosci. 2015 Feb 9;9:26.

Chapter 2: How to Manage Your Busy Brain

[1] Personal Inner Values—A Key to Effective Face-to-Face Business Communication. Manning CA, Waldman MR, Lindsey WE, Newberg AB, Cotter-Lockard D. J Executive Ed. 2012 July 11(1):37-65. Available at: http://digitalcommons.kennesaw.edu/jee/vol11/iss1/3.

[2] Incentive salience: novel treatment strategies for major depression. Soskin DP, Holt DJ, Sacco GR, Fava M. CNS Spectr. 2013 Dec;18(6):307-14.

Dynamics of the dopaminergic system as a key component to the understanding of depression. Yadid G, Friedman A. Prog Brain Res. 2008;172:265-86.

[3] Viral over-expression of D1 dopamine receptors in the prefrontal cortex increase high-risk behaviors in adults: comparison with adolescents. Sonntag KC, Brenhouse HC, Freund N, Thompson BS, Puhl M, Andersen SL. Psychopharmacology (Berl). 2014 Apr;231(8):1615-26.

[4] Context, emotion, and the strategic pursuit of goals: interactions among multiple brain systems controlling motivated behavior. Gruber AJ, McDonald RJ. Front Behav Neurosci. 2012 Aug 3;6:50.

[5] Contributions of subregions of the prefrontal cortex to the theory of mind and decision making. Xi C, Zhu Y, Niu C, Zhu C, Lee TM, Tian Y, Wang K. Behav Brain Res. 2011 Aug 10;221(2):587-93.

[6] Always Approach the Bright Side of Life: A General Positivity Training Reduces Stress Reactions in Vulnerable Individuals. Becker ES, Ferentzi H, Ferrari G, Möbius M, Brugman S, Custers J, Geurtzen N, Wouters J, Rinck M. Cognit Ther Res. 2016;40:57-71.

Dopamine and extinction: a convergence of theory with fear and reward circuitry. Abraham AD, Neve KA, Lattal KM. Neurobiol Learn Mem. 2014 Feb;108:65-77.

[7] Do meditators have higher awareness of their intentions to act?

Jo HG, Hinterberger T, Wittmann M, Schmidt S. Cortex. 2015 Apr;65:149-58.

[8] Functional cortical connectivity analysis of mental fatigue unmasks hemispheric asymmetry and changes in small-world networks. Sun Y, Lim J, Kwok K, Bezerianos A. Brain Cogn. 2014 Mar;85:220-30.

[9] Nondirective meditation activates default mode network and areas associated with memory retrieval and emotional processing. Xu J, Vik A, Groote IR, Lagopoulos J, Holen A, Ellingsen O, Håberg AK, Davanger S. Front Hum Neurosci. 2014 Feb 26;8:86.

[10] A default mode of brain function. Raichle ME, MacLeod AM, Snyder AZ, Powers WJ, Gusnard DA, Shulman GL. Proc Natl Acad Sci U S A. 2001 Jan 16;98(2):676-82.

[11] Brain connectivity during resting state and subsequent working memory task predicts behavioural performance. Sala-Llonch R, Peña-Gómez C, Arenaza-Urquijo EM, Vidal-Piñeiro D, Bargalló N, Junqué C, Bartrés-Faz D. Cortex. 2012 Oct;48(9):1187-96.

[12] Resting-state networks in awake five- to eight-year old children. de Bie HM, Boersma M, Adriaanse S, Veltman DJ, Wink AM, Roosendaal SD, Barkhof F, Stam CJ, Oostrom KJ, Delemarre-van de Waal HA, Sanz-Arigita EJ. Hum Brain Mapp. 2012 May;33(5):1189-201.

[13] Creativity and the default network: A functional connectivity analysis of the creative brain at rest. Beaty RE, Benedek M, Wilkins RW, Jauk E, Fink A, Silvia PJ, Hodges DA, Koschutnig K, Neubauer AC. Neuropsychologia. 2014 Sep 20;64C:92-98.

[14] Meta-awareness, perceptual decoupling and the wandering mind. Schooler JW, Smallwood J, Christoff K, Handy TC, Reichle ED, Sayette MA. Trends Cogn Sci. 2011 Jul;15(7):319-26.

[15] Cognitive, behavioral, and autonomic correlates of mind wandering and perseverative cognition in major depression. Ottaviani C, Shahabi L, Tarvainen M, Cook I, Abrams M, Shapiro D. Front Neurosci. 2015 Jan 5;8:433.

[16] Ode to positive constructive daydreaming. McMillan RL, Kaufman SB, Singer JL. Front Psychol. 2013 Sep 23;4:626.

[17] The interplay between spontaneous and controlled processing in creative cognition. Mok LW. Front Hum Neurosci. 2014 Aug 28;8:663.

[18] High-expanding cortical regions in human development and

evolution are related to higher intellectual abilities. Fjell AM, Westlye LT, Amlien I, Tamnes CK, Grydeland H, Engvig A, Espeseth T, Reinvang I, Lundervold AJ, Lundervold A, Walhovd KB. Cereb Cortex. 2015 Jan;25(1):26-34.

See also: Newberg AS and Waldman MR, *How God Changes Your Brain,* Ballantine 2009.

[19]   Neural development of mentalizing in moral judgment from adolescence to adulthood. Harenski CL, Harenski KA, Shane MS, Kiehl KA. Dev Cogn Neurosci. 2012 Jan;2(1):162-73.

[20]   Andrew Newberg and Mark Waldman. *How God Changes Your Brain.* Ballantine, 2009.

[21]   Effects of brief and sham mindfulness meditation on mood and cardiovascular variables. Zeidan F, Johnson SK, Gordon NS, Goolkasian P. J Altern Complement Med. 2010 Aug;16(8):867-73.

Mindfulness meditation improves cognition: evidence of brief mental training. Zeidan F, Johnson SK, Diamond BJ, David Z, Goolkasian P. Conscious Cogn. 2010 Jun;19(2):597-605.

The effects of brief mindfulness meditation training on experimentally induced pain. Zeidan F, Gordon NS, Merchant J, Goolkasian P. J Pain. 2010 Mar;11(3):199-209.

[22]   For a thorough investigation into the neuroscience of insights and "aha" experiences see *How Enlightenment Changes Your Brain* by Newberg and Waldman. Also: *The Eureka Factor* by Kounios and Beeman.

[23]   Moral intuition: its neural substrates and normative significance. Woodward J, Allman J. J Physiol Paris. 2007 Jul-Nov;101(4-6):179-202.

[24]   Interoception drives increased rational decision-making in meditators playing the ultimatum game. Kirk U, Downar J, Montague PR. Front Neurosci. 2011 Apr 18;5:49.

[25]   Neural components of altruistic punishment. Du E, Chang SW. Front Neurosci. 2015 Feb 9;9:26.

Punishing unfairness: rewarding or the organization of a reactively aggressive response? White SF, Brislin SJ, Sinclair S, Blair JR. Hum Brain Mapp. 2014 May;35(5):2137-47.

Beyond revenge: neural and genetic bases of altruistic punishment. Strobel A, Zimmermann J, Schmitz A, Reuter M, Lis S, Windmann S, Kirsch P. Neuroimage. 2011 Jan 1;54(1):671-80.

[26]   Insights into the experiences of older workers and change: through

the lens of selection, optimization, and compensation. Unson C, Richardson M. Gerontologist. 2013 Jun;53(3):484-94.

[27] Demands, values, and burnout: relevance for physicians. Leiter MP, Frank E, Matheson TJ. Can Fam Physician. 2009 Dec;55(12):1224-1225, 1225.e1-6.

[28] Mindfulness Training and Classroom Behavior Among Lower-Income and Ethnic Minority Elementary School Children. Black DS, Fernando R. J Child Fam Stud. 2014 Oct;23(7):1242-1246.

[29] Managing the demands of professional life. Dickey J, Ungerleider R. Cardiol Young. 2007 Sep;17 Suppl 2:138-44.

[30] Chade-Meng Tan. *Search Inside Yourself.* HarperOne, 2012.

[31] Review of the effects of mindfulness meditation on mental and physical health and its mechanisms of action. Ngô TL. Sante Ment Que. 2013 Autumn;38(2):19-34.

[32] Preventing occupational stress in healthcare workers. Ruotsalainen JH, Verbeek JH, Mariné A, Serra C. Cochrane Database Syst Rev. 2015 Apr 7;4:CD002892.

Short-term effects of a randomized controlled worksite relaxation intervention in Greece. Alexopoulos EC, Zisi M, Manola G, Darviri C. Ann Agric Environ Med. 2014;21(2):382-7.

[33] Endogenous reward mechanisms and their importance in stress reduction, exercise and the brain. Esch T, Stefano GB. Arch Med Sci. 2010 Jun 30;6(3):447-55.

[34] The neurobiology of stress management. Esch T, Stefano GB. Neuro Endocrinol Lett. 2010;31(1):19-39.

[35] Gabriele Oettingen. *Rethinking Positive Thinking.* Current/Penguin, 2014.

[36] From Fantasy to Action: Mental Contrasting with Implementation Intentions (MCII) Improves Academic Performance in Children. Duckworth AL, Kirby T, Gollwitzer A, Oettingen G. Soc Psychol Personal Sci. 2013 Nov 1;4(6):745-753.

[37] Mental contrasting and transfer of energization. Sevincer AT, Busatta PD, Oettingen G. Pers Soc Psychol Bull. 2014 Feb;40(2):139-52.

[38] Mental contrasting and the self-regulation of responding to negative feedback. Kappes A, Oettingen G, Pak H. Pers Soc Psychol Bull. 2012 Jul;38(7):845-57.

[39] Mind wandering via mental contrasting as a tool for behavior change. Oettingen G, Schwörer B. Front Psychol. 2013 Sep 2;4:562.

[40] Mechanisms underlying encoding of short-lived versus durable episodic memories. Sneve MH, Grydeland H, Nyberg L, Bowles B, Amlien IK, Langnes E, Walhovd KB, Fjell AM. J Neurosci. 2015 Apr 1;35(13):5202-12.

[41] Boosting long-term memory via wakeful rest: intentional rehearsal is not necessary, consolidation is sufficient. Dewar M, Alber J, Cowan N, Della Sala S. PLoS One. 2014 Oct 15;9(10):e109542.

[42] The silver lining of a mind in the clouds: interesting musings are associated with positive mood while mind-wandering. Franklin MS, Mrazek MD, Anderson CL, Smallwood J, Kingstone A, Schooler JW. Front Psychol. 2013 Aug 27;4:583.

[43] Positive emotionality is associated with baseline metabolism in orbitofrontal cortex and in regions of the default network. Volkow ND, Tomasi D, Wang GJ, Fowler JS, Telang F, Goldstein RZ, Alia-Klein N, Woicik P, Wong C, Logan J, Millard J, Alexoff D. Mol Psychiatry. 2011 Aug;16(8):818-25.

[44] Neural correlates of personal goal processing during episodic future thinking and mind-wandering: An ALE meta-analysis. Stawarczyk D, D'Argembeau A. Hum Brain Mapp. 2015 Apr 30.

[45] Rest Boosts the Long-term Retention of Spatial Associative and Temporal Order Information. Craig M, Dewar M, Della Sala S, Wolbers T. Hippocampus. 2015 Jan 24.
    Brief wakeful resting boosts new memories over the long term. Dewar M, Alber J, Butler C, Cowan N, Della Sala S. Psychol Sci. 2012 Sep 1;23(9):955-60.

[46] Mind wandering, sleep quality, affect and chronotype: an exploratory study. Carciofo R, Du F, Song N, Zhang K. PLoS One. 2014 Mar 7;9(3):e91285.

[47] The role of edge-sensing in experiential psychotherapy. Glanzer D, Early A. Am J Psychother. 2012;66(4):391-406.

[48] Better without (lateral) frontal cortex? Insight problems solved by frontal patients. Reverberi C, Toraldo A, D'Agostini S, Skrap M. Brain. 2005 Dec;128(Pt 12):2882-90.

[49] Intuition in clinical decision-making: a psychological penumbra. Nyatanga B, Vocht Hd. Int J Palliat Nurs. 2008 Oct;14(10):492-6.

[50] Effect of audible and visual reminders on adherence in glaucoma patients using a commercially available dosing aid. Ho LY, Camejo L, Kahook MY, Noecker R. Clin Ophthalmol. 2008 Dec;2(4):769-72.

[51] Physiological and psychological effects of a Himalayan singing bowl in meditation practice: a quantitative analysis. Landry JM. Am J Health Promot. 2014 May-Jun;28(5):306-9.

[52] Activity of striatal neurons reflects dynamic encoding and recoding of procedural memories. Barnes TD, Kubota Y, Hu D, Jin DZ, Graybiel AM. Nature. 2005 Oct 20;437(7062):1158-61.

[53] Brief wakeful resting boosts new memories over the long term. Dewar M, Alber J, Butler C, Cowan N, Della Sala S. Psychol Sci. 2012 Sep 1;23(9):955-60.

Regional cerebral blood flow increases during wakeful rest following cognitive training. Mazoyer B, Houdé O, Joliot M, Mellet E, Tzourio-Mazoyer N. Brain Res Bull. 2009 Sep 28;80(3):133-8.

[54] The brain correlates of the effects of monetary and verbal rewards on intrinsic motivation. Albrecht K, Abeler J, Weber B, Falk A. Front Neurosci. 2014 Sep 18;8:303.

[55] Value signals in the prefrontal cortex predict individual preferences across reward categories. Gross J, Woelbert E, Zimmermann J, Okamoto-Barth S, Riedl A, Goebel R. J Neurosci. 2014 May 28;34(22):7580-6.

Anticipatory pleasure predicts motivation for reward in major depression. Sherdell L, Waugh CE, Gotlib IH. J Abnorm Psychol. 2012 Feb;121(1):51-60.

[56] Neural sensitivity to eudaimonic and hedonic rewards differentially predict adolescent depressive symptoms over time. Telzer EH, Fuligni AJ, Lieberman MD, Galván A. Proc Natl Acad Sci U S A. 2014 May 6;111(18):6600-5.

[57] Effects of optimism on motivation in rats. Rygula R, Golebiowska J, Kregiel J, Kubik J, Popik P. Front Behav Neurosci. 2015 Feb 25;9:32.

[58] For a summary of the research on optimism see Newberg and Waldman's book *How God Changes Your Brain.* Ballantine Books, 2009.

Chapter 3: Preparing to Succeed

[1] Mental contrasting and transfer of energization. Sevincer AT, Busatta PD, Oettingen G. Pers Soc Psychol Bull. 2014 Feb;40(2):139-52.

[2] Strategies of intention formation are reflected in continuous MEG activity. Achtziger A, Fehr T, Oettingen G, Gollwitzer PM, Rockstroh B. Soc Neurosci. 2009;4(1):11-27.

[3] Library of Congress documentation of the value of yawning (along with early photographic evidence of its use in the classroom):http://www.loc.gov/rr/scitech/mysteries/yawn.html.

[4] A thermal window for yawning in humans: yawning as a brain cooling mechanism. Massen JJ, Dusch K, Eldakar OT, Gallup AC. Physiol Behav. 2014 May 10;130:145-8.

Yawning: unsuspected avenue for a better understanding of arousal and interoception. Walusinski O. Med Hypotheses. 2006;67(1):6-14.

[5] Yawning, fatigue, and cortisol: expanding the Thompson Cortisol Hypothesis. Thompson SB. Med Hypotheses. 2014 Oct;83(4):494-6.

The thermoregulatory theory of yawning: what we know from over 5 years of research. Gallup AC, Eldakar OT. Front Neurosci. 2013 Jan 2;6:188.

[6] Yawning and its physiological significance. Gupta S, Mittal S. Int J Appl Basic Med Res. 2013 Jan;3(1):11-5.

[7] Yawning throughout life. Giganti F, Salzarulo P. Front Neurol Neurosci. 2010;28:26-31.

[8] How yawning switches the default-mode network to the attentional network by activating the cerebrospinal fluid flow. Walusinski O. Clin Anat. 2014 Mar;27(2):201-9.

[9] Daquin G, Micallef J, Blin O. Yawning. Sleep Med Rev. 2001 Aug;5(4):299-312.

[10] Social modulation of contagious yawning in wolves. Romero T, Ito M, Saito A, Hasegawa T. PLoS One. 2014 Aug 27;9(8):e105963.

[11] Yawning: from birth to senescence. Walusinski O. Psychol Neuropsychiatr Vieil. 2006 Mar;4(1):39-46.

[12] Estradiol, dopamine and motivation. Yoest KE, Cummings JA, Becker JB. Cent Nerv Syst Agents Med Chem. 2014;14(2):83-9.

[13] Coherence between emotional experience and physiology: does body awareness training have an impact? Sze JA, Gyurak A, Yuan JW, Levenson RW. Emotion. 2010 Dec;10(6):803-14.

[14] The effectiveness of the feldenkrais method: a systematic review of the evidence. Hillier S, Worley A. Evid Based Complement Alternat Med. 2015;2015:752160.

Coherence between emotional experience and physiology: does body awareness training have an impact? Sze JA, Gyurak A, Yuan JW, Levenson RW. Emotion. 2010 Dec;10(6):803-14.

[15] Effects of Feldenkrais method on chronic neck/scapular pain in people with visual impairment: a randomized controlled trial with one-year follow-up. Lundqvist LO, Zetterlund C, Richter HO. Arch Phys Med Rehabil. 2014 Sep;95(9):1656-61.

Moving with ease: feldenkrais method classes for people with osteoarthritis. Webb R, Cofré Lizama LE, Galea MP. Evid Based Complement Alternat Med. 2013;2013:479142.

[16] Feldenkrais method-based exercise improves quality of life in individuals with Parkinson's disease: a controlled, randomized clinical trial. Teixeira-Machado L, Araújo FM, Cunha FA, Menezes M, Menezes T, Melo DeSantana J. Altern Ther Health Med. 2015 Jan-Feb;21(1):8-14.

Self-reported interoceptive awareness in primary care patients with past or current low back pain. Mehling WE, Daubenmier J, Price CJ, Acree M, Bartmess E, Stewart AL. J Pain Res. 2013 May 28;6:403-18.

[17] Mood alterations in mindful versus aerobic exercise modes. Netz Y, Lidor R. J Psychol. 2003 Sep;137(5):405-19.

[18] Using an ambulatory stress monitoring device to identify relaxation due to untrained deep breathing. Khan HM, Ahmed B, Choi J, Gutierrez-Osuna R. Conf Proc IEEE Eng Med Biol Soc. 2013;2013:1744-7.

Slow recovery from voluntary hyperventilation in panic disorder. Wilhelm FH, Gerlach AL, Roth WT. Psychosom Med. 2001 Jul-Aug;63(4):638-49.

[19] Effect of slow- and fast-breathing exercises on autonomic functions in patients with essential hypertension. Mourya M, Mahajan AS, Singh NP, Jain AK. J Altern Complement Med. 2009 Jul;15(7):711-7.

[20] The thermoregulatory theory of yawning: what we know from over 5 years of research. Andrew C. Gallup, Omar T. Eldakar. Front Neurosci. 2012; 6: 188.

[21] Tan CM. *Search Inside Yourself.* HarperOne, 2012.

[22] Neural correlates of focused attention during a brief mindfulness induction. Dickenson J, Berkman ET, Arch J, Lieberman MD. Soc Cogn Affect Neurosci. 2013 Jan;8(1):40-7.

[23] Neural correlates of mindfulness meditation-related anxiety

relief. Zeidan F, Martucci KT, Kraft RA, McHaffie JG, Coghill RC. Soc Cogn Affect Neurosci. 2014 Jun;9(6):751-9.

Psychological and neural mechanisms of trait mindfulness in reducing depression vulnerability. Paul NA, Stanton SJ, Greeson JM, Smoski MJ, Wang L. Soc Cogn Affect Neurosci. 2013 Jan;8(1):56-64.

[24] Dynamical properties of BOLD activity from the ventral posteromedial cortex associated with meditation and attentional skills. Pagnoni G. J Neurosci. 2012 Apr 11;32(15):5242-9.

[25] At the beginning of each new school year, we ask our students to do the inner values exercise for 10 days and to then fill out a brief questionnaire asking them how the exercise affected their day at work. Our findings were published in the Journal of Executive Education. 2012 July 11(1):37-65. Available at:http://digitalcommons.kennesaw.edu/jee/vol11/iss1/3.

[26] Arousing "gentle passions" in young adolescents: Sustained experimental effects of value affirmations on prosocial feelings and behaviors. Thomaes S, Bushman BJ, de Castro BO, Reijntjes A. Dev Psychol. 2012 Jan;48(1):103-10.

[27] Affirmation of personal values buffers neuroendocrine and psychological stress responses. Creswell JD, Welch WT, Taylor SE, Sherman DK, Gruenewald TL, Mann T. Psychol Sci. 2005 Nov;16(11):846-51.

[28] Relaxation response induces temporal transcriptome changes in energy metabolism, insulin secretion and inflammatory pathways. Bhasin MK, Dusek JA, Chang BH, Joseph MG, Denninger JW, Fricchione GL, Benson H, Libermann TA. PLoS One. 2013 May 1;8(5):e62817.

Genomic counter-stress changes induced by the relaxation response. Dusek JA, Otu HH, Wohlhueter AL, Bhasin M, Zerbini LF, Joseph MG, Benson H, Libermann TA. PLoS One. 2008 Jul 2;3(7):e2576.

[29] The cessation of rumination through self-affirmation. Koole, SL, Smeets K, van Knippenberg a, Dijksterhuis. Am J Personality Soc Pysch. 1999; 77: 111-25.

[30] Preserving integrity in the face of performance threat: self-affirmation enhances neurophysiological responsiveness to errors. Legault L, Al-Khindi T, Inzlicht M. Psychol Sci. 2012 Dec;23(12):1455-60.

[31] A multidimensional approach to measuring well-being in

students: Application of the PERMA framework. Kern ML, Waters LE, Adler A, White MA. J Posit Psychol. 2015 May 4;10(3):262-271.

The effects of counting blessings on subjective well-being: a gratitude intervention in a Spanish sample. Martínez-Martí ML, Avia MD, Hernández-Lloreda MJ. Span J Psychol. 2010 Nov;13(2):886-96.

Positive psychology progress: empirical validation of interventions. Seligman ME, Steen TA, Park N, Peterson C. Am Psychol. 2005 Jul-Aug;60(5):410-21.

A balanced psychology and a full life. Seligman ME, Parks AC, Steen T. Philos Trans R Soc Lond B Biol Sci. 2004 Sep 29;359(1449):1379-81.

[32] Stress at the Workplace. World Health Organizaton. http://www.who.int/occupational_health/topics/stressatwp/en/.

[33] Stress, PTSD, and dementia. Greenberg MS, Tanev K, Marin MF, Pitman RK. Alzheimers Dement. 2014 Jun;10(3 Suppl):S155-65.

Chapter 4: Motivation—The First Pillar of Wealth

[1] Development of in-group favoritism in children's third-party punishment of selfishness. Jordan JJ, McAuliffe K, Warneken F. Proc Natl Acad Sci U S A. 2014 Sep 2;111(35):12710-5.

[2] Individual differences in decision making: Drive and Reward Responsiveness affect strategic bargaining in economic games. Scheres A, Sanfey AG. Behav Brain Funct. 2006 Oct 18;2:35.

[3] Full pockets, empty lives: a psychoanalytic exploration of the contemporary culture of greed. Wachtel PL. Am J Psychoanal. 2003 Jun;63(2):103-22.

[4] Emotions and cooperation in economic games. Haselhuhn MP, Mellers BA. Brain Res Cogn Brain Res. 2005 Apr;23(1):24-33.

[5] Dispositional greed. Seuntjens TG, Zeelenberg M, van de Ven N, Breugelmans SM. J Pers Soc Psychol. 2015 Jun;108(6):917-33.

[6] Statistical fluctuations in population bargaining in the ultimatum game: static and evolutionary aspects. da Silva R, Kellermann GA, Lamb LC. J Theor Biol. 2009 May 21;258(2):208-18.

[7]   Empathy leads to fairness. Page KM, Nowak MA. Bull Math Biol. 2002 Nov;64(6):1101-16.

[8]   Metacognitions in desire thinking: a preliminary investigation. Caselli G, Spada MM. Behav Cogn Psychother. 2010 Oct;38(5):629-37.

[9]   Brain. Conscious and Unconscious Mechanisms of Cognition, Emotions, and Language. Leonid Perlovsky, Roman Ilin. Brain Sci. 2012 December; 2(4): 790-834.

[10]   Wishful seeing: more desired objects are seen as closer. Balcetis E, Dunning D. Psychol Sci. 2010 Jan;21(1):147-52.

[11]   What is Bottom-Up and What is Top-Down in Predictive Coding? Rauss K, Pourtois G. Front Psychol. 2013 May 17;4:276.

[12]   Dopamine and extinction: a convergence of theory with fear and reward circuitry. Abraham AD, Neve KA, Lattal KM. Neurobiol Learn Mem. 2014 Feb;108:65-77.

[13]   A frontal dopamine system for reflective exploratory behavior. Blanco NJ, Love BC, Cooper JA, McGeary JE, Knopik VS, Maddox WT. Neurobiol Learn Mem. 2015 May 22;123:84-91.

[14]   Emotional imagery: assessing pleasure and arousal in the brain's reward circuitry. Costa VD, Lang PJ, Sabatinelli D, Versace F, Bradley MM. Hum Brain Mapp. 2010 Sep;31(9):1446-57.

[15]   Nucleus accumbens and impulsivity. Basar K, Sesia T, Groenewegen H, Steinbusch HW, Visser-Vandewalle V, Temel Y. Prog Neurobiol. 2010 Dec;92(4):533-57.

[16]   Modulation of frontostriatal interaction aligns with reduced primary reward processing under serotonergic drugs. Abler B, Grön G, Hartmann A, Metzger C, Walter M. J Neurosci. 2012 Jan 25;32(4):1329-35.

[17]   Deep brain stimulation for treatment-resistant depression: efficacy, safety and mechanisms of action. Anderson RJ, Frye MA, Abulseoud OA, Lee KH, McGillivray JA, Berk M, Tye SJ. Neurosci Biobehav Rev. 2012 Sep;36(8):1920-33. doi: 10.1016/j.neubiorev.2012.06.001.

[18]   Nucleus accumbens dopamine release is necessary and sufficient to promote the behavioral response to reward-predictive cues. Nicola SM, Taha SA, Kim SW, Fields HL. Neuroscience. 2005;135(4):1025-33.

[19]   The reward circuit: linking primate anatomy and human

imaging. Haber SN, Knutson B. Neuropsychopharmacology. 2010 Jan;35(1):4-26. doi: 10.1038/npp.2009.129.

[20] Emotional modulation of control dilemmas: the role of positive affect, reward, and dopamine in cognitive stability and flexibility. Goschke T, Bolte A. Neuropsychologia. 2014 Sep;62:403-23.

[21] The mysterious motivational functions of mesolimbic dopamine. Salamone JD, Correa M. Neuron. 2012 Nov 8;76(3):470-85.

[22] Overlapping neural systems represent cognitive effort and reward anticipation. Vassena E, Silvetti M, Boehler CN, Achten E, Fias W, Verguts T. PLoS One. 2014 Mar 7;9(3):e91008.

[23] Spontaneous mental contrasting and selective goal pursuit. Sevincer AT, Oettingen G. Pers Soc Psychol Bull. 2013 Sep;39(9):1240-54.

[24] Wishful information preference: positive fantasies mimic the effects of intentions. Kappes HB, Oettingen G. Pers Soc Psychol Bull. 2012 Jul;38(7):870-81.

[25] Strategies of intention formation are reflected in continuous MEG activity. Achtziger A, Fehr T, Oettingen G, Gollwitzer PM, Rockstroh B. Soc Neurosci. 2009;4(1):11-27.

[26] Approach/avoidance in dreams. Malcolm-Smith S, Koopowitz S, Pantelis E, Solms M. Conscious Cogn. 2012 Mar;21(1):408-12. doi: 10.1016/j.concog.2011.11.004.

[27] Music and emotions: from enchantment to entrainment. Vuilleumier P, Trost W. Ann N Y Acad Sci. 2015 Mar;1337:212-22.

[28] The motive for sensory pleasure. Eisenberger R, Sucharski IL, Yalowitz S, Kent RJ, Loomis RJ, Jones JR, Paylor S, Aselage J, Mueller MS, McLaughlin JP. J Pers. 2010 Apr;78(2):599-638.

[29] Do rats really express neophobia towards novel objects? Experimental evidence from exposure to novelty and to an object recognition task in an open space and an enclosed space. Ennaceur A, Michalikova S, Chazot PL. Behav Brain Res. 2009 Feb 11;197(2):417-34.

Motivated exploratory behaviour in the rat: the role of hippocampus and the histaminergic neurotransmission. Alvarez EO, Alvarez PA. Behav Brain Res. 2008 Jan 10;186(1):118-25.

[30] Deficits in novelty exploration after controlled cortical impact. Wagner AK, Postal BA, Darrah SD, Chen X, Khan AS. J Neurotrauma. 2007 Aug;24(8):1308-20.

[31] Short- and long-lasting consequences of novelty, deviance and

surprise on brain and cognition. Schomaker J, Meeter M. Neurosci Biobehav Rev. 2015 May 12;55:268-279.

[32] Information-seeking, curiosity, and attention: computational and neural mechanisms. Gottlieb J, Oudeyer PY, Lopes M, Baranes A. Trends Cogn Sci. 2013 Nov;17(11):585-93.

[33] Neuromarketing and consumer neuroscience: contributions to neurology. Javor A, Koller M, Lee N, Chamberlain L, Ransmayr G. BMC Neurol. 2013 Feb 6;13(1):13.

[34] Aesthetic evolution by mate choice: Darwin's really dangerous idea. Prum RO. Philos Trans R Soc Lond B Biol Sci. 2012 Aug 19;367(1600):2253-65.

[35] Kandel, E. *In Search of Memory.* Norton, 2006.

[36] Neural correlates of mindfulness meditation-related anxiety relief. Zeidan F, Martucci KT, Kraft RA, McHaffie JG, Coghill RC. Soc Cogn Affect Neurosci. 2014 Jun;9(6):751-9.

[37] Dispositional mindfulness co-varies with smaller amygdala and caudate volumes in community adults. Taren AA, Creswell JD, Gianaros PJ. PLoS One. 2013 May 22;8(5):e64574.

[38] Self-efficacy as a moderator of information-seeking effectiveness. Brown SP, Ganesan S, Challagalla G. J Appl Psychol. 2001 Oct;86(5):1043-51.

[39] The influence of positive affect on the components of expectancy motivation. Erez A, Isen AM. J Appl Psychol. 2002 Dec;87(6):1055-67.

[40] Lord RG, Klimoski RJ, Kanfer R, eds. *Emotions in the Workplace: Understanding the Structure and Role of Emotions in Organizational Behavior.* Jossey-Bass, 2002 (pp. 5-19).

[41] Compassion-based emotion regulation up-regulates experienced positive affect and associated neural networks. Engen HG, Singer T. Soc Cogn Affect Neurosci. 2015 Feb 19.

[42] The cooperative brain. Stallen M, Sanfey AG. Neuroscientist. 2013 Jun;19(3):292-303. doi: 10.1177/1073858412469728.

[43] The brain's emotional foundations of human personality and the Affective Neuroscience Personality Scales. Davis KL, Panksepp J. Neurosci Biobehav Rev. 2011 Oct;35(9):1946-58. doi: 10.1016/j.neubiorev.2011.04.004.

[44] The SEEKING mind: primal neuro-affective substrates for appetitive incentive states and their pathological dynamics in addictions and depression. Alcaro A, Panksepp J. Neurosci

Biobehav Rev. 2011 Oct;35(9):1805-20. doi: 10.1016/j. neubiorev.2011.03.002.

[45] Measuring hedonia and eudaimonia as motives for activities: cross-national investigation through traditional and Bayesian structural equation modeling. Bujacz A, Vittersø J, Huta V, Kaczmarek LD. Front Psychol. 2014 Sep 8;5:984.

[46] Dopamine modulates egalitarian behavior in humans. Sáez I, Zhu L, Set E, Kayser A, Hsu M. Curr Biol. 2015 Mar 30;25(7):912-9.

Chapter 5: Turning On the M-Drive

[1] Mind-sets matter: a meta-analytic review of implicit theories and self-regulation. Burnette JL, O'Boyle EH, VanEpps EM, Pollack JM, Finkel EJ. Psychol Bull. 2013 May;139(3):655-701.

[2] Distributed value representation in the medial prefrontal cortex during intertemporal choices. Wang Q, Luo S, Monterosso J, Zhang J, Fang X, Dong Q, Xue G. J Neurosci. 2014 May 28;34(22):7522-30.

[3] When desire collides with reason: functional interactions between anteroventral prefrontal cortex and nucleus accumbens underlie the human ability to resist impulsive desires. Diekhof EK, Gruber O. J Neurosci. 2010 Jan 27;30(4):1488-93.

[4] Rapid dopamine dynamics in the accumbens core and shell: learning and action. Saddoris MP, Sugam JA, Cacciapaglia F, Carelli RM. Front Biosci (Elite Ed). 2013 Jan 1;5:273-88.

[5] Understanding entrepreneurial intent in late adolescence: the role of intentional self-regulation and innovation. Geldhof GJ, Weiner M, Agans JP, Mueller MK, Lerner RM. J Youth Adolesc. 2014 Jan;43(1):81-91.

Occupational dreams, choices and aspirations: adolescents' entrepreneurial prospects and orientations. Schmitt-Rodermund E, Vondracek FW. J Adolesc. 2002 Feb;25(1):65-78.

[6] Neuroanatomical correlates of the sense of control: Gray and white matter volumes associated with an internal locus of control. Hashimoto T, Takeuchi H, Taki Y, Sekiguchi A, Nouchi R, Kotozaki Y, Nakagawa S, Miyauchi CM, Iizuka K, Yokoyama R, Shinada T, Yamamoto Y, Hanawa S, Araki T, Hashizume H, Kunitoki K, Kawashima R. Neuroimage. 2015 Oct 1;119:146-51.

[7]   Dissociating motivation from reward in human striatal activity. Miller EM, Shankar MU, Knutson B, McClure SM. J Cogn Neurosci. 2014 May;26(5):1075-84.

[8]   Neural correlates of episodic memory: associative memory and confidence drive hippocampus activations. Kuchinke L, Fritzemeier S, Hofmann MJ, Jacobs AM. Behav Brain Res. 2013 Oct 1;254:92-101.

[9]   Cognitive and attentional mechanisms in delay of gratification. Mischel W, Ebbesen EB, Zeiss AR. J Pers Soc Psychol. 1972 Feb;21(2):204-18.

[10] Delay of gratification in children. Mischel W, Shoda Y, Rodriguez MI. Science. 1989 May 26;244(4907):933-8.

[11] Preschoolers' delay of gratification predicts their body mass 30 years later. Schlam TR, Wilson NL, Shoda Y, Mischel W, Ayduk O. J Pediatr. 2013 Jan;162(1):90-3.

[12] Interventions shown to aid executive function development in children 4 to 12 years old. Diamond A, Lee K. Science. 2011 Aug 19;333(6045):959-64.

[13] Circuitry of self-control and its role in reducing addiction. Tang YY, Posner MI, Rothbart MK, Volkow ND. Trends Cogn Sci. 2015 Jul 13. pii: S1364-6613(15)00144-8.

[14] Caudate responses to reward anticipation associated with delay discounting behavior in healthy youth. Benningfield MM, Blackford JU, Ellsworth ME, Samanez-Larkin GR, Martin PR, Cowan RL, Zald DH. Dev Cogn Neurosci. 2014 Jan;7:43-52.

[15] Rational snacking: young children's decision making on the marshmallow task is moderated by beliefs about environmental reliability. Kidd C, Palmeri H, Aslin RN. Cognition. 2013 Jan;126(1):109-14.

[16] The neurobiology of intertemporal choice: insight from imaging and lesion studies. Sellitto M, Ciaramelli E, di Pellegrino G. Rev Neurosci. 2011;22(5):565-74.

[17] Rewards and creative performance: a meta-analytic test of theoretically derived hypotheses. Byron K, Khazanchi S. Psychol Bull. 2012 Jul;138(4):809-30.

[18] Modeling effects of intrinsic and extrinsic rewards on the competition between striatal learning systems. Boedecker J, Lampe T, Riedmiller M. Front Psychol. 2013 Oct 16;4:739.

[19] States of curiosity modulate hippocampus-dependent learning

via the dopaminergic circuit. Gruber MJ, Gelman BD, Ranganath C. Neuron. 2014 Oct 22;84(2):486-96.

[20] The SEEKING mind: primal neuro-affective substrates for appetitive incentive states and their pathological dynamics in addictions and depression. Alcaro A, Panksepp J. Neurosci Biobehav Rev. 2011 Oct;35(9):1805-20.

[21] Personality, effective goal-striving, and enhanced well-being: comparing 10 candidate personality strengths. Sheldon KM, Jose PE, Kashdan TB, Jarden A. Pers Soc Psychol Bull. 2015 Apr;41(4):575-85.

[22] Mechanisms of hippocampal long-term depression are required for memory enhancement by novelty exploration. Dong Z, Gong B, Li H, Bai Y, Wu X, Huang Y, He W, Li T, Wang YT. J Neurosci. 2012 Aug 29;32(35):11980-90.

[23] Different developmental trajectories for anticipation and receipt of reward during adolescence. Hoogendam JM, Kahn RS, Hillegers MH, van Buuren M, Vink M. Dev Cogn Neurosci. 2013 Oct;6:113-24.

[24] Strategies of intention formation are reflected in continuous MEG activity. Achtziger A, Fehr T, Oettingen G, Gollwitzer PM, Rockstroh B. Soc Neurosci. 2009;4(1):11-27.

[25] Positive fantasies about idealized futures sap energy. Kappes, HB, & Oettingen, G. J Experimental Soc Psychol. 2011 (47): 719-729.

[26] Wishful information preference: positive fantasies mimic the effects of intentions. Kappes HB, Oettingen G. Pers Soc Psychol Bull. 2012 Jul;38(7):870-81.

[27] Recalling happy memories in remitted depression: a neuroimaging investigation of the repair of sad mood. Foland-Ross LC, Cooney RE, Joormann J, Henry ML, Gotlib IH. Cogn Affect Behav Neurosci. 2014 Jun;14(2):818-26.

[28] For a comprehensive overview of Oettingen's research and goal-achievement formula, read her popular book *Rethinking Positive Thinking.* Current: 2014.

[29] Mind wandering via mental contrasting as a tool for behavior change. Oettingen G, Schwörer B. Front Psychol. 2013 Sep 2;4:562.

[30] Functions of the frontal lobes: relation to executive functions. Stuss DT. J Int Neuropsychol Soc. 2011 Sep;17(5):759-65.

[31] Mental contrasting and transfer of energization. Sevincer

AT, Busatta PD, Oettingen G. Pers Soc Psychol Bull. 2014 Feb;40(2):139-52.

[32] For a student/teacher manual and a free online training course using Oettingen's "WOOP" strategy, go to https://characterlab. org/goal-setting.

[33] Norcross JC. *Changeology.* Simon and Schuster: 2012.

[34] The role of goal specificity in the goal-setting process. Klein HJ, Whitener, EM, Ilgen DR. Motivation and Emotion. 1990;14(3):179-93.

[35] Demands, values, and burnout: relevance for physicians. Leiter MP, Frank E, Matheson TJ. Can Fam Physician. 2009 Dec;55(12):1224-1225, 1225.e1-6.
    Burnout and nurses' personal and professional values. Altun I. Nurs Ethics. 2002 May;9(3):269-78.

[36] Psychobiological changes from relaxation response elicitation: long-term practitioners vs. novices. Chang BH, Dusek JA, Benson H. Psychosomatics. 2011 Nov-Dec;52(6):550-9.
    Genomic counter-stress changes induced by the relaxation response. Dusek JA, Otu HH, Wohlhueter AL, Bhasin M, Zerbini LF, Joseph MG, Benson H, Libermann TA. PLoS One. 2008 Jul 2;3(7):e2576.

[37] Neural basis of individualistic and collectivistic views of self. Chiao JY, Harada T, Komeda H, Li Z, Mano Y, Saito D, Parrish TB, Sadato N, Iidaka T. Hum Brain Mapp. 2009 Sep;30(9):2813-20.

[38] Absolute versus relative values: effects on medical decisions and personality of patients and physicians. Neumann JK, Olive KE, McVeigh SD. South Med J. 1999 Sep;92(9):871-6.

[39] Newberg A, and Waldman M. *How God Changes Your Brain.* Ballantine, 2009.

[40] True Grit: Trait-level Perseverance and Passion for Long-term Goals Predicts Effectiveness and Retention among Novice Teachers. Robertson-Kraft C, Duckworth AL. Teach Coll Rec (1970). 2014;116(3).

[41] Job satisfaction, occupational commitment and intent to stay among Chinese nurses: a cross-sectional questionnaire survey. Wang L, Tao H, Ellenbecker CH, Liu X. J Adv Nurs. 2012 Mar;68(3):539-49.

[42] Dopaminergic control of cognitive flexibility in humans and

animals. Klanker M, Feenstra M, Denys D. Front Neurosci. 2013 Nov 5;7:201.

Rolling the dice: the importance of mesolimbic dopamine signaling in risky decision making. Sugam JA, Carelli RM. Neuropsychopharmacology. 2013 Jan;38(1):248.

[43] Passion and coping: relationships with changes in burnout and goal attainment in collegiate volleyball players. Schellenberg BJ, Gaudreau P, Crocker PR. J Sport Exerc Psychol. 2013 Jun;35(3):270-80.

[44] From autonomy to creativity: a multilevel investigation of the mediating role of harmonious passion. Liu D, Chen XP, Yao X. J Appl Psychol. 2011 Mar;96(2):294-309.

[45] The relationship between grit and resident well-being. Salles A, Cohen GL, Mueller CM. Am J Surg. 2014 Feb;207(2):251-4.

[46] True Grit: Trait-level Perseverance and Passion for Long-term Goals Predicts Effectiveness and Retention among Novice Teachers. Robertson-Kraft C, Duckworth AL. Teach Coll Rec (1970). 2014;116(3).

[47] The neurobiology of stress management. Esch T, Stefano GB. Neuro Endocrinol Lett. 2010;31(1):19-39.

[48] Calculating utility: preclinical evidence for cost-benefit analysis by mesolimbic dopamine. Phillips PE, Walton ME, Jhou TC. Psychopharmacology (Berl). 2007 Apr;191(3):483-95.

[49] Are you working too hard? A conversation with mind/body researcher Herbert Benson. Benson H. Harv Bus Rev. 2005 Nov;83(11):53-8, 165.

[50] Happiness unpacked: positive emotions increase life satisfaction by building resilience. Cohn MA, Fredrickson BL, Brown SL, Mikels JA, Conway AM. Emotion. 2009 Jun;9(3):361-8.

[51] Modulators of decision making. Doya K. Nat Neurosci. 2008 Apr;11(4):410-6. doi: 10.1038/nn2077.

[52] The nucleus accumbens: an interface between cognition, emotion, and action. Floresco SB. Annu Rev Psychol. 2015 Jan 3;66:25-52.

[53] The brain's conversation with itself: neural substrates of dialogic inner speech. Alderson-Day B, Weis S, McCarthy-Jones S, Moseley P, Smailes D, Fernyhough C. Soc Cogn Affect Neurosci. 2016 Jan;11(1):110-20.

Toward a phenomenology of inner speaking. Hurlburt RT, Heavey CL, Kelsey JM. Conscious Cogn. 2013 Dec;22(4):1477-94.

[54] Interoceptive predictions in the brain. Barrett LF, Simmons WK. Nat Rev Neurosci. 2015 Jul;16(7):419-29.

Chapter 6: Decision Making—The Second Pillar of Wealth

[1] Kaufman JC and Sternberg RJ (editors).The Cambridge Handbook of Creativity. Cambridge University Press, 2010.

[2] Miller BL and Cummings JL (editors). *The Human Frontal Lobes, Second Edition.* Guilford Press, 2006.

[3] The frontal lobe contains many interconnected substructures, including the motor cortex, prefrontal cortex, and orbitofrontal cortex. Everyday consciousness, memory recall, impulse control, and decision-making processes primarily take place in the prefrontal cortex, the area just behind your forehead. The left half of the frontal lobe is more specialized for language and memory processing, abstract thinking, and positivity, while the right half is oriented toward social cognition, spatial awareness, and the processing of negative feelings and thoughts.

[4] What is that little voice inside my head? Inner speech phenomenology, its role in cognitive performance, and its relation to self-monitoring. Perrone-Bertolotti M, Rapin L, Lachaux JP, Baciu M, Lœvenbruck H. Behav Brain Res. 2014 Mar 15;261:220-39.

[5] The neural correlate of consciousness. Bodovitz S. J Theor Biol. 2008 Oct 7;254(3):594-8. The brainscan image is courtesy of the National Institutes of Health.

[6] The neural basis of optimism and pessimism. Hecht D. Exp Neurobiol. 2013 Sep;22(3):173-99.

How unrealistic optimism is maintained in the face of reality. Sharot T, Korn CW, Dolan RJ. Nat Neurosci. 2011 Oct 9;14(11):1475-9.

[7] Measuring emotion in advertising research: prefrontal brain activity. Silberstein RB, Nield GE. IEEE Pulse. 2012 May-Jun;3(3):24-7.

[8] Dispositional optimism. Carver CS, Scheier MF. Trends Cogn Sci. 2014 Jun;18(6):293-9.

[9] An examination of optimism/pessimism and suicide risk in primary care patients: Does belief in a changeable future make a

difference? Chang EC, Yu EA, Lee JY, Hirsch JK, Kupfermann Y, Kahle ER. Cognit Ther Res. 2013;37:796-804.

[10] Are optimists oriented uniquely toward the future? Investigating dispositional optimism from a temporally-expanded perspective. Busseri MA, Malinowski A, Choma BL. J Res Pers. 2013;47:533-538.

[11] Neural mechanisms mediating optimism bias. Sharot T, Riccardi AM, Raio CM, Phelps EA. Nature. 2007 Nov 1;450(7166):102-5.

[12] A two-factor model of defensive pessimism and its relations with achievement motives. Lim L. J Psychol. 2009 May;143(3):318-36.

[13] Dispositional optimism and thoughts of well-being determine sensitivity to an experimental pain task. Geers AL, Wellman JA, Helfer SG, Fowler SL, France CR. Ann Behav Med. 2008 Dec;36(3):304-13.

[14] Become more optimistic by imagining a best possible self: effects of a two week intervention. Meevissen YM, Peters ML, Alberts HJ. J Behav Ther Exp Psychiatry. 2011 Sep;42(3):371-8.

[15] Effects of a best-possible-self mental imagery exercise on mood and dysfunctional attitudes. Renner F, Schwarz P, Peters ML, Huibers MJ. Psychiatry Res. 2014 Jan 30;215(1):105-10.

[16] Mental imagery and emotion in treatment across disorders: using the example of depression. Holmes EA, Lang TJ, Deeprose C. Cogn Behav Ther. 2009;38 Suppl 1:21-8.

[17] Positive interpretation training: effects of mental imagery versus verbal training on positive mood. Holmes EA, Mathews A, Dalgleish T, Mackintosh B. Behav Ther. 2006 Sep;37(3):237-47.

[18] Mental imagery as an emotional amplifier: application to bipolar disorder. Holmes EA, Geddes JR, Colom F, Goodwin GM. Behav Res Ther. 2008 Dec;46(12):1251-8.

[19] Giving off a rosy glow: the manipulation of an optimistic orientation. Fosnaugh J, Geers AL, Wellman JA. J Soc Psychol. 2009 Jun;149(3):349-64.

[20] Treatment of childhood memories: theory and practice. Arntz A, Weertman A. Behav Res Ther. 1999 Aug;37(8):715-40.

[21] Seligman M. Learned Optimism. Free Press, 1997.

[22] Enhancing well-being and alleviating depressive symptoms with positive psychology interventions: a practice-friendly meta-analysis. Sin NL, Lyubomirsky S. J Clin Psychol. 2009 May;65(5):467-87.

[23] Optimism. Carver CS, Scheier MF, Segerstrom SC. Clin Psychol Rev. 2010 Nov;30(7):879-89.

[24] Well-being and affective style: neural substrates and biobehavioural correlates. Davidson RJ. Philos Trans R Soc Lond B Biol Sci. 2004 Sep 29;359(1449):1395-411.

[25] The debate over dopamine's role in reward: the case for incentive salience. Berridge KC. Psychopharmacology (Berl). 2007 Apr;191(3):391-431.

[26] Dopaminergic action beyond its effects on motor function: imaging studies. Brooks DJ. J Neurol. 2006 Aug;253 Suppl 4:IV8-15.

[27] How dopamine enhances an optimism bias in humans. Sharot T, Guitart-Masip M, Korn CW, Chowdhury R, Dolan RJ. Curr Biol. 2012 Aug 21;22(16):1477-81.

[28] Frontotemporal and dopaminergic control of idea generation and creative drive. Flaherty AW. J Comp Neurol. 2005 Dec 5;493(1):147-53.

[29] Prediction of all-cause mortality by the Minnesota Multiphasic Personality Inventory Optimism-Pessimism Scale scores: study of a college sample during a 40-year follow-up period. Brummett BH, Helms MJ, Dahlstrom WG, Siegler IC. Mayo Clin Proc. 2006 Dec;81(12):1541-4.

[30] The Power of Personality: The Comparative Validity of Personality Traits, Socioeconomic Status, and Cognitive Ability for Predicting Important Life Outcomes. Roberts BW, Kuncel NR, Shiner R, Caspi A, Goldberg LR. Perspect Psychol Sci. 2007 Dec;2(4):313-45.

Optimism-pessimism assessed in the 1960s and self-reported health status 30 years later. Maruta T, Colligan RC, Malinchoc M, Offord KP. Mayo Clin Proc. 2002 Aug;77(8):748-53.

[31] Perceptions of self-concept and self-presentation by procrastinators: further evidence. Ferrari JR, Díaz-Morales JF. Span J Psychol. 2007 May;10(1):91-6.

[32] Writing apprehension and academic procrastination among graduate students. Onwuegbuzie AJ, Collins KM. Percept Mot Skills. 2001 Apr;92(2):560-2.

[33] Why not procrastinate? Development and validation of a new active procrastination scale. Choi JN, Moran SV. J Soc Psychol. 2009 Apr;149(2):195-211.

[34] Lateralization is predicted by reduced coupling from the left to right prefrontal cortex during semantic decisions on written

words. Seghier ML, Josse G, Leff AP, Price CJ. Cereb Cortex. 2011 Jul;21(7):1519-31.

[35] Neurobiology and treatment of compulsive hoarding. Saxena S. CNS Spectr. 2008 Sep;13(9 Suppl 14):29-36.

[36] An investigation of the efficacy of acceptance-based behavioral therapy for academic procrastination. Glick DM, Orsillo SM. J Exp Psychol Gen. 2015 Apr;144(2):400-9. doi: 10.1037/xge0000050.

Multilevel growth curve analyses of treatment effects of a Web-based intervention for stress reduction: randomized controlled trial. Drozd F, Raeder S, Kraft P, Bjørkli CA. J Med Internet Res. 2013 Apr 22;15(4):e84.

[37] Rethinking procrastination: positive effects of "active" procrastination behavior on attitudes and performance. Chu AH, Choi JN. J Soc Psychol. 2005 Jun;145(3):245-64.

Procrastination at work and time management training. Van Eerde W. J Psychol. 2003 Sep;137(5):421-34.

[38] Procrastination, deadlines, and performance: self-control by precommitment. Ariely D, Wertenbroch K. Psychol Sci. 2002 May;13(3):219-24.

[39] Perfectionism as a transdiagnostic process: a clinical review. Egan SJ, Wade TD, Shafran R. Clin Psychol Rev. 2011 Mar;31(2):203-12.

[40] Multidimensional Perfectionism and Burnout: A Meta-Analysis. Hill AP, Curran T. Pers Soc Psychol Rev. 2015 Jul 31.

[41] Neural correlates of obsessive-compulsive related dysfunctional beliefs. Alonso P, Orbegozo A, Pujol J, López-Solà C, Fullana MÀ, Segalàs C, Real E, Subirà M, Martínez-Zalacaín I, Menchón JM, Harrison BJ, Cardoner N, Soriano-Mas C. Prog Neuropsychopharmacol Biol Psychiatry. 2013 Dec 2;47:25-32.

[42] Brown, R. *The Gifts of Imperfection*. Hazelden, 2010.

[43] Hierarchically organized behavior and its neural foundations: a reinforcement learning perspective. Botvinick MM, Niv Y, Barto AC. Cognition. 2009 Dec;113(3):262-80.

[44] Do you have a voting plan?: implementation intentions, voter turnout, and organic plan making. Nickerson DW, Rogers T. Psychol Sci. 2010 Feb;21(2):194-9.

Harnessing Our Inner Angels and Demons: What We Have Learned About Want/Should Conflicts and How That Knowledge Can Help Us Reduce Short-Sighted Decision

Making. Milkman KL, Rogers T, Bazerman MH. Perspect Psychol Sci. 2008 Jul;3(4):324-38.

[45] From Fantasy to Action: Mental Contrasting with Implementation Intentions (MCII) Improves Academic Performance in Children. Duckworth AL, Kirby T, Gollwitzer A, Oettingen G. Soc Psychol Personal Sci. 2013 Nov 1;4(6):745-753.

[46] Promoting the translation of intentions into action by implementation intentions: behavioral effects and physiological correlates. Wieber F, Thürmer JL, Gollwitzer PM. Front Hum Neurosci. 2015 Jul 14;9:395.

The neural correlates of emotion regulation by implementation intentions. Hallam GP, Webb TL, Sheeran P, Miles E, Wilkinson ID, Hunter MD, Barker AT, Woodruff PW, Totterdell P, Lindquist KA, Farrow TF. PLoS One. 2015 Mar 23;10(3):e0119500.

[47] Get your team to do what it says it's going to do. Grant H. Harv Bus Rev. 2014 May;92(5):82-7, 133.

[48] Recovery after work: the role of work beliefs in the unwinding process. Zoupanou Z, Cropley M, Rydstedt LW. PLoS One. 2013 Dec 11;8(12):e81381.

[49] Neural precursors of delayed insight. Darsaud A, Wagner U, Balteau E, Desseilles M, Sterpenich V, Vandewalle G, Albouy G, Dang-Vu T, Collette F, Boly M, Schabus M, Degueldre C, Luxen A, Maquet P. J Cogn Neurosci. 2011 Aug;23(8):1900-10.

Chapter 7: Sharpening Your Decision-Making Skills

[1] Miller BL, Cummings JL (editors). *The Human Frontal Lobes, Second Edition*. Guilford Press, 2007.

[2] Mindfulness meditation improves cognition: evidence of brief mental training. Zeidan F, Johnson SK, Diamond BJ, David Z, Goolkasian P. Conscious Cogn. 2010 Jun;19(2):597-605.

[3] The effect of focused attention and open monitoring meditation on attention network function in healthy volunteers. Ainsworth B, Eddershaw R, Meron D, Baldwin DS, Garner M. Psychiatry Res. 2013 Dec 30;210(3):1226-31.

[4] Effective and viable mind-body stress reduction in the workplace: a randomized controlled trial. Wolever RQ, Bobinet

KJ, McCabe K, Mackenzie ER, Fekete E, Kusnick CA, Baime M. J Occup Health Psychol. 2012 Apr;17(2):246-58.

[5] Matthews G. Her findings were presented at Ninth Annual International Conference of the Psychology Research Unit of Athens Institute for Education and Research, 2015. The study is published online: http://www.dominican.edu/dominicannews/study-highlights-strategies-for-achieving-goals.

[6] Making health habitual: the psychology of 'habit-formation' and general practice. Gardner B, Lally P, Wardle J. Br J Gen Pract. 2012 Dec;62(605):664-6.

[7] Behavioral and neural substrates of habit formation in rats intravenously self-administering nicotine. Clemens KJ, Castino MR, Cornish JL, Goodchild AK, Holmes NM. Neuropsychopharmacology. 2014 Oct;39(11):2584-93.

Regulation of prefrontal excitatory neurotransmission by dopamine in the nucleus accumbens core. Wang W, Dever D, Lowe J, Storey GP, Bhansali A, Eck EK, Nitulescu I, Weimer J, Bamford NS. J Physiol. 2012 Aug 15;590(Pt 16):3743-69.

[8] Mental contrasting and transfer of energization. Sevincer AT, Busatta PD, Oettingen G. Pers Soc Psychol Bull. 2014 Feb;40(2):139-52.

[9] Self-affirmation activates brain systems associated with self-related processing and reward and is reinforced by future orientation. Cascio CN, O'Donnell MB, Tinney FJ, Lieberman MD, Taylor SE, Strecher VJ, Falk EB. Soc Cogn Affect Neurosci. 2015 Nov 5. pii: nsv136.

[10] Self-affirmation improves problem-solving under stress. Creswell JD, Dutcher JM, Klein WM, Harris PR, Levine JM. PLoS One. 2013 May 1;8(5):e62593.

[11] What drives self-affirmation effects? On the importance of differentiating value affirmation and attribute affirmation. Stapel DA, van der Linde LA. J Pers Soc Psychol. 2011 Jul;101(1):34-45.

[12] Arousing "gentle passions" in young adolescents: Sustained experimental effects of value affirmations on prosocial feelings and behaviors. Thomaes S, Bushman BJ, de Castro BO, Reijntjes A. Dev Psychol. 2012 Jan;48(1):103-10.

[13] Positive psychology progress: empirical validation of interventions. Seligman ME, Steen TA, Park N, Peterson C. Am Psychol. 2005 Jul-Aug;60(5):410-21.

[14] Neural correlates of gratitude. Fox GR, Kaplan J, Damasio H, Damasio A. Front Psychol. 2015 Sep 30;6:1491.

[15] The effects of two novel gratitude and mindfulness interventions on well-being. O'Leary K, Dockray S. J Altern Complement Med. 2015 Apr;21(4):243-5.

[16] The brain on stress: vulnerability and plasticity of the prefrontal cortex over the life course. McEwen BS, Morrison JH. Neuron. 2013 Jul 10;79(1):16-29.

[17] Reset a task set after five minutes of mindfulness practice. Kuo CY, Yeh YY. Conscious Cogn. 2015 Sep;35:98-109.

[18] Cultivating multiple aspects of attention through mindfulness meditation accounts for psychological well-being through decreased rumination. Wolkin JR. Psychol Res Behav Manag. 2015 Jun 29;8:171-80.

      Psychological and neural mechanisms of trait mindfulness in reducing depression vulnerability. Paul NA, Stanton SJ, Greeson JM, Smoski MJ, Wang L. Soc Cogn Affect Neurosci. 2013 Jan;8(1):56-64.

[19] Fredrickson B. *Positivity.* Three Rivers Press, 2009.

[20] Losada, M. & Heaphy, E. (2004). The role of positivity and connectivity in the performance of business teams: A nonlinear dynamics model. Losada M, Heaphy E. Am Behav Scientist. 2004 47 (6):740–765. *Note:* Losada's data has been called into question; see this study: Positive psychology and romantic scientism. Brown NJ, Sokal AD, Friedman HL. Am Psychol. 2014 Sep;69(6):636-7.

[21] Gottman J. *What Predicts Divorce?: The Relationship Between Marital Processes and Marital Outcomes.* Psychology Press, 1993.

[22] Optimal and normal affect balance in psychotherapy of major depression: Evaluation of the balanced states of mind model. Schwartz RM, Reynolds CF, Thase ME, Frank E, Fasiczka, AL, Haaga, David AF. Behav Cogn Psychother. 2002 Oct; 30(4):439-450.

[23] Prioritizing positivity: an effective approach to pursuing happiness? Catalino LI, Algoe SB, Fredrickson BL. Emotion. 2014 Dec;14(6):1155-61.

      Updated thinking on positivity ratios. Fredrickson BL. Am Psychol. 2013 Dec;68(9):814-22.

[24] Embodied cognition and beyond: acting and sensing the body. Borghi AM, Cimatti F. Neuropsychologia. 2010 Feb;48(3):763-73.

Voice: a pathway to consciousness as "social contact to oneself." Bertau MC. Integr Psychol Behav Sci. 2008 Mar;42(1):92-113.

[25]   The voice of self-control: blocking the inner voice increases impulsive responding.Tullett AM, Inzlicht M. Acta Psychol (Amst). 2010 Oct;135(2):252-6.

[26]   Private speech in adolescents. Kronk CM. Adolescence. 1994 Winter;29(116):781-804.

[27]   "Right hemispheric self-awareness: a critical assessment. Morin A. Conscious Cogn. 2002 Sep;11(3):396-401.

[28]   Self-awareness and the left inferior frontal gyrus: inner speech use during self-related processing. Morin A, Michaud J. Brain Res Bull. 2007 Nov 1;74(6):387-96.

[29]   Self-compassion influences PTSD symptoms in the process of change in trauma-focused cognitive-behavioral therapies: a study of within-person processes. Hoffart A, Øktedalen T, Langkaas TF. Front Psychol. 2015 Aug 27;6:1273.

[30]   The effects of mindfulness-based stress reduction therapy on mental health of adults with a chronic medical disease: a meta-analysis. Bohlmeijer E, Prenger R, Taal E, Cuijpers P. J Psychosom Res. 2010 Jun;68(6):539-44.

[31]   Inner speech as a retrieval aid for task goals: the effects of cue type and articulatory suppression in the random task cuing paradigm. Miyake A, Emerson MJ, Padilla F, Ahn JC. Acta Psychol (Amst). 2004 Feb-Mar;115(2-3):123-42.

[32]   The phenomena of inner experience. Heavey CL, Hurlburt RT. Conscious Cogn. 2008 Sep;17(3):798-810.

[33]   Studying the effects of self-talk on thought content with male adult tennis players. Latinjak AT, Torregrosa M, Renom J. Percept Mot Skills. 2010 Aug;111(1):249-60.

Effects of instructional and motivational self-talk on the vertical jump. Tod DA, Thatcher R, McGuigan M, Thatcher J. J Strength Cond Res. 2009 Jan;23(1):196-202.

[34]   Interpretation of self-talk and post-lecture affective states of higher education students: a self-determination theory perspective. Oliver EJ, Markland D, Hardy J. Br J Educ Psychol. 2010 Jun;80(Pt 2):307-23.

[35]   Using self-talk to enhance career satisfaction and performance. White SJ. Am J Health Syst Pharm. 2008 Mar 15;65(6):514, 516, 519.

[36]   "Aha!": The neural correlates of verbal insight solutions. Aziz-

Zadeh L, Kaplan JT, Iacoboni M. Hum Brain Mapp. 2009 Mar;30(3):908-16.

Neural correlates of the 'Aha! reaction'. Luo J, Niki K, Phillips S. Neuroreport. 2004 Sep 15;15(13):2013-7.

Neural activity when people solve verbal problems with insight. Jung-Beeman M, Bowden EM, Haberman J, Frymiare JL, Arambel-Liu S, Greenblatt R, Reber PJ, Kounios J. PLoS Biol. 2004 Apr;2(4):E97.

[37] A longitudinal investigation of repressive coping and ageing. Erskine J, Kvavilashvili L, Myers L, Leggett S, Davies S, Hiskey S, Hogg J, Yeo S, Georgiou G. Aging Ment Health. 2015 Jul 3:1-11.

[38] Psychopathology and thought suppression: a quantitative review. Magee JC, Harden KP, Teachman BA. Clin Psychol Rev. 2012 Apr;32(3):189-201.

[39] Better control with less effort: The advantage of using focused-breathing strategy over focused-distraction strategy on thought suppression. Ju YJ, Lien YW. Conscious Cogn. 2015 Dec 21;40:9-16.

[40] Design and Implementation of an fMRI Study Examining Thought Suppression in Young Women with, and At-risk, for Depression. Carew CL, Tatham EL, Milne AM, MacQueen GM, Hall GB. J Vis Exp. 2015 May 19;(99):e52061.

Chapter 8: Creativity—The Third Pillar of Wealth

[1] Meditate to create: the impact of focused-attention and open-monitoring training on convergent and divergent thinking. Colzato LS, Ozturk A, Hommel B. Front Psychol. 2012 Apr 18;3:116.

Neural correlates of focused attention and cognitive monitoring in meditation. Manna A, Raffone A, Perrucci MG, Nardo D, Ferretti A, Tartaro A, Londei A, Del Gratta C, Belardinelli MO, Romani GL. Brain Res Bull. 2010 Apr 29;82(1-2):46-56.

[2] Evolutionary aspects of self- and world consciousness in vertebrates. Fabbro F, Aglioti SM, Bergamasco M, Clarici A, Panksepp J. Front Hum Neurosci. 2015 Mar 26;9:157.

The remote roots of consciousness in fruit-fly selective attention? Swinderen Bv. Bioessays. 2005 Mar;27(3):321-30.

[3] Honey bees selectively avoid difficult choices. Perry CJ, Barron AB. Proc Natl Acad Sci U S A. 2013 Nov 19;110(47):19155-9.

[4] Cephalopod consciousness: behavioural evidence. Mather JA. Conscious Cogn. 2008 Mar;17(1):37-48.

[5] Reorganization of large-scale cognitive networks during automation of imagination of a complex sequential movement. Sauvage C, De Greef N, Manto M, Jissendi P, Nioche C, Habas C. J Neuroradiol. 2015 Apr;42(2):115-25.

[6] The brain's default network: anatomy, function, and relevance to disease. Buckner RL, Andrews-Hanna JR, Schacter DL. Ann N Y Acad Sci. 2008 Mar;1124:1-38.

[7] The neural substrate for dreaming: is it a subsystem of the default network? William Domhoff G. Conscious Cogn. 2011 Dec;20(4):1163-74.

[8] The neuroscience of musical improvisation. Beaty RE. Neurosci Biobehav Rev. 2015 Apr;51:108-17.

[9] Personality and complex brain networks: The role of openness to experience in default network efficiency. Beaty RE, Kaufman SB, Benedek M, Jung RE, Kenett YN, Jauk E, Neubauer AC, Silvia PJ. Hum Brain Mapp. 2015 Nov 26.

Brain structure links trait creativity to openness to experience. Li W, Li X, Huang L, Kong X, Yang W, Wei D, Li J, Cheng H, Zhang Q, Qiu J, Liu J. Soc Cogn Affect Neurosci. 2015 Feb;10(2):191-8.

[10] Resting state and task-related brain dynamics supporting insight. Wu YC, Jung M, Lock D, Chao E, Swartz J, Jung TP. Conf Proc IEEE Eng Med Biol Soc. 2014;2014:5454-7.

[11] Wei D, Yang J, Li W, Wang K, Zhang Q, Qiu J. Increased resting functional connectivity of the medial prefrontal cortex in creativity by means of cognitive stimulation. Cortex. 2014;51:92-102.

[12] Zhao Q, Zhou Z, Xu H, Chen S, Xu F, Fan W, Han L. Dynamic neural network of insight: a functional magnetic resonance imaging study on solving Chinese "chengyu" riddles. PLoS One. 2013;8(3):e59351.

[13] Neural correlates of the 'Aha! reaction'. Luo J, Niki K, Phillips S. Neuroreport. 2004 Sep 15;15(13):2013-7.

[14] Multisensory brain mechanisms of bodily self-consciousness. Blanke O. Nat Rev Neurosci. 2012 Jul 18;13(8):556-71.

[15] Exploring the neural correlates of visual creativity. Aziz-Zadeh L, Liew SL, Dandekar F. Soc Cogn Affect Neurosci. 2012 Mar 9.

[16] Cortical regions involved in the generation of musical structures during improvisation in pianists. Bengtsson SL, Csikszentmihalyi M, Ullén F. J Cogn Neurosci. 2007 May;19(5):830-42.

[17] Can clouds dance? Neural correlates of passive conceptual expansion using a metaphor processing task: Implications for creative cognition. Rutter B, Kröger S, Stark R, Schweckendiek J, Windmann S, Hermann C, Abraham A. Brain Cogn. 2012 Mar;78(2):114-22.

[18] Cooperation between the default mode network and the frontal-parietal network in the production of an internal train of thought. Smallwood J, Brown K, Baird B, Schooler JW. Brain Res. 2012 Jan 5;1428:60-70.

[19] The default network and self-generated thought: component processes, dynamic control, and clinical relevance. Andrews-Hanna JR, Smallwood J, Spreng RN. Ann N Y Acad Sci. 2014 May;1316:29-52.

[20] The costs and benefits of mind wandering: a review. Mooneyham BW, Schooler JW. Can J Exp Psychol. 2013 Mar;67(1):11-8.

[21] Mental illness, suicide and creativity: 40-year prospective total population study. Kyaga S, Landén M, Boman M, Hultman CM, Långström N, Lichtenstein P. J Psychiatr Res. 2013 Jan;47(1):83-90.

[22] The dreaming brain/mind, consciousness and psychosis. Limosani I, D'Agostino A, Manzone ML, Scarone S. Conscious Cogn. 2011 Dec;20(4):987-92.

[23] Organization of intrinsic functional brain connectivity predicts decisions to reciprocate social behavior. Cáceda R, James GA, Gutman DA, Kilts CD. Behav Brain Res. 2015 Oct 1;292:478-83.

[24] "Not in their right mind": the relation of psychopathology to the quantity and quality of creative thought. Ramey CH, Chrysikou EG. Front Psychol. 2014 Jul 30;5:835.

[25] Antagonistic neural networks underlying differentiated leadership roles. Boyatzis RE, Rochford K, Jack AI. Front Hum Neurosci. 2014 Mar 4;8:114.

[26] Stepping out of history: mindfulness improves insight problem solving. Ostafin BD, Kassman KT. Conscious Cogn. 2012 Jun;21(2):1031-6.

[27] Specific Mindfulness Skills Differentially Predict Creative

Performance. Baas M, Nevicka B, Ten Velden FS. Pers Soc Psychol Bull. 2014 May 23;40(9):1092-1106.

[28]   Motivating meta-awareness of mind wandering: A way to catch the mind in flight? Zedelius CM, Broadway JM, Schooler JW. Conscious Cogn. 2015 Nov;36:44-53.

[29]   Mindful creativity: the influence of mindfulness meditation on creative thinking. Capurso V, Fabbro F, Crescentini C. Front Psychol. 2014 Jan 10;4:1020.

[30]   Paul AM. Researchers Find That Frequent Tests Can Boost Learning. Scientific American, Aug 1, 2015. www.scientificamerican.com/article/researchers-find-that-frequent-tests-can-boost-learning.

[31]   Kaplan M, Silver N, LaVaque-Manty D, Meizlish D (editors). *Using Reflection and Metacognition to Improve Student Learning.* Stylus Publishing, 2013.

Promoting cognitive and metacognitive reflective reasoning skills in nursing practice: self-regulated learning theory. Kuiper RA, Pesut DJ. J Adv Nurs. 2004 Feb;45(4):381-91.

Chapter 9: Thinking Outside the Box

[1]   Aldag R and Kuzuhara L. *Creating High Performance Teams: Applied Strategies and Tools for Managers.* Routledge, 2015.

[2]   Aesthetic, emotion and empathetic imagination: beyond innovation to creativity in the health and social care workforce. Munt D, Hargreaves J. Health Care Anal. 2009 Dec;17(4):285-95.

[3]   The last of the magicians? Children, scientists, and the invocation of hidden causal powers. Harris PL. Child Dev. 1997 Dec;68(6):1018-20.

[4]   Can PLAY diminish ADHD and facilitate the construction of the social brain? Panksepp J. J Can Acad Child Adolesc Psychiatry. 2007 May;16(2):57-66.

[5]   Quoted in FBIS Daily Report: East Europe, April 4, 1995.

[6]   Aha! experiences leave a mark: facilitated recall of insight solutions. Danek AH, Fraps T, von Müller A, Grothe B, Ollinger M. Psychol Res. 2013 Sep;77(5):659-69.

[7]   Csikszentmihalyi M. *Creativity.* HarperCollins, 1996.

[8]   Generating original ideas: The neural underpinning of originality.

Mayseless N, Eran A, Shamay-Tsoory SG. Neuroimage. 2015 Aug 1;116:232-9.

[9] Default and Executive Network Coupling Supports Creative Idea Production. Beaty RE, Benedek M, Kaufman SB, Silvia PJ. Sci Rep. 2015 Jun 17;5:10964.

[10] Neurohemodynamic correlates of 'OM' chanting: A pilot functional magnetic resonance imaging study. Kalyani BG, Venkatasubramanian G, Arasappa R, Rao NP, Kalmady SV, Behere RV, Rao H, Vasudev MK, Gangadhar BN. Int J Yoga. 2011;4(1):3-6.

[11] Newberg A and Waldman M. *How Enlightenment Changes Your Brain.* Avery, 2016.

[12] A framework for understanding the relationship between externally and internally directed cognition. Dixon ML, Fox KC, Christoff K. Neuropsychologia. 2014 Sep;62:321-30.

[13] Focused attention, open monitoring and loving kindness meditation: effects on attention, conflict monitoring, and creativity - A review. Lippelt DP, Hommel B, Colzato LS. Front Psychol. 2014 Sep 23;5:1083.

Mindful creativity: the influence of mindfulness meditation on creative thinking. Capurso V, Fabbro F, Crescentini C. Front Psychol. 2014 Jan 10;4:1020.

[14] Specific Mindfulness Skills Differentially Predict Creative Performance. Baas M, Nevicka B, Ten Velden FS. Pers Soc Psychol Bull. 2014 May 23;40(9):1092-1106.

Chapter 10: Awareness—The Fourth Pillar of Wealth

[1] Developmental Changes in Memory-Related Linguistic Skills and Their Relationship to Episodic Recall in Children. Uehara I. PLoS One. 2015 Sep 2;10(9):e0137220.

[2] The nature of goal-directed action representations in infancy. Sommerville JA, Upshaw MB, Loucks J. Adv Child Dev Behav. 2012;43:351-87.

[3] A neural model of mechanisms of empathy deficits in narcissism. Jankowiak-Siuda K, Zajkowski W. Med Sci Monit. 2013 Nov 5;19:934-41.

[4] Narcissism is associated with weakened frontostriatal

connectivity: a DTI study. Chester DS, Lynam DR, Powell DK, DeWall CN. Soc Cogn Affect Neurosci. 2015 Jun 5.

[5] The neuronal basis of empathy and fairness. Singer T. Novartis Found Symp. 2007;278:20-30.

[6] Compassion, guilt and innocence: An fMRI study of responses to victims who are responsible for their fate. Fehse K, Silveira S, Elvers K, Blautzik J. Soc Neurosci. 2015;10(3):243-52.

[7] Neuroscience, moral reasoning, and the law. Knabb JJ, Welsh RK, Ziebell JG, Reimer KS. Behav Sci Law. 2009 Mar-Apr;27(2):219-36.
   Neural foundations to moral reasoning and antisocial behavior. Raine A, Yang Y. Soc Cogn Affect Neurosci. 2006 Dec;1(3):203-13.

[8] Social mindfulness: skill and will to navigate the social world. Van Doesum NJ, Van Lange DA, Van Lange PA. J Pers Soc Psychol. 2013 Jul;105(1):86-103.

[9] Interventions shown to aid executive function development in children 4 to 12 years old. Diamond A, Lee K. Science. 2011 Aug 19;333(6045):959-64.

[10] Being present at school: implementing mindfulness in schools. Bostic JQ, Nevarez MD, Potter MP, Prince JB, Benningfield MM, Aguirre BA. Child Adolesc Psychiatr Clin N Am. 2015 Apr;24(2):245-59.

[11] Mindfulness Training and Classroom Behavior Among Lower-Income and Ethnic Minority Elementary School Children. Black DS, Fernando R. J Child Fam Stud. 2014 Oct;23(7):1242-1246.

[12] Mindfulness Training and Classroom Behavior Among Lower-Income and Ethnic Minority Elementary School Children. Black DS, Fernando R. J Child Fam Stud. 2014 Oct;23(7):1242-1246.

[13] Watching my mind unfold versus yours: an fMRI study using a novel camera technology to examine neural differences in self-projection of self versus other perspectives. St Jacques PL, Conway MA, Lowder MW, Cabeza R. J Cogn Neurosci. 2011 Jun;23(6):1275-84.

[14] Spectral power and functional connectivity changes during mindfulness meditation with eyes open: A magnetoencephalography (MEG) study in long-term meditators. Wong WP, Camfield DA, Woods W, Sarris J, Pipingas A. Int J Psychophysiol. 2015 Oct;98(1):95-111.

[15] Newberg AS and Waldman MR. *How God Changes Your Brain.* Ballantine, 2010.

[16]   Williams M, Teasdale J, Segal, Kabat-Zinn J. *The Mindful Way Through Depression*. Guilford, 2007.

[17]   Mindful walking in psychologically distressed individuals: a randomized controlled trial. Teut M, Roesner EJ, Ortiz M, Reese F, Binting S, Roll S, Fischer HF, Michalsen A, Willich SN, Brinkhaus B. Evid Based Complement Alternat Med. 2013;2013:489856.

[18]   Effects of a mindfulness-based intervention on mindful eating, sweets consumption, and fasting glucose levels in obese adults: data from the SHINE randomized controlled trial. Mason AE, Epel ES, Kristeller J, Moran PJ, Dallman M, Lustig RH, Acree M, Bacchetti P, Laraia BA, Hecht FM, Daubenmier J. J Behav Med. 2015 Nov 12.

[19]   Nash, Jf. From *Les Prix Nobel. The Nobel Prizes 1994.* edited by Tore Frängsmyr. Nobel Foundation, 1995.

[20]   Motivating forces of human actions. Neuroimaging reward and social interaction. Walter H, Abler B, Ciaramidaro A, Erk S. Brain Res Bull. 2005 Nov 15;67(5):368-81.

[21]   Social decision making: insights from game theory and neuroscience. Sanfey AG. Science. 2007 Oct 26;318(5850):598-602.

[22]   From reciprocity to unconditional altruism through signalling benefits. Lotem A, Fishman MA, Stone L. Proc Biol Sci. 2003 Jan 22;270(1511):199-205.

[23]   Why be nice? Psychological constraints on the evolution of cooperation. Stevens JR, Hauser MD. Trends Cogn Sci. 2004 Feb;8(2):60-5.

[24]   Reciprocal altruism. Silk JB. Curr Biol. 2013 Sep 23;23(18):R827-8.

[25]   The neurobiology of moral behavior: review and neuropsychiatric implications. Mendez MF. CNS Spectr. 2009 Nov;14(11):608-20.

[26]   Cues of being watched enhance cooperation in a real-world setting. Bateson M, Nettle D, Roberts G. Biol Lett. 2006 Sep 22;2(3):412-4.

[27]   Social control, social learning, and cheating: Evidence from lab and online experiments on dishonesty. Kroher M, Wolbring T. Soc Sci Res. 2015 Sep;53:311-24.

[28]   In a very different voice: unmasking moral hypocrisy. Batson CD, Kobrynowicz D, Dinnerstein JL, Kampf HC, Wilson AD. J Pers Soc Psychol. 1997 Jun;72(6):1335-48.

[29] "...As you would have them do unto you": Does imagining yourself in the other's place stimulate moral action? Batson CD, Lishner DA, Carpenter A, Dulin L, Harjusola-Webb S, Stocks EL, Gale S, Hassan O, Sampat B. Pers Soc Psychol Bull. 2003 Sep;29(9):1190-201.

[30] Social mindfulness: skill and will to navigate the social world. Van Doesum NJ, Van Lange DA, Van Lange PA. J Pers Soc Psychol. 2013 Jul;105(1):86-103.

[31] Dispositional greed. Seuntjens TG, Zeelenberg M, van de Ven N, Breugelmans SM. J Pers Soc Psychol. 2015 Jun;108(6):917-33.

[32] Defining greed. Seuntjens TG, Zeelenberg M, Breugelmans SM, van de Ven N. Br J Psychol. 2015 Aug;106(3):505-25.

[33] Cognitive motivations of free riding and cooperation and impaired strategic decision making in schizophrenia during a public goods game. Chung D, Kim YT, Jeong J. Schizophr Bull. 2013 Jan;39(1):112-9.

[34] Perceptions of moral character modulate the neural systems of reward during the trust game. Delgado MR, Frank RH, Phelps EA. Nat Neurosci. 2005 Nov;8(11):1611-8.

[35] Organization of intrinsic functional brain connectivity predicts decisions to reciprocate social behavior. Cáceda R, James GA, Gutman DA, Kilts CD. Behav Brain Res. 2015 Oct 1;292:478-83.

[36] Relationship between platelet serotonin content and rejections of unfair offers in the ultimatum game. Emanuele E, Brondino N, Bertona M, Re S, Geroldi D. Neurosci Lett. 2008 May 30;437(2):158-61.

[37] State- and trait-greed, its impact on risky decision making and underlying neural mechanisms. Mussel P, Reiter AM, Osinsky R, Hewig J. Soc Neurosci. 2015 Apr;10(2):126-34.

[38] The neural bases of cognitive conflict and control in moral judgment. Greene JD, Nystrom LE, Engell AD, Darley JM, Cohen JD. Neuron. 2004 Oct 14;44(2):389-400.

[39] How primates (including us!) respond to inequity. Brosnan SF. Adv Health Econ Health Serv Res. 2008;20:99-124.

[40] A study of sharing and reciprocity in grey parrots. Péron F, John M, Sapowicz S, Bovet D, Pepperberg IM. Anim Cogn. 2013 Mar;16(2):197-210.

[41] In search of the neurobiological substrates for social playfulness in mammalian brains. Siviy SM, Panksepp J. Neurosci Biobehav Rev. 2011 Oct;35(9):1821-30.

[42] Can natural selection favour altruism between species? Wyatt GA, West SA, Gardner A. J Evol Biol. 2013 Sep;26(9):1854-65.

[43] Plant cooperation. Dudley SA. AoB Plants. 2015 Sep 25;7. pii: plv113.

[44] Interoception drives increased rational decision making in meditators playing the ultimatum game. Kirk U, Downar J, Montague PR. Front Neurosci. 2011 Apr 18;5:49.

[45] Interoception drives increased rational decision making in meditators playing the ultimatum game. Kirk U, Downar J, Montague PR. Front Neurosci. 2011 Apr 18;5:49.

[46] Game Theory Paradigm: A New Tool for Investigating Social Dysfunction in Major Depressive Disorders. Wang Y, Yang LQ, Li S, Zhou Y. Front Psychiatry. 2015 Sep 15;6:128.

[47] Money talks: neural substrate of modulation of fairness by monetary incentives. Zhou Y, Wang Y, Rao LL, Yang LQ, Li S. Front Behav Neurosci. 2014 May 5;8:150.

[48] How much is our fairness worth? The effect of raising stakes on offers by Proposers and minimum acceptable offers in Dictator and Ultimatum Games. Novakova J, Flegr J. PLoS One. 2013 Apr 8;8(4):e60966.

[49] The role of self-interest in elite bargaining. LeVeck BL, Hughes DA, Fowler JH, Hafner-Burton E, Victor DG. Proc Natl Acad Sci U S A. 2014 Dec 30;111(52):18536-41.

[50] Proportion offered in the Dictator and Ultimatum Games decreases with amount and social distance. Bechler C, Green L, Myerson J. Behav Processes. 2015 Jun;115:149-55.

[51] 60 Minutes. CBS television, July 20, 2014.

[52] Rapid evolution of cooperation in group-living animals. Franz M, Schülke O, Ostner J. BMC Evol Biol. 2013 Oct 29;13:235.

[53] Evolution, epigenetics and cooperation. Bateson P. J Biosci. 2014 Apr;39(2):191-200.

[54] Zunz O. Philanthropy in America: A History. Princeton University Press, 2014.

Chapter 11: Developing Your Social Brain

[1] Enhancing cognitive and social-emotional development through a simple-to-administer mindfulness-based school program for elementary school children: a randomized controlled

trial. Schonert-Reichl KA, Oberle E, Lawlor MS, Abbott D, Thomson K, Oberlander TF, Diamond A. Dev Psychol. 2015 Jan;51(1):52-66.

[2]   Playing charades in the fMRI: Are mirror and/or mentalizing areas involved in gestural communication? Schippers MB, Gazzola V, Goebel R, Keysers C. PLoS One. 2009 Aug 27; 4(8):e6801.

[3]   The power of simulation: imagining one's own and other's behavior. Decety J, Grèzes J. Brain Res. 2006 Mar 24;1079(1):4-14.

[4]   The neural substrates of cognitive empathy. Preston SD, Bechara A, Damasio H, Grabowski TJ, Stansfield RB, Mehta S, Damasio AR. Soc Neurosci. 2007;2(3-4):254-75.

[5]   The effect of empathy on accuracy of behavior prediction in social exchange situation. Tanida S, Yamagishi T. Shinrigaku Kenkyu. 2004 Feb;74(6):512-20.

[6]   Control your anger! The neural basis of aggression regulation in response to negative social feedback. Achterberg M, van Duijvenvoorde AC, Bakermans-Kranenburg MJ, Crone EA. Soc Cogn Affect Neurosci. 2016 Jan 10. pii: nsv154.

[7]   Don't look back in anger: neural correlates of reappraisal, analytical rumination, and angry rumination during recall of an anger-inducing autobiographical memory. Fabiansson EC, Denson TF, Moulds ML, Grisham JR, Schira MM. Neuroimage. 2012 Feb 1;59(3):2974-81.

[8]   Linguistically mediated visual search: the critical role of speech rate. Gibson BS, Eberhard KM, Bryant TA. Psychon Bull Rev. 2005 Apr;12(2):276-81.

        The influence of voice volume, pitch, and speech rate on progressive relaxation training: application of methods from speech pathology and audiology. Applied Psychophysiology and Biofeedback, 31, 173-85.

[9]   Working memory capacity for spoken sentences decreases with adult ageing: recall of fewer but not smaller chunks in older adults. Gilchrist AL, Cowan N, Naveh-Benjamin M. Memory. 2008 Oct;16(7):773-87.

[10]   Synchronized brain activity during rehearsal and short-term memory disruption by irrelevant speech is affected by recall mode. Kopp F, Schröger E, Lipka S. Int J Psychophysiol. 2006 Aug;61(2):188-203.

[11]   Irrelevant speech effects and statistical learning. Neath I, Guérard

K, Jalbert A, Bireta TJ, Surprenant AM. Q J Exp Psychol (Hove). 2009 Aug;62(8):1551-9.

[12] Effects of target-masker contextual similarity on the multimasker penalty in a three-talker diotic listening task. Iyer N, Brungart DS, Simpson BD. J Acoust Soc Am. 2010 Nov;128(5):2998-10.

[13] Cross-modal distraction by background speech: what role for meaning? Marsh JE, Jones DM. Noise Health. 2010 Oct-Dec;12(49):210-6.

[14] Effects of road traffic noise and irrelevant speech on children's reading and mathematical performance. Ljung R, Sörqvist P, Hygge S. Noise Health. 2009 Oct-Dec;11(45):194-8.

[15] Linguistically mediated visual search: the critical role of speech rate. Gibson BS, Eberhard KM, Bryant TA. Psychon Bull Rev. 2005 Apr;12(2):276-81.

[16] The influence of voice volume, pitch, and speech rate on progressive relaxation training: application of methods from speech pathology and audiology. Knowlton GE, Larkin KT. Appl Psychophysiol Biofeedback. 2006 Jun;31(2):173-85.

[17] Celerity and cajolery: Rapid speech may promote or inhibit persuasion through its impact on message elaboration." Smith SM, Shaffer DR. Personality Soc Psych Bull. 1991: Dec:17(6):663-69.

[18] Voices of fear and anxiety and sadness and depression: the effects of speech rate and loudness on fear and anxiety and sadness and depression. Siegman AW, Boyle S. J Abnorm Psychol. 1993 Aug;102(3):430-7.

The angry voice: its effects on the experience of anger and cardiovascular reactivity. Siegman AW, Anderson RA, Berger T. Psychosom Med. 1990 Nov-Dec;52(6):631-43.

[19] The effect of rate control on speech rate and intelligibility of dysarthric speech. Van Nuffelen G, De Bodt M, Wuyts F, Van de Heyning P. Folia Phoniatr Logop. 2009;61(2):69-75.

Influences of rate, length, and complexity on speech disfluency in a single-speech sample in preschool children who stutter. Sawyer J, Chon H, Ambrose NG. J Fluency Disord. 2008 Sep;33(3):220-40.

[20] Heffner KL, Loving TJ, Kiecolt-Glaser JK, Himawan LK, Glaser R, Malarkey WB. Older spouses' cortisol responses to marital conflict: associations with demand/withdraw communication patterns. J Behav Med. 2006 Aug;29(4):317-25.

[21] Newberg A, and Waldman M. *Words Can Change Your Brain*. Hudson Street Press, 2012.

[22] Voice analysis during bad news discussion in oncology: reduced pitch, decreased speaking rate, and nonverbal communication of empathy. McHenry M, Parker PA, Baile WF, Lenzi R. Support Care Cancer. 2012 May;20(5):1073-8.

[23] Leadership = Communication? The Relations of Leaders' Communication Styles with Leadership Styles, Knowledge Sharing and Leadership Outcomes. de Vries RE, Bakker-Pieper A, Oostenveld W. J Bus Psychol. 2010 Sep;25(3):367-380.

[24] The interventional effects of loving-kindness meditation on positive emotions and interpersonal interactions. He X, Shi W, Han X, Wang N, Zhang N, Wang X. Neuropsychiatr Dis Treat. 2015 May 25;11:1273-7.

Short-term compassion training increases prosocial behavior in a newly developed prosocial game. Leiberg S, Klimecki O, Singer T. PLoS One. 2011 Mar 9;6(3):e17798.

[25] BOLD signal and functional connectivity associated with loving kindness meditation. Garrison KA, Scheinost D, Constable RT, Brewer JA. Brain Behav. 2014 May;4(3):337-47.

Brain activation during compassion meditation: a case study. Engström M, Söderfeldt B. J Altern Complement Med. 2010 May;16(5):597-9.

[26] Loving-kindness meditation for posttraumatic stress disorder: a pilot study. Kearney DJ, Malte CA, McManus C, Martinez ME, Felleman B, Simpson TL. J Trauma Stress. 2013 Aug;26(4):426-34.

A yoga and compassion meditation program reduces stress in familial caregivers of Alzheimer's disease patients. Danucalov MA, Kozasa EH, Ribas KT, Galduróz JC, Garcia MC, Verreschi IT, Oliveira KC, Romani de Oliveira L, Leite JR. Evid Based Complement Alternat Med. 2013;2013:513149.

The theoretical and empirical basis for meditation as an intervention for PTSD. Lang AJ, Strauss JL, Bomyea J, Bormann JE, Hickman SD, Good RC, Essex M. Behav Modif. 2012 Nov;36(6):759-86.

[27] A wait-list randomized controlled trial of loving-kindness meditation programme for self-criticism. Shahar B, Szsepsenwol O, Zilcha-Mano S, Haim N, Zamir O, Levi-Yeshuvi S, Levit-Binnun N. Clin Psychol Psychother. 2015 Jul-Aug;22(4):346-56.

[28] Loving-kindness meditation and the broaden-and-build theory

of positive emotions among veterans with posttraumatic stress disorder. Kearney DJ, McManus C, Malte CA, Martinez ME, Felleman B, Simpson TL. Med Care. 2014 Dec;52(12 Suppl 5):S32-8.

[29] Loving-kindness meditation's effects on nitric oxide and perceived well-being: a pilot study in experienced and inexperienced meditators. Kemper KJ, Powell D, Helms CC, Kim-Shapiro DB. Explore (NY). 2015 Jan-Feb;11(1):32-9.

Effect of compassion meditation on neuroendocrine, innate immune and behavioral responses to psychosocial stress. Pace TW, Negi LT, Adame DD, Cole SP, Sivilli TI, Brown TD, Issa MJ, Raison CL. Psychoneuroendocrinology. 2009 Jan;34(1):87-98.

[30] Loving-kindness and compassion meditation: potential for psychological interventions. Hofmann SG, Grossman P, Hinton DE. Clin Psychol Rev. 2011 Nov;31(7):1126-32.

[31] Focused attention, open monitoring and loving kindness meditation: effects on attention, conflict monitoring, and creativity - A review. Lippelt DP, Hommel B, Colzato LS. Front Psychol. 2014 Sep 23;5:1083.

[32] Loving-kindness meditation increases social connectedness. Hutcherson CA, Seppala EM, Gross JJ. Emotion. 2008 Oct;8(5):720-4.

[33] Compassion Training Alters Altruism and Neural Responses to Suffering. Weng HY, Fox AS, Shackman AJ, Stodola DE, Caldwell JZ, Olson MC, Rogers GM, Davidson RJ. Psychol Sci. 2013 May 21.

[34] Meditation-based treatment yielding immediate relief for meditation-naïve migraineurs. Tonelli ME, Wachholtz AB. Pain Manag Nurs. 2014 Mar;15(1):36-40.

[35] Loving-Kindness Meditation practice associated with longer telomeres in women. Hoge EA, Chen MM, Orr E, Metcalf CA, Fischer LE, Pollack MH, De Vivo I, Simon NM. Brain Behav Immun. 2013 Aug;32:159-63.

A meta-analytic review of the effects of mindfulness meditation on telomerase activity. Schutte NS, Malouff JM. Psychoneuroendocrinology. 2014 Apr;42:45-8.

Telomere lengthening after three weeks of an intensive insight meditation retreat. Conklin Q, King B, Zanesco A, Pokorny J, Hamidi A, Lin J, Epel E, Blackburn E, Saron C. Psychoneuroendocrinology. 2015 Nov;61:26-7.

[36]   Happy people become happier through kindness: a counting kind-
       nesses intervention. Otake K, Shimai S, Tanaka-Matsumi J, Otsui K,
       Fredrickson BL. J Happiness Stud. 2006 Sep;7(3):361-375.
[37]   Positive psychology progress: empirical validation of interven-
       tions. Seligman ME, Steen TA, Park N, Peterson C. Am Psychol.
       2005 Jul-Aug;60(5):410-21.
[38]   Two distinct neural mechanisms underlying indirect reciprocity.
       Watanabe T, Takezawa M, Nakawake Y, Kunimatsu A, Yamasue
       H, Nakamura M, Miyashita Y, Masuda N. Proc Natl Acad Sci U
       S A. 2014 Mar 18;111(11):3990-5.
[39]   Practice positive activities to help overcome depression: Acts
       of kindness and a sense of optimism may help when meds or
       other treatments don't work, or are financially unavailable.
       DukeMedicine Healthnews 2011, 17 (11): 5-6.
[40]   Bolton GE, Katok e, Zwick R. Dictator game giving: rules of
       fairness versus acts of kindness. Intl J of Game Theory. 1998
       Aug:27(2):269-299.
[41]   Kindness counts: prompting prosocial behavior in preadolescents
       boosts peer acceptance and well-being. Layous K, Nelson SK,
       Oberle E, Schonert-Reichl KA, Lyubomirsky S. PLoS One.
       2012;7(12):e51380.
[42]   On being grateful and kind: results of two randomized controlled
       trials on study-related emotions and academic engagement.
       Ouweneel E, Le Blanc PM, Schaufeli WB. J Psychol. 2014 Jan-
       Feb;148(1):37-60.
[43]   Paying it forward: generalized reciprocity and the limits of
       generosity. Gray K, Ward AF, Norton MI. J Exp Psychol Gen.
       2014 Feb;143(1):247-54.
[44]   Spontaneous giving and calculated greed. Rand DG, Greene JD,
       Nowak MA. Nature. 2012 Sep 20;489(7416):427-30.
[45]   Meditation improves self-regulation over the life span. Tang
       YY, Posner MI, Rothbart MK. Ann N Y Acad Sci. 2014
       Jan;1307:104-11.
[46]   Neural correlates of receiving an apology and active forgiveness:
       an FMRI study. Strang S, Utikal V, Fischbacher U, Weber B,
       Falk A. PLoS One. 2014 Feb 5;9(2):e87654.
[47]   The strength of a remorseful heart: psychological and neural
       basis of how apology emolliates reactive aggression and promotes
       forgiveness. Beyens U, Yu H, Han T, Zhang L, Zhou X. Front
       Psychol. 2015 Oct 27;6:1611.

[48] "An eye for an eye"? Neural correlates of retribution and forgiveness. Brüne M, Juckel G, Enzi B. PLoS One. 2013 Aug 29;8(8):e73519.

[49] Forgiveness, health, and well-being: a review of evidence for emotional versus decisional forgiveness, dispositional forgivingness, and reduced unforgiveness. Worthington EL Jr, Witvliet CV, Pietrini P, Miller AJ. J Behav Med. 2007 Aug;30(4):291-302.

[50] Effects of a group forgiveness intervention on forgiveness, perceived stress, and trait-anger. Harris AH, Luskin F, Norman SB, Standard S, Bruning J, Evans S, Thoresen CE. J Clin Psychol. 2006 Jun;62(6):715-33.

[51] Dispositional forgiveness of self, others, and situations. Thompson LY, Snyder CR, Hoffman L, Michael ST, Rasmussen HN, Billings LS, Heinze L, Neufeld JE, Shorey HS, Roberts JC, Roberts DE. J Pers. 2005 Apr;73(2):313-59.

[52] The unique effects of forgiveness on health: an exploration of pathways. Lawler KA, Younger JW, Piferi RL, Jobe RL, Edmondson KA, Jones WH. J Behav Med. 2005 Apr;28(2):157-67.

[53] Forgiveness, feeling connected to others, and well-being: two longitudinal studies. Bono G, McCullough ME, Root LM. Pers Soc Psychol Bull. 2008 Feb;34(2):182-95.

[54] The road to forgiveness: a meta-analytic synthesis of its situational and dispositional correlates. Fehr R, Gelfand MJ, Nag M. Psychol Bull. 2010 Sep;136(5):894-914.

[55] Effect of Training of Emotional Competence in Financial Services Advisors. Luskin F, Aberman R, DeLorenzo AE.http://learningtoforgive.com/research/effect-of-training-of-emotional-competence-in-financial-services-advisors/.

[56] Effects of a group forgiveness intervention on forgiveness, perceived stress, and trait-anger. Harris AH, Luskin F, Norman SB, Standard S, Bruning J, Evans S, Thoresen CE. J Clin Psychol. 2006 Jun;62(6):715-33.

[57] Efficacy of psychotherapeutic interventions to promote forgiveness: a meta-analysis. Wade NG, Hoyt WT, Kidwell JE, Worthington EL. J Consult Clin Psychol. 2014 Feb;82(1):154-70.

[58] Forgiving usually takes time: A lesson learned by studying interventions to promote forgiveness. Worthington Jr EL, Kurusu TA, Collins W, Berry JW, Ripley JS, Baier SN. J Psych and Theology. 2000:28(1):3-20.

[59] More frequent partner hugs and higher oxytocin levels are linked to lower blood pressure and heart rate in premenopausal women. Light KC, Grewen KM, Amico JA. Biol Psychol. 2005 Apr;69(1):5-21.

[60] Profiling of serum proteins influenced by warm partner contact in healthy couples. Matsunaga M, Sato S, Isowa T, Tsuboi H, Konagaya T, Kaneko H, Ohira H. Neuro Endocrinol Lett. 2009;30(2):227-36.

[61] Maslow A. *The Farther Reaches of Human Nature.* McGraw-Hill, 1971.

[62] Neural correlates of gratitude. Fox GR, Kaplan J, Damasio H, Damasio A. Front Psychol. 2015 Sep 30;6:1491.

[63] Gratitude and well-being: a review and theoretical integration. Wood AM, Froh JJ, Geraghty AW. Clin Psychol Rev. 2010 Nov;30(7):890-905.

[64] The effects of counting blessings on subjective well-being: a gratitude intervention in a Spanish sample. Martínez-Martí ML, Avia MD, Hernández-Lloreda MJ. Span J Psychol. 2010 Nov;13(2):886-96.

Counting blessings in early adolescents: an experimental study of gratitude and subjective well-being. Froh JJ, Sefick WJ, Emmons RA. J Sch Psychol. 2008 Apr;46(2):213-33.

Counting blessings versus burdens: an experimental investigation of gratitude and subjective well-being in daily life. Emmons RA, McCullough ME. J Pers Soc Psychol. 2003 Feb;84(2):377-89.

[65] Expressing gratitude to a partner leads to more relationship maintenance behavior. Lambert NM, Fincham FD. Emotion. 2011 Feb;11(1):52-60.

Benefits of expressing gratitude: expressing gratitude to a partner changes one's view of the relationship. Lambert NM, Clark MS, Durtschi J, Fincham FD, Graham SM. Psychol Sci. 2010 Apr 1;21(4):574-80.

[66] Gratitude orientation reduces death anxiety but not positive and negative affect. Lau RW, Cheng ST. Omega (Westport). 2012-2013;66(1):79-88.

[67] A little thanks goes a long way: Explaining why gratitude expressions motivate prosocial behavior. Grant AM, Gino F. J Pers Soc Psychol. 2010 Jun;98(6):946-55.

[68] Psychological "gel" to bind individuals' goal pursuit: gratitude

facilitates goal contagion. Jia L, Tong EM, Lee LN. Emotion. 2014 Aug;14(4):748-60.

[69] Gratitude is associated with greater levels of protective factors and lower levels of risks in African American adolescents. Ma M, Kibler JL, Sly K. J Adolesc. 2013 Oct;36(5):983-91.

[70] The impact of a brief gratitude intervention on subjective well-being, biology and sleep. Jackowska M, Brown J, Ronaldson A, Steptoe A. J Health Psychol. 2015 Mar 2. pii: 1359105315572455.

[71] A little thanks goes a long way: Explaining why gratitude expressions motivate prosocial behavior. Grant AM, Gino F. J Pers Soc Psychol. 2010 Jun;98(6):946-55.

Counting blessings in early adolescents: an experimental study of gratitude and subjective well-being. Froh JJ, Sefick WJ, Emmons RA. J Sch Psychol. 2008 Apr;46(2):213-33.

[72] The reward of a good joke: neural correlates of viewing dynamic displays of stand-up comedy. Franklin RG Jr, Adams RB Jr. Cogn Affect Behav Neurosci. 2011 Dec;11(4):508-15.

Mark Robert Waldman has authored 14 books, including the national bestseller *How God Changes Your Brain*. Mark is on the Executive MBA faculty at Loyola Marymount University and serves on the faculty of Holmes Institute. His research has been published in numerous neuroscience and psychology journals, and his work has been featured in *Time*, the *Washington Post*, the *New York Times, Forbes, Entrepreneur, Oprah Magazine*, and many others. He has appeared on hundreds of radio and television programs, including PBS and NPR. Mark has an international practice offering personal and professional NeuroCoaching services and training/certification programs, and he travels throughout the world lecturing and teaching workshops in mindfulness, NeuroLeadership, and NeuroWisdom to schools, health centers, and corporations. For more information visit **www.MarkRobertWaldman.com**.

Chris Manning, MBA, PhD, is a professor in the College of Business at Loyola Marymount University teaching entrepreneurship, finance, and real estate investment, and he is one of the founders of LMU's Executive MBA program. Chris has served as President of the American Real Estate Society. He is on the editorial board of the *Journal of Real Estate Research* and has been published in many academic journals. He was a managing partner of a national financial consulting firm, worked for Bank of America as a corporate lending officer, and has coached thousands of corporate leaders. Chris served as an officer in the United States Army in Vietnam and was awarded the Bronze Star Medal. Further details on his career can be found in Marquis' *Who's Who in America* (70th Edition, 2016) or Marquis' *Who's Who in the World* (33rd Edition, 2016).

Printed in the USA
CPSIA information can be obtained
at www.ICGtesting.com
JSHW031708140824
68134JS00038B/3581

9 781635 766684